Chicago Public Library

05

ns for career

IT

D1311870

DISCARD

Women with Attitude

Have you ever wondered how top-ranking women directors made it to the top, what they think of their success, and how it affects their lives? *Women with Attitude* answers all of these questions and more, as nineteen top-achieving businesswomen tell the stories of their career success. All winners of the Veuve Clicquot Business Woman of the Year Award, their diverse lives have been brought together here for the first time.

A groundbreaking study of women in management, entrepreneurship and the politics of leadership, *Women with Attitude* includes interviews with Barbara Cassani of Go Fly Airlines, Camelot's Dianne Thompson, Pearson's Dame Marjorie Scardino and Anita Roddick of The Body Shop fame. It brings individual stories of success together with expert research into the emergence of women entrepreneurs, aspects of leadership, and the politics of breaking into the boardroom.

A fascinating insight into the minds and lives of some of the world's top businesswomen, *Women with Attitude* is a must-read for anybody who wants advice from women who have progressed to the top.

Susan Vinnicombe is Professor of Organizational Behaviour and Diversity Management at Cranfield School of Management. She is internationally known for her research and consultancy work, and is an active campaigner for getting more women on major corporate boards.

John Bank left the United States to lecture at the London Business School. He is now a management consultant with international experience and lectures in Human Resources at Cranfield School of Management. He has published widely.

Women with Attitude

Lessons for career management

**Susan Vinnicombe
and John Bank**

Routledge
Taylor & Francis Group

LONDON AND NEW YORK

First published 2003 by Routledge
11 New Fetter Lane, London EC4P 4EE

Simultaneously published in the USA and Canada
by Routledge
29 West 35th Street, New York, NY 10001

Routledge is an imprint of the Taylor & Francis Group

© 2003 Susan Vinnicombe and John Bank

The right of Susan Vinnicombe and John Bank to be identified as the
Authors of this Work has been asserted by them in accordance with
the Copyright, Designs and Patents Act 1988

Typeset in Times New Roman by
Florence Production Ltd, Stoodleigh, Devon
Printed and bound in Great Britain by
TJ International Ltd, Padstow, Cornwall

British Library Cataloguing in Publication Data
A catalogue record for this book is available from the British Library

Library of Congress Cataloging in Publication Data
A catalog record for this book has been requested

ISBN 0–415–28742–1

For our daughters Jade and Rebecca as they
strive to be women with attitude, and our sons
Alex, Nicholas, and Daniel who respect what
their sisters are doing

Performance

I starred last night, I shone:
I was footwork and firework in one,

a rocket that wriggled up and shot
darkness with a parasol of brilliants
and a peewee descant on a flung bit;
I was busters of glitter-bombs expanding
to mantle and aurora from a crown,
I was flouettés, falls of blazing paint,
para-flares spot welding cloudy heaven,
loose gold off fierce toeholds of white,
a finale red-tongued as a haka leap:
that too was a butt of all right!

As usual after any triumph, I was
of course inconsolable.

Les Murray, *Superhuman Redneck Poems*
Winner of the T.S. Eliot Prize, 1997. Printed with
permission of Carcanet Press Limited, Manchester.

Contents

Foreword

In 1972, Veuve Clicquot celebrated its bicentenary. When François Clicquot, the founder's son, died suddenly in 1805, such a landmark must have seemed very unlikely, but his widow, Nicole-Barbe, decided against the odds to continue to run the business. In fact, she not only continued the business but developed it both commercially, with expanding sales to distant markets such as Russia, and technically, with the great innovation of *remuage*. This technique, inadequately translated into English as 'riddling', is the process by which all champagne is clarified to this day. By the time of her death in 1866 at the great age of 88, after more than sixty years of running this house with passion, dedication to excellence and strong leadership, she was a legendary figure, known throughout the region and beyond as 'La Grande Dame de la Champagne'.

Two centuries after our foundation in 1772 we launched an award to recognize women who had faced and successfully overcome similar odds in the world of business. The Veuve Clicquot Award is now run in twelve countries around the world, from its origins in France and the United Kingdom, to new markets like Japan and Brazil. It is hard to imagine, just a generation later, how restricted were the opportunities for women in business, even in sophisticated Europe, and I hope I do not claim too much when I say that this award has played its part in changing perceptions. I am nevertheless convinced that strong support and new initiatives are still needed before the topic fades.

Therefore, it is my great pleasure to introduce this study of these nineteen remarkable businesswomen, in the hope that their stories will provide role models for the future in the same way that Nicole-Barbe Clicquot has for nearly two centuries.

Cécile Bonnefond
President
Veuve Clicquot Ponsardin s.a.

Preface by Rt Hon. Harriet Harman, QC, MP

Whenever anyone says anything about senior women in management there are always two things that are said in response – 'This is all elitist – women at the top of business can look after themselves. You should be concentrating on women at the bottom of the heap', and 'This is all irrelevant – what business needs is the best people in management. It doesn't matter whether they are men or women.'

The reason why the issues addressed in this book, *Women with Attitude*, are important is that it does matter that there are so few women in top management and we must work to change it.

First, to tackle the argument that the issues in this book are elitist. As a matter of principle, sex discrimination is wrong. It is just as wrong if it happens in the boardroom as on the shop floor. But also, it is my strong view that women in low-paid, low-skilled jobs – women 'at the bottom of the pile' – do benefit if women are at the top of their company. It reminds all those in the company that women do have a vital contribution to make to its success, a major theme of this book. What message does it send to women in the workforce that the top levels are men only? An all-male board reinforces in the minds of the women lower down the organization that only men in that company count. Women in top management are, like their female colleagues lower down the organization, likely to be balancing home and work responsibilities, as their stories in this book aptly illustrate. They are much more likely to understand the need for family-friendly work patterns and for flexibility and to recognize the importance of their earnings to the family budget. And to focus on the lack of women in top management is by no means to preclude the important campaigns for women who are low paid.

Second, any campaign to get more women into top management positions is somehow seen to detract from the real need of business, which is to have the best people in the top jobs. This raises the question of how you assess merit. Merit is not just about your qualities as an individual but also what you bring to a team. An all-male team will, inevitably, lack the insights that it will need if it is managing a workforce which has, as most do, a percentage of women, or if women are the purchasers of the goods or services it provides. A diverse management team has shown itself able to draw on a diverse range of talents. As the nineteen career case studies demonstrate, drawn as they are from across many different industries, women have the ability to run successful organizations at the highest level.

It is inconceivable now that there should ever again be an all-male Cabinet. Public opinion would find it unconvincing to be told that the country could be governed by men alone. So too, the days of the all-male boardroom are numbered. Many of the women, whose life stories are vividly recounted in the book, have made trail-blazing contributions in their positions of leadership. They are wonderful exceptions.

British business will be confidently looking to the future when women in the boardroom and in top management are not the exception but the norm.

Authors' preface

In Veuve Clicquot's vineyards, a two-hour drive east of Paris, Dianne Thompson pours a bottle of champagne over a vine named in her honour. The vine is named after her as a living, lasting tribute to Dianne Thompson's leadership as CEO of Camelot. She is the Veuve Clicquot Business Woman of the Year for 2000 for the United Kingdom.

She is introduced to award-winning women from other European countries and Japan. Together they tour the vineyards by helicopter, hold a round-table discussion about their shared concerns, and that evening attended a formal dinner in 'the Pavilion' in the Rue du Marc, an elegant old house belonging to the owners' family, now used as a hospitality suite, in the cathedral city of Rheims.

A few months earlier, at a reception at London's Claridges, Dianne Thompson had won the award. She was praised for her outstanding leadership that secured for Camelot a new licence to run the British national lottery. It was a highly visible leadership exercised in the glare of national media coverage. She had taken on Richard Branson's People's Lottery and won a famous victory in the High Court over his challenge to Camelot's right to run the lottery. She saw herself as the protector of Camelot's 900 employees. She convinced both the High Court and the head of the lottery commission, Lord Burns, that Camelot was the best alternative to run the nation's lucrative lottery.

By April 2003 thirty women will have shared this honour of being named Veuve Clicquot Business Women of the Year in the United Kingdom. They are rightly celebrated as role models for women business leaders.

What have these women in common? What strategies did they use to reach the top of their organizations? What motivated many of them to set up their own businesses? What advice do they have for women wanting to reach the top? Were there similar factors in their family backgrounds and education that turned them into high achievers? How do they define success and how do they balance their demanding careers with their personal lives? Did they encounter any gender-based obstacles to their advancement, any glass walls or glass ceilings? How did some of these women become executive and non-executive directors on major corporate boards? Do these women lead their organizations differently from men? Is there any evidence from them for the so-called 'female advantage'? How best can a company build a business case for greater gender diversity in the workplace to gain its contributions to the bottom line, while breaking the traditional white male mould? What can be done now to create a more positive environment of men and women working together?

To answer these questions we interviewed sixteen winners of the Veuve Clicquot Business Woman of the Year Award in the UK, a rich sample of women business leaders over three decades. Six of these women appeared in a list of the fifty most powerful women in the UK last year, including Dame Marjorie Scardino in the number two spot.[1]

We also spoke with Cécile Bonnefond, first female President of Veuve Clicquot Ponsardin since the company's founder Madame Clicquot, in Paris. We offer a brief history of Madame Clicquot, which more than justifies the award carrying her name. We explain how the award developed in the UK. To add an international dimension, we interviewed three Veuve Clicquot Business Women of the Year Award winners for the year 2001 from Denmark, Norway and Sweden.

For the most part, although we were using semi-structured interviewing techniques, we allowed the women to tell their own stories. To do so was in keeping with a tradition in the women's movement beautifully illustrated in Mary Catherine Bateson's book *Composing a Life*.[2] In this book the lives of five extraordinary women are viewed as improvisations – work in progress. As Catherine Bateson puts it:

> Each of us constructs a life that is her own central metaphor for thinking about the world. But of course these lives do not look like parables or allegories. Mostly, they look like ongoing improvisations, quite ordinary sequences of day-to-day events. They continue to unfold . . . The compositions we create in these times of change are filled with interlocking messages of our commitments and decisions. Each one is a message of possibility.[3]

Similarly, we treated the lives of the nineteen award-winning women we interviewed as 'work in progress', and we facilitated the telling of their life stories – so far. Their individual stories are inspiring and filled with improvisations, chance and opportunism; but they are also records of outstanding effort and achievement. Their insights may illuminate the way for other women, clarify some of the issues that are theorized about and make a contribution to the wider discussion about the role women should play in Britain's economic life.

[1] 'Power and the Glory: Officially the 50 Most Powerful Women', 27 April 2001, *Daily Record*.
[2] Mary Catherine Bateson, *Composing a Life*, New York: Plume, Penguin Books (1990).
[3] Ibid., p. 241.

Collectively they build a powerful business case for greater gender diversity in all our enterprises. Their views provide invaluable advice for both businesswomen and businessmen.

These nineteen interviews have been turned into profiles of each woman for Part II of the book. They are listed in reverse chronological order from the UK award winner for the year 2001. The three northern European award winners are grouped at the end of Part II. Because they are all current winners and from Scandinavia, there is no attempt to integrate these three profiles in the analysis in Part III. We simply do not know enough about their national working cultures.

In Part III of the book we attempt to link the lives of the sixteen Veuve Clicquot Business Women of the Year Award winners in the UK to our own research and to that of others in the area of 'women in management'. We offer an up-to-date overview of the academic literature on this subject. Because it is such a wide area we have restricted the themes we cover to five: careers, entrepreneurship, success, leadership and boardroom participation.

In the first chapter of Part III, 'Making it to the top', the sample is restricted to the six women in corporate or public sector careers. (We exclude the ten women who are entrepreneurs from this discussion.) This chapter explores the concept of careers for women and offers a model of the ten key factors for success that have emerged from the experiences of the corporate women. They are: (1) confidence, (2) self-promotion, (3) risk-taking, (4) visibility, (5) career acceleration, (6) mentoring, (7) portfolio careers, (8) international experience, (9) positive role models, (10) a management style compatible with that of male colleagues.

The second chapter, 'Emerging women entrepreneurs', focuses on the ten women who have created their own businesses. In this chapter we look at the phenomenal rise in the numbers of women entrepreneurs, both in America and in the UK, and the reasons behind it. We explore the types of women entrepreneurs and try to fit those in our sample into a typology that illustrates the diversity of the drive to create one's own business.

'Personal definitions of success', the third chapter, puts the personal meanings of success of the sixteen women award winners in the context of the research on gender and life development. Understandably, women's experience of management is significantly different from men's because of the particular roles they fill both at work and within life in general. A model developed at Cranfield School of Management on how male and female managers saw their own career success serves as the basis of analysing the women in our sample as 'climbers', 'experts', 'influencers' or 'self-realizers'.

The next chapter, 'Leadership with a difference', explores the idea of a particular leadership style for women managers. If it is different from men's leadership, why and how is it different? The research on this topic is mixed. We explain why that is so and then, drawing on our own data from the award-winning women and other research, we assert that women are developing distinctive styles of leadership that are not only effective but actually more appropriate for leading modern companies.

Our fifth chapter, 'Breaking into the corporate boardroom', deals with women on corporate boards. As we are part of the campaign to increase the numbers of women on the FTSE corporate boards we 'declare an interest' and admit to a possible bias here. Only one woman out of our sample of sixteen – Dame Marjorie Scardino – is a CEO of a FTSE 100 company. Others, however, have been non-executive directors on a range of boards and this chapter includes their advice on how to get there and how to be an effective board member.

'Career strategy checklist' is designed to involve the reader in a self-assessment based on the ten key factors of career success explained in the first chapter.

Linking the profiles of these distinguished women to the research and literature on 'women in management' has, we admit, been difficult and demanding. Each woman has seen her own profile to correct for any factual errors before publication. They have not seen the linkages in Part III. We trust that they will welcome our attempt to analyse and distil the data they have generated. We believe strongly that the careers of women managers in progress must form the basis of imaginative research in this field. At the same time, research should illuminate some of the difficulties these women encounter as many of them carve out Protean careers for themselves in a business world that must swiftly prepare itself for their leadership.

Susan Vinnicombe and John Bank

Acknowledgements

Having an idea for a book is the easiest step to take in writing one. We discussed the idea with Moira Collins and John West at Veuve Clicquot and won their support, for which we are very grateful.

The idea has to take shape in a proposal for a book that a publisher wants to publish. From the idea to the proposal stage we sought out Malcolm Stern, who helped us define and shape the book in search of a publisher. Malcolm Stern stayed with the project from start to finish, even to editing the manuscript over the Easter holiday 2002. His expertise and encouragement were invaluable throughout the year it took to bring the work to completion. Thank you immensely, Malcolm.

We were fortunate to find a commissioning editor in Francesca Poynter at Routledge who shared our passion for 'women with attitude'. She sorted out the politics of publishing and marketing whilst we got on with the interviewing and the writing. She had the idea for the Andy Warhol-styled jacket and other good suggestions for improving the book, for which we are thankful.

Cranfield School of Management gave us a supportive network. Dr Val Singh co-authored many of the Cranfield research papers referred to in Part III. Bill Prince helped us with the mini-disk recorded interviews. Jean Hutton transcribed the interviews, typed the profiles and many drafts of the book, including the manuscript. Angela Wood provided a fresh pair of eyes and quality control in preparing the final manuscript. Heather Peake and Julie Tate, at the Management Information Resource Centre, supplied the background materials on the nineteen women we interviewed and their companies. Thank you, colleagues!

Our biggest vote of thanks goes to the nineteen women themselves for being so positive, generous and open with us during the interviews. They were award winners when we met them, accomplished businesswomen and role models, so we expected to be impressed. But we found each one insightful, inspiring, motivating and very personable. It is their stories that are at the heart of the book and to them goes our heartfelt thanks.

Part I

The Veuve Clicquot dimension

The story of Madame Clicquot

The Veuve Clicquot Business Woman of the Year Award was appropriately named for Madame Clicquot who was a businesswoman ahead of her time at the start of the nineteenth century. She embodied many of the leadership qualities celebrated by the award today. While never reckless, she took risks. She seized opportunities. In 1814 she organized her first shipment of champagne to Russia, despite the fact that it tied up much of her capital. The Imperial Russian Court became one of her best customers. To satisfy Russian demand for her champagne, Madame Clicquot beat England's blockade of the seas.

She also invented a new process for perfecting champagne, leaving it brilliantly clear. Her technique, called *remuage*, was soon adopted by all the other champagne houses. Fittingly, the trophy held by the winner of the Veuve Clicquot Business Woman of the Year Award for twelve months is a scale model of a *pupitre*, the instrument used for the *remuage* process.

Madame Clicquot was born Nicole-Barbe Ponsardin in 1777. Her father, Nicolas Ponsardin, was a successful businessman and she was brought up in a middle-class family used to financial independence. She married François-Marie Clicquot in 1798. She was 21 and he 24. The following year they had a daughter, Clementine.

François Clicquot had become involved in his father's champagne business in Rheims only eighteen months before the marriage. He started to work for his father, Philippe Clicquot, just before Christmas in 1796. In June the next year he was sent out as a sales representative for the company to open new markets. His father delayed his own plans to retire until 1802. Three years later his son fell fatally ill – just seven years after his marriage to Nicole-Barbe. François had possessed a weak constitution since his youth. It did not stop him from expanding the business and travelling all over Europe. When he came down with a fever it was not regarded as serious. Twelve days later he was dead. It devastated both his father and his young wife. While still in the shock of his bereavement Philippe Clicquot announced that he and his daughter-in-law were going to wind up the business by the end of the year 1805.

Then Widow Clicquot made the amazing decision to carry on her husband's business. It was an extraordinary act for a young woman at that time, made within a few weeks of her husband's death. Her motive was not to earn a living. Her own father, Nicolas Ponsardin, was rich and would have gladly supported his daughter and her child. In fact, during the difficult early years of the business, Madame Clicquot subsidized the business from her own personal finances.

Her administration of the champagne company was far from an overnight success. She had eight difficult years at the outset, from 1806 to 1814, before the business became a commercial success. Four months after her husband's death she entered into a partnership with another local Rheims wine-producer, Jerome Alexandre Fourneaux, to form Veuve Clicquot Fourneaux et Cie. The partnership gave her an opportunity to learn about the champagne business whilst running the small company.

Their traditional markets, however, fell victim to the political turmoil of the times. In response to threats from Napoleon in March 1806, England used its powerful navy to blockade France. Trying to run the blockade, Madame Clicquot and her partner lost 50,000 bottles of champagne, more than a third of their annual production. England's blockade of Prussian ports closed those markets to the struggling partnership. An effort to use Amsterdam as a way of breaching the blockade also failed.

But the resilient sales force Madame Clicquot employed continued to fight on against the odds and sold 80,000 bottles of champagne in Russia, Northern Europe and Germany. In the face of the turbulent market conditions due to the ongoing Napoleonic Wars (1793–1815), the champagne partnership company decided to run the blockade by shipping its champagne overland to Russia. The trip was risky, expensive and time consuming, but in the end the champagne arrived safely in Russia and sold for great profit.

Her partnership company paid half the cost of outfitting a merchant ship, the *Pactole*, only to lose the investment. As the war reached its full-scale disruption of Europe, the champagne company gave up its policy of trying to get the wine to market at any cost and went into a semi-dormant period. Sales plummeted to a mere tens of thousands of bottles. In 1810 Madame Clicquot's partnership with Alexandre Fourneaux was dissolved.

Undaunted by the hostile environment, Madame Clicquot formed a new company, Veuve Clicquot-Ponsardin. When she had taken over her husband's company, it was a growing concern, the business climate was good and she had her personal desire to preserve his memory. Four years later, the environment could not have been less favourable for a business start-up. Europe was moving to the climax of the Napoleonic Wars. Whole countries had closed their frontiers. Her father-in-law was too old to help her with the new venture, apart from investing some money. She had split with her business partner. Her sales force was totally demoralized. She herself was under no illusions about the difficulties of running a business. Yet she chose to start the new company and to persevere.

That her business was ultimately successful was largely due to her own abilities. She was a good judge of character and had an instinctive feel for business. She liked to look at problems from all angles before taking decisions. She continually sought the advice of others – her loyal salesmen, people like Louis Bohne (whom her husband met on his travels and made one of his salesmen in 1801) – mostly through letters, and other regular correspondents. But once this extensive consultative period was finished, she took decisions and implemented them with resolution. Nothing would deter her from following through with her plans, and she was single-minded in pursuing her goals.

A year after starting the new company she had her sales force on the road again, including her star salesman Louis Bohne. She wrote to him: 'All my hopes are centred on you, on your enthusiasm and industry, convinced that if you cannot succeed no one can.'

His reply dashed her hopes: 'You have no idea of the misery to be found everywhere. In the Tyrol I was told I deserved to be hanged for daring to offer them a luxury item like champagne, after the damage the French had done to their country.'

When traditional markets in Holland and Belgium yielded virtually no business, Madame Clicquot sent her salesmen to Italy and Malta but could find little business there. In the whole of 1811 only 17,000 bottles of champagne were sold. The following year, while Napoleon was initiating his Russian campaign, she downsized her entire sales force, keeping only Louis Bohne full-time and salaried. She sold her champagne on a commission basis through salesmen who carried other lines as well. As the First Empire collapsed around her, she showed her determination to fight on and prevail. Rheims itself was overrun by allied forces. Although Cossacks, Prussians and Russian troops occupied her home town, Madame Clicquot's fears of having her winery sacked proved groundless as the troops were disciplined.

She and Louis Bohne decided to steal a march on rival champagne houses. Taking advantage of the chaos surrounding the ending of hostilities, she chartered a ship and sent it with 8,000 bottles of champagne to a Baltic port. She sent Louis Bohne on board the same ship with the precious cargo. An avid reader herself, she gave him a copy of *Don Quixote* to read on the voyage. He sold out the entire shipment in St Petersburg at record prices, and a few months later another entire shipment of 13,000 bottles was sold out as soon as it arrived. The sales in Russia seriously depleted Madame Clicquot's stocks. The business was on the rise.

The Russian market continued to grow exponentially until three years after her death. It was a market she dominated by sheer daring and perseverance.

Her qualities and managerial behaviour made her a role model for modern women in business. She was quick-thinking. She showed courage in taking calculated risks. She enjoyed the challenge of entrepreneurship, and had a love of adventure. In her management style she was not autocratic at a time when the divine right to manage was unchallenged. Rather, she encouraged open, two-way communication. She was a good listener. Correspondence between her and her salesmen in the field show her to be empathetic to their concerns, even to their family problems. She was also open to their ideas and suggestions, enjoying their success stories and sympathizing with their setbacks. Her enthusiasm and commitment to life-long learning built confidence among her workforce. She had the ability to anticipate events and to persuade people to do things her way.

She failed in two business ventures away from her mainline concern with the Champagne House. Both were run by Georges Kessler – the Clicquot Bank and mill investments. When they went into liquidation she honoured her obligations, but discharged them through a proxy, Edouard Werle. This left her free to stay focused on the champagne company, which demanded her energy and full commitment. It also distanced herself from events that might have hurt her business reputation.

She was kind and generous towards her rather quiet daughter, Clementine, and to Clementine's attractive and romantic husband Louis de Chevigne whose company she enjoyed. But she was always careful not to involve either of them in the champagne business.

One of the qualities required of a successful senior manager or chief executive is the ability to identify talent and to develop people, and Madame Clicquot had this competency. She recognized the managerial potential of Edouard Werle who arrived in Rheims from Germany in 1821. She gave him increasing levels of responsibility in the running of the business and, when he proved competent, kept promoting him. After twelve years in her employment she made him a partner in the business. This judgement – to give an equity stakeholding in the business (something denied to members of her family) to outsiders on the basis of merit – showed her strength of character.

La Veuve Clicquot died at age 88. Her legacy of a successful company with 650 acres of some of the finest vineyards in Champagne speaks for itself. Her motto – 'One quality . . . the finest' – still guides the company today.

The Business Woman of the Year Award

The Veuve Clicquot Business Woman of the Year Award is three decades old. Its original title reflects the ambience of 1973, the year it was first presented; it was called 'Woman in a Man's World Award'. The first winner of the award was Stella Brumell, managing director of Benford Ltd, the largest manufacturer of concrete mixing equipment in the UK. The award continued with that dubious title until 1978, when it became The Veuve Clicquot Business Woman of the Year Award. For the first nine years of the award Veuve Clicquot worked in partnership with *The Times* newspaper. 'The first editor we worked with in 1973 was Sir William Rees Mogg and the last was Harry Evans', explained Moira Collins, who conceived the idea of the award at Veuve Clicquot. The link between the award and *The Times* was broken in 1982.

Veuve Clicquot found a new partner for the award in The Institute of Directors. 'We ran it with the IOD beginning with Sir Walter Goldsmith, then Sir John Hoskyns and finally Peter Morgan', Moira Collins said. 'Since 1990 we have gone it alone and held the event at Claridges.'

What is the selection process for choosing the Veuve Clicquot Business Woman of the Year Award winner?

It starts in early autumn when Veuve Clicquot UK, from its Central London offices on St George Street, sends out by post 6,000 booklets printed in the champagne company's distinctive yellow and deep purple colours. The FTSE 100 companies are on the mailing list, as are a number of women's organizations and the wider Veuve Clicquot network of business contacts built up over the years. The attractive booklet, with the use of many photos, explains the purpose of the award, gives a little history about it, and lists the winners during the past thirty years. There is a photo of the immediate past winner and some words from her. There is a sketch of the founder Madame Clicquot. Most importantly the booklet explains how to nominate someone for the award and provides a tear-off entry form. People who nominate candidates for the award are promised a dozen magnums of Veuve Clicquot should their candidate win. They are asked to include supportive documents about her in the form of company reports and press clippings and other evidence of the candidate's worthiness.

Veuve Clicquot UK receives over a hundred nominations for Business Woman of the Year from the business community in this manner each year. The nominations arrive to be sorted in January and February.

In February or March a panel of ten, selected by Veuve Clicquot to broadly represent the business community, then meets to consider each of the nominations and to debate their merits and make a shortlist of five candidates. These five candidates receive an interview from John West, managing director of Veuve Clicquot UK, and Moira Collins, the founder and current director of the award. They spend about an hour and a half with each shortlisted candidate. It is a supportive interview in which the candidates are encouraged to tell their stories in an open manner. They may be asked questions about items concerning themselves or their businesses that the panel members wanted clarified. The shortlist of candidates for the award is then announced to the national press sometime in mid-March or early April.

Who are the panel members? Sky Business News journalists, Simon Bucks and Michael Wilson; BBC Economic Unit's Nigel Cassidy; *The Sunday Times* ex-business editor, John Jay; journalist Kirsty Hamilton; and business editor, Rory Godson. There is Dame Judith Wilcox, past chairman of the Consumers Council, who is a member of the House of Lords and pays particular attention to consumer affairs. Stephen Quinn, editor of *Vogue*, adds a bit of style to the panel. BT's Patricia Vaz, a former winner of the award, is on the panel to represent corporate business. The previous year's award winner is also invited to sit on the panel. This year it was Dianne Thompson, CEO of Camelot, who won the award for the year 2000.

The panel of ten, which is chaired by Moira Collins, then reconvenes to select the winner of the award. All the shortlisted candidates are invited to a reception at Claridges in London late in April. Here, the five candidates are presented with a bouquet of flowers and the award winner is presented with the silver trophy.

The twenty-ninth winner of the Veuve Clicquot Business Woman of the Year Award for 2001 was announced on 25 April 2002 as Barbara Cassani.

Part II
The profiles

Barbara Cassani

Barbara Cassani, CEO, Go Fly

Barbara Cassani, as CEO of Go Fly airlines since it began in 1998, has become one of the most inspirational women business leaders in Britain. She predicts that the positions of the low-cost airlines and the conventional airlines will shift irrevocably.

'Low-cost airlines are already taking the place of the conventional airlines. The transformation is underway. Take the air travel market between London and Glasgow. Low-cost airlines have gone from zero to about 50 per cent of the market. BA and British Midland have now a relatively small proportion of flights between those two cities. In the place of these conventional airlines as major contenders for that route are easyJet, Go and Ryanair.

'It is only a matter of time before the low-cost carriers become the dominant players on many domestic and European routes', she said. 'The roles of the low-cost carriers and the traditional carriers will be reversed. We will become the mainstream carriers while the traditional airlines become niche players charging a premium for additional services.

'Customers don't want to pay a lot for short trips. They don't need very much from a product standpoint. They don't want a hot towel and a glass of champagne. They just want to get there on time at a reasonable cost.

'I always knew the low-cost airline sector had potential but I thought that it would take ten years for the traditional airlines to be forced to come to grips with the reality of the new economics that drives the airline business. September 11 has caused traditional airlines to rethink their own businesses. They are a lot less profitable. Airlines like BA were making money on other parts of their network such as the North Atlantic – but they were using these to cross-subsidize loss-making routes in Europe. As a result of losing the North Atlantic profits, they have had to wake up and adjust their networks in a way that was sensible, given the fact that they have a high-cost structure.'

The extent of the damage to conventional airlines is considerable. Since the terrorist attacks and the downturn in business, airlines have grounded and mothballed unneeded aircraft. Research from Boeing suggests that two-thirds of the 2,000 jets grounded after the attack – about 1,300 planes – will not return to service, but will be scrapped at a cost of $1.3 billion.

Barbara Cassani is quick to point out that the essentials of the low-cost model are important. 'We are discounters and the more we can lower our prices the more we can grow our market, which is just the opposite of the traditional airlines. This year our capacity grew by 30 per cent. We have added 30 per cent more aircraft and so we would expect to add at least that much in revenue every year as well', she told a business conference in Belfast. She knows what she is talking about. Her low-cost airline carried 310,000 passengers to Northern Ireland from its base at Stansted in one year.

'When we do business planning within Go, the issue is can we cope internally with this level of growth and ensure that we still have our high standards on punctuality, that we are employing good people, training people satisfactorily, and that we are running a safe and secure airline', she said.

The dynamic 41-year-old Italian-Irish American executive heads an exciting new venture. The management buy-out is now the nation's third largest low-cost airline behind Ryanair and easyJet.

She has been with the project from its start under the protective umbrella of British Airways. She expected losses in its first two years. But the extent of the start-up losses did frighten her – £20 million in the red for year one and the same for year two. But against all expectations Go posted a £4.2 million profit in year three and is on course for profit in the current year four of its existence.

She has led the fastest airline start-up in Europe and has reasons to be optimistic. During the six months to 30 September 2001, passenger numbers for Go soared to 2.1 million, up 41 per cent on the same period the year before. Barbara Cassani has expanded her staff from 750 to 900, opening up new routes for Go and buying more jets – either 737s from Boeing, to add to the 18 it already has in its fleet, or switching to the rival Airbus. She makes sure her pilots can fly every type of plane Go has.

She had already won the Entrepreneur of the Year Award before winning the Veuve Clicquot Business Woman of the Year Award for 2001, announced in April 2002.

Writing in the *Sunday Herald*, Kenny Kemp said: 'Her mix of hard-edged good sense, a genuine compassion for her people and a forensic appreciation of the fickleness of the flying public is a balance rarely achieved in the UK. Frankly, Britain needs a 737-400 series load more of her ilk.'[1]

[1] 'High hopes and will of iron as Go's Barbara Cassani basks in the success of the low-budget airline', 9 December 2001.

Under British Airways' umbrella

She built her low-cost airline from a solid base of its three-year history under its former parent company and her former employer British Airways. After ten years as a senior manager with British Airways, Barbara Cassani was ready to move on to another challenging job. The headhunters were already approaching her. She herself was looking to companies that needed someone to start up a new business for them.

Then Bob Ayling, the chief executive of BA at the time, gave her every reason to stay with BA. As Barbara Cassani recalled, 'Bob Ayling and Charles Gurassa, now chief executive of the Thompson Group, approached me and asked me if I had a minute. I said: "For you two I have an hour." We sat down and they said, "We were wondering if you would like to set out a business plan to see if BA should set up a low-cost airline?"'

At the time she was general manager for BA in the US, based in New York City. Conveniently the bank her husband was working for was also headquartered in New York.

Mindful of the axiom 'Be careful, you might get what you ask for', she seemed to have found a perfect answer to what she had been looking for. 'It came at the right moment. I had a consultancy background and knew how to set up a business plan. I understood the airline business. They knew that they could trust me to give them a straight story. I would have told them if it were a dumb idea. I wouldn't have cooked the books to make it work. I would not want to waste my time on something I knew would be unsuccessful.'

Barbara Cassani left her family in New York and began to commute on the Concorde back and forth to London. She was aware of the irony of doing a business plan for a low-cost airline whilst commuting on the world's most expensive supersonic jet. The project of writing a business plan took her from April to November 1997, but by August she knew it was going to go forward and relocated her family back in London. She won the £25 million from BA needed to launch the new airline.

'After a couple of months I established that there was a hole in the market and room for a low-cost airline that I had in mind. I envisioned one where you offered low fares but still provided good service, like a cup of good coffee that the customer is willing to pay for. We crafted every bit of the airline and there was sweat all over the place', Barbara Cassani recalled. 'I wanted to take away the best from a role model airline like Southwest Airlines and add my own ideas. Southwest Airlines managed to please the customers by offering a friendly service. They have a robust operation with super punctuality. Southwest does not lose bags. They have a brilliant safety record and are super in terms of profitability. Moreover, they have a wonderful relationship with their people as an employer. That's success!

'Success is going home at night knowing that people are managed in a way that is consistent with your value set. Knowing that meeting the customers' requirements is our first priority, not creating a bigger office or doing something purely political like having drinks with the Prime Minister. That's not what we're here for. We're here to transport people safely, really cheaply and with a genuine smile.'

The first flight was in May 1998. She complained that easyJet tried to get a court injunction to stop the flight; but they failed to get the order. Someone sent ten people in orange boiler suits to sit in the back of the airplane to disrupt the flight.

Go provoked controversy among the other low-cost airlines who cried 'foul', attacking BA's sponsorship of the airline as unfair to competition. They objected to BA's logistical as well as financial support for Go, which meant the start-up airline could draw on BA's massive fleet if it ran into problems with its own jets and schedules.

Management buy-out

Then in June 2001 Rod Eddington, the new chief executive of BA, decided that the low-cost airline did not fit in with BA's core business. (It was internal competition; it blurred the BA brand, and was a distraction for management.) He decided to sell Go to venture capitalists. Reasoning that any venture capitalists would want to keep the management team in place, Barbara Cassani spoke to her employees at Go about a management buy-out. She constructed a £110 million buy-out deal that BA accepted. Partners in the deal were venture capitalists 3i (66.3 per cent), Barclay Capital (11.2 per cent) and the executives and employees (22.5 per cent). She was one of the few Go executives to have made money from the sale with a 4 per cent stakeholding in the business, making her a paper millionaire. She felt uneasy about it. 'To be honest, it was a moral question. So I wanted to show my commitment and I put nearly all that money back into the airline', she said.

Growing the business is, of course, her intention. But she insists on wise decision-making as to where and how to grow the business. She strengthened her management team at all levels, starting at the top. She was pleased to have Keith Hamill as chairman of her board, comfortable with his experiences as financial director at WH Smith and Forte Hotels. She secured Paul Sterbenz, a retired vice-president from Southwest Airlines, as a non-executive director. 'He wrote a great letter about two years ago offering to help. And when I was looking for someone with a strategic brain who knew the airline business, his name came up. He agreed to take it on and he and his wife flew our network, reporting on what they saw with fresh eyes.'

She runs her airline from Enterprise House at Stansted Airport. Her executive office is a smallish room, just off the operational offices. She is often not there. Not far from her offices is a room where Go pilots stop to get coffee and a sandwich before their flights. The offices have a family atmosphere – there are no class boundaries between staff and management.

Under her direction Go has set up a Bristol hub and a third base in the East Midlands, a catchment area with 6 million potential customers for its low-cost flights. Initially it will fly to six destinations from the East Midlands airport. 'We are trying to make up our minds where our growth should be for the next year – should we be adding to the routes where the big guys have exited or should we be going to new places and finding the right blend of new growth on existing routes. In Northern Ireland, the biggest opportunity we have is to make what we have work well.'

The strategic plan is to double the size of the company every couple of years – something not possible under BA's umbrella – and to float the company within a few years. Expectations are that such a flotation would be at least as successful as easyJet's which raised £750 million in 2001.

Barbara Cassani is quick to talk about turnround times of each aircraft, cut to about 25 minutes, and 'sweating the assets' of her planes, expecting a 30 per cent return in 2002. She sees her airline as part of a move towards low-cost everything. She puts Go in the same league as other discounters such as Wal-Mart – where driving costs down is the main priority. She insists on maintaining the highest standards for safety and punctuality, while driving out all the other unnecessary costs.

'When I was at BA we were always looking at how we could charge more for a premium service. Now at Go we are looking at how we can keep the costs down. It is the customer who dictates our success and we need to attract them with lower fares.

'BA offers cheap deals on 750,000 seats a year, just 3 per cent of capacity. BA cannot afford more because its costs are so high', she said.

At Go everything is geared to efficiency. The low-cost airline, like its rivals, sells seats cheaply but requires very high load factors, flexibility and fierce competition. Giving the customer a no-frills, low-cost option means that they pay for all the extras, including a cup of Costa coffee. 'There's one thing I would like to take credit for – our good coffee on board. I cannot take full responsibility for the name [the name 'Go' was created by a joint team from Wolff Olins and HHCL, but they also suggested 'Bus', which she vetoed], for the advertising, for the uniform – for anything except the coffee. For me the essence of this airline is that if you're going to charge someone £1.50 for a cup of coffee you can't give them some crummy instant coffee. We can't afford to give it to you free, but if I'm going to charge you, I'm going to give you nice cafetière coffee', she said.

One cost she is attacking constantly is the landing fees that airports charge. She feels that it is unfair that one company such as BAA can control 85 per cent of the UK's airports. European airports have the same responsibilities to provide fire services, security and safety as UK airports; and yet their costs are lower.

Family background and education

Barbara Cassani was born on 22 July 1960, in Boston, Massachusetts to a salesman, Italian-American father and an Irish mother. She was the youngest of three children. They were not poor, but also not well off.

She inherits her business drive from her father who trained as a bacteriologist before setting off on a career selling lab equipment. Her 'gift of the gab' comes from her mother, whom she describes as 'an unembarrassed Irish American, who can talk to anyone'. The family moved around a lot with her father's work – Boston, San Francisco, the Midwest, New Hampshire. Between ages 14 and 18 Barbara Cassani went to three different high schools.

The children's education was very important to the family. They were told that they were responsible for their own future. She had a double dose of the immigrant work ethic. She was her father's girl in that her relationship with him is 'really, really strong'. At 74 he is still working three days a week. He checks the Go website to see how his daughter is doing. 'The first thing my dad asks me when we speak on the phone every week is: "how's sales?" When I got into sales with BA, I knew I was my father's daughter.'

She worked to earn spending money. 'I worked in Burger King, in a card shop, as a waitress. I did all sorts of things, babysitting, cleaning people's houses – for no other reason than expediency, and that I needed money. I had a great love of horse-riding and it's a very expensive sport.' Her parents thought she'd grow out of the riding at 16, when she discovered boys, but it did not happen.

She learned customer service the hard way as a waitress in a restaurant, a car hop in a fast-food place. 'I wasn't a great waitress. But what I worked out early on was that if I was super-friendly to customers I could get away with it – and I got great tips.'

She claims to have had many 'customer service recovery moments' because of her clumsiness. On one occasion she tipped a tray of milkshakes through the window of a brand-new pickup truck onto the lap of the new owner. Another time she lost a tray of lobster dinners when she stumbled at a table and sent the lot into the sea in front of the stunned diners.

She was expected to do well and did. She graduated from Mount Holyoke College in Massachusetts with a BA *magna cum laude* honours degree in International Relations. She is now a trustee of Mount Holyoke College. 'I didn't choose it because it was an all-women's college, but because it was a very good school for my undergraduate work. I enjoyed myself at college. Intellectually I just exploded. My parents paid my tuition and board throughout college and I paid my expenses. It was quite a lot of money for me to raise, so I did a wide assortment of jobs.'

She won a scholarship to Princeton University, Woodrow Wilson School, New Jersey, where she earned a Masters in Public and International Affairs.

'I just followed my heart instead of being career-minded. I thought international affairs would be interesting – and besides, Princeton paid for everything for which I was grateful.' She met her British-born husband at Princeton where he was studying economics. 'He had two degrees from Oxford and was supposed to be working on his Ph.D. when we met,' she recalled.

In the summers between the two years of her graduate studies at Princeton she worked in the economics section of the United States Embassy in Stockholm. 'I had a really good time there, but realized I was not part of that world. I didn't have the personality for the diplomatic corps. I was too action-oriented, too impatient, too forward. I wasn't into protocol enough. It was too slow moving.'

Work experience

She has translated her own work experiences at the sharp end of customer service into clear expectation from her staff in the new airline. She believes passionately in serving the customer and demands the same commitment to service from others.

Her first proper job after university was as a management consultant, and then as a senior consultant with Coopers & Lybrand in Washington DC from 1984 to 1987. The consultancy firm was filled with sharp, young MBAs who made up with brashness for their lack of business experience. She fitted in nicely. Personally she had her doubts. 'I was doing something described as international business, yet I had never lived or worked abroad (apart from summer jobs in Stockholm).' She and her husband decided to return to his native UK. She tried to arrange a transfer with Coopers & Lybrand to the London office, but the US branch of the company baulked at it, not wanting to pay her moving costs, she felt. So she had to join the firm afresh in London. It was a different company in London from the US firm, with much older consultants who based their advice on ten to twenty years' experience. She stayed with it for just a year. Ultimately she was not happy with management consultancy as a career. 'Too much observing; not enough doing. You tell people what you think they should do and then you leave', she said. 'You write reports, you analyse problems and make recommendations and in 80 per cent of the cases sadly nothing happens. Either your report was written for political purposes or there was a problem of implementation.'

She decided she wanted to work in a company. 'I was so arrogant, I had great ideas that needed a real company for testing. I wanted to work somewhere I could figure out what needed to be changed and then implement the change.' She answered an obscure wanted ad in the *Sunday Times* from a company looking for a strategic marketing person with imagination. 'It read: "do you want to be a marketing challenger in a global service business?" And I said, "Yes, please!" I thought it was a bank, because it was at the time of the Big Bang in the financial sector. You could have knocked me over when I found out after my third interview that it was British Airways.'

She got the job in 1987 just as BA was privatized and stayed ten years. She had a series of jobs, first as internal consultant and then as project leader in Distribution (1987–88). She insisted on a real job in line management and got it. She was made General Manager, Market Development (1988–89), UK Corporate Sales Manager (1989–92), General Manager, Sales and Marketing, Gatwick (1992–93) and General Manager USA (1993–97). Once she got into BA she realized that it had many 'rubic cube-type business problems' that fascinated her. She introduced systems of measurement wherever she could. One group did not understand the cost of sale because they were not measuring it. The organization was just awakening to its new life as a public company instead of a government-sponsored industry. She came into her own when she had people to manage, sales targets to reach, deals to be cut with corporate clients and the travel agencies. During the decade as a BA manager she discovered that she really enjoyed managing people and that she loved being accountable for her part of the business. It was excellent preparation for the future.

She has been CEO of Go Fly Ltd since its start-up in 1997 till the present. Go's strategy, brand and business model were founded and developed by Barbara Cassani. Today she draws on her four-year experience with Go and her decade with BA in strategy, sales and marketing and general management to lead the low-cost airline into its second year as a management buy-out. Since the buy-out in June 2001 the company has gone from strength to strength, posting record passenger numbers and profits. One of its goals is punctuality, something not necessarily associated with budget airlines. In November 2001 Go was one of the most punctual airlines in the UK: 85 per cent of Go's flights took off on time.

Management style

Barbara Cassani takes an immediate and personal view of her low-cost airline. She believes in team working. It was on that basis that she constructed the management buy-out knowing that venture capitalists would need a management team in place to secure the airline's future. She had already spent three years building the management team. 'I felt from the beginning this is our company. It's the people that have created it. We have always had a very strong, independent, tough mentality. We are such a different place to BA. We had a baptism of fire that made us resilient and committed and convinced that we were right.'

Instead of standing by and watching BA sell Go to another airline, which would have 'devastated' her, Barbara Cassani thought why not turn the tables and have her management team find their own venture capitalists and do a management buy-out? It was an audacious move, a costly one at £110 million, one of the most expensive investments 3i had made. It showed her faith in her own team, which was reciprocal, and the venture capitalists' faith in Barbara Cassani and her management team.

A former colleague at BA summed up her management style in these words: 'She had a critical quality to be a manager. She was brave. She was ready to say what she thought and not just to blow with the wind. She is not touchy-feely, but she is very good with staff. She motivates, she is straight, she tells them what is what and they love her.'[2]

Bob Ayling first noticed her talent on a BA management course when he was human resources director: 'She impressed me because of her energy, her strong intelligence, her motivational skills and her ambition', he said. 'She thinks about things deeply but is very upfront and has no fear of telling you what's what. It's immensely refreshing.' Much later, when she told him she was thinking about leaving BA to run her own business, he created the blue-sky project and asked her to run it with the aim to start up a low-cost airline within BA. He met her ambition with a challenge, a six-month deadline and a £25 million budget. But she is the first to admit that Go is not entirely her own creation.

She believes in sharing the credit. Early on she said, 'The Go brand is not just me, I would say it was David Magliano's personality (he's the marketing director) and Ed's in operations and John's, who's our chief pilot. We're all very straightforward people. You wouldn't make it in Go if you had airs. You wouldn't make it in Go without a sense of humour. You wouldn't make it in Go if you weren't absolutely driven to do the best job you can.

'People say "Are you always going to be in the airline business?" and I say "Absolutely not" – but I think the customer-facing thing is now engrained in me. I enjoy it because if I ever have a bad day, with the paperwork and all the guff of being a CEO, I go to the check-in or I get on a plane or I go to the call centre. And as soon as I spend time with the people who deliver our service, or the customers, I feel rejuvenated and can come back to anything.'

'I think there are a lot of really crummy managers out there and the way they manage is through fear and obfuscation', says Cassani. 'That's dumb. If your role is leader then you should try to simplify things and help other people understand things when they are complicated.'[3]

She is strong in her beliefs about employee recognition. It is part of the job she most enjoys. She gave each member of staff a Go watch to thank them for excellent service. She presents Go badges as signs of extraordinary customer service. She encourages the 'Go-mad (go make a difference)'

[2] Kevin Done, 'Go may be ready for take-off after £100m management buy-out', *Financial Times*, 16 June 2001.

[3] Andrew Davidson, 'Barbara Cassani: interview with Go's chief executive', *Management Today*, 1 August 1999.

peer group awards her line managers alone hand out to staff for extra efforts. She sends each of her 900 staff a special Go birthday card on the day. Each staff member has £50 spent on him or her each year as a recognition award. The team may go out for a Chinese dinner or to an amusement park. Or the award can be very individual, as when one person was given a ticket to a Sting concert because she was a fan.

Barbara Cassani is open to employee suggestions. Everyone has access to her e-mail address and to her mobile phone number. Her office is open to all the staff. Each week she tries to do a round-up audiotape to communicate Go's most important events to the employees who dial in for the report. She sees to it that other reports of the key new events of the company, and indicators like punctuality and messages from its personnel, are available on Go TV, a power-point presentation accessed by computers. 'Out of the 900 staff, about 700 hundred of them are not working here. They pop in for a while and then are gone. The sky is their workplace. We have to keep that in mind when we try to keep them in touch with the key indicators of the business,' she explained.

Every six months staff views are solicited formally through an employee survey in which everyone is asked for his or her views on how well they are being managed.

Her most favourite outside management activity is direct contact with the passengers on Go flights. 'The part of my job that I really enjoy is going on the aircraft and walking up and down the aisle talking to the customers. I love it. You have no idea what you're going to get – you get it all. You get compliments, criticisms, irrational comments, and people who are trying to pitch a business idea to you.'

Dealing with the media

In an interview for *Bloomberg News*, Guy Collins probed Barbara Cassani on Go's future.

GUY COLLINS: I want to look at profit outlook and also prospects of flotation. You lost £15 million in the year ending in March 2000. What's your more recent performance? What's the outlook and are you going to float?

BARBARA CASSANI: Well I have a big grin on my face because we've just had our first profits announced. In the year that ends 31 March 2001 we made over £4 million pre-tax profits, and that was despite the fuel prices and the dollar, which were horrendous. So we've now got a business that has an underlying profitable base to it. We had £159 million in revenues and since then the company has grown 20–30 per cent already. So we are expecting significant growth, both on the top line, and also in the profits for the year that we're in now.

GUY COLLINS: And the flotation prospect?

BARBARA CASSANI: Well, as you would imagine, as somebody who's exhausted from the strains of an MBO [management buy-out], I'm not making precise predictions, but both 3i and ourselves are very hopeful that we'll do it in the next couple of years.[4]

The flotation issue is still very much alive and something everyone at Go is working towards, as it raises the service bar in delivering to its customers. Already the airline is excelling in its use of the Internet for bookings. An independent website performance study by Qualiope in April 2001 ranked Go first for speed and first for availability among the low-cost airlines. This performance was validated by customer satisfaction ratings: in a May 2001 survey conducted by NOP of 15,905 online users, 94 per cent of UK respondents would recommend Go to a friend; 86 per cent rated the site as good or excellent and 94 per cent would book a Go flight online in the future.

Risk-taking

When Barbara Cassani was putting together the venture capital that would give her the £110 million she needed to buy the airline from British Airways, her two rivals in the low-cost airline business were pouring scorn on her Go airlines. Ryanair's chief executive Michael O'Leary cheered BA's decision to sell Go. 'This is a dog, it's a chronic loss maker. If it gets sold, it will not get sold for very much. I don't think Go could ever make money in its present form', he said.

Stelios Haji-Ioannou, founder and former chairman of easyJet, was just as disdainful of Go's prospects. He ran a competition on easyJet's website to guess the size of Go's losses. Earlier he had attacked the airline in the High Court when it was owned by British Airways, claiming that BA's cross-subsidization of Go was illegal, a case filed in January 1998.

'What is interesting is that most legal actions that were brought against Go have been dropped. One that was taken to the European Commission was easyJet's, which said "their prices on Edinburgh are too low, they must be pricing below cost. It will harm our business and therefore it will hurt competition." And they dropped it a few months later when they said "Ahem, actually we're doing fine." '

Personal meaning of success

'For me success is about feeling useful and doing things that make a difference. At home it could be having a discussion with my daughter about the piano test she has coming up, and encouraging her and challenging her. In the business it's coming into work every morning and saying "Right,

[4] From an unofficial transcript, *Bloomberg News*, 18 June 2001 (11:45 a.m. eastern time).

what are all the problems, what are all the opportunities? Are we lined up in the right direction?"

'I spend my time trying to move forward on my little goal posts. I don't look too far in advance. I cannot tell you what I'll be doing in ten years' time. I have no idea and I really don't care. Do you jump out of bed or do you roll over and go uggh? These days I leap out of bed. But if I roll over I'll have to change something in my life.'

Work/life balance

She is married to investment banker Guy Davis and they live in Barnes, south-west London, with their two children, a 9-year-old girl and a 6-year-old boy. 'Look, my whole being is not wrapped up in Go. I am a mother, a daughter. I am someone who likes to read and to horse-ride', she says. She admits to preferring modern fiction and biographies of US presidents. She's reading about Adams now. She enjoys eventing.

'Having a supportive husband is half the battle. At the end of the day the kids have a special relationship with the mother and that adds pressure for me. But that's life and it's a good thing. But it is pressure and if you have additional pressure from a partner who isn't supportive of the balancing act you're trying to do, it will tip you over.

'My husband has known me since I was 21 or 22. He knows what I'm like. He knows I'm oriented toward the outside world. That's why he likes me. We're best friends and we've always been that way. You'd never hold your best friend back. That's just the way we work it out. Sure we have our ups and downs.

'People ask me, "What would you do if your children were really ill?" I'd quit. Bingo! My work is still my work and my family is my family. It's all about priorities. People who manage the best are those who have made explicit choices with themselves and their partners. The people who have the most trouble are those who are kidding themselves. I actually think it goes for men as well. A lot of the benefits of the so-called women's movement have been to give men the ability to make choices as well. Not everyone is cut out to run businesses or to be career-minded. Some people are just better at having equally strong influences balanced in their lives. I'm not a feminist. I'm a humanist.'

She likes to breakfast with her husband before setting off for Stansted Airport. Sometimes she drives herself in her car. Sometimes she gets a ride. Sometimes she takes a combination of London tube and rail. It depends on her schedule. She tries to be home before 8 p.m. in time to read her children a bedtime story. She hurried home from her £110 million management buy-out deal to play Monopoly with her children, rather than celebrate with friends. She felt guilty at having been away from them too much during the excessive time it took to put the complicated deal together.

'I'm not going to throw myself in front of the press and say: "Aren't I wonderful. I'm a mother and have a really high-profile job." I've got the wherewithal to make money smooth my path; the women who are really amazing are those who make £20,000 a year, have two kids in school and a husband who works shifts.

'We're lucky we both have the money to hire extremely qualified, intelligent women to work in our house with our kids and us. (We're usually home together. If one of us has to go off, the other is usually there.) We always treat them with respect when they are with us and we stay in touch with them when they eventually leave us. They're great. I'm going to help one of them open her own business in Colchester in two weeks' time. She's taken over her parents' curtain business. She came to us when she was 19 and stayed for two years. She went off to university and got a degree and now she is a small business person.

'You know better than anyone else when that balance has got out of whack. You just listen to that little voice and you fix it. If you ignore the little voice, that's when trouble starts.

'I'm happy to be a sounding board on what are important issues the government should be dealing with, but I'm not putting my name out there. I'd rather spend time here at work or at home with my kids.'

When she took three months off to have her first child – her daughter – in 1992 she told BA: '"I don't want to come back and do the job I did. I loved it, but I'll be back in three months to do whatever's available." This was considered risky from a career perspective, but if there'd been nothing good to do, I'd have gone to something else somewhere else. Both of my children boast of travelling Concorde – while in their mummy's tummy.

'I try to leave the office by 6.30 p.m., to get home in time to tuck in the kids. I do have to take work home at weekends: I go through my in-tray on Sunday afternoons to prepare for the week. I'm always connected to bleepers, phones and faxes. I'm fully functioning online all the time. But I relax by reading and riding and I take all my holiday, which I spend with the children. That's when I really unwind.'

Ethical issues

What was her role in the BA marketing scams that Virgin Atlantic exposed and won damages for? (A BA sales team in 1990 analysed rivals' confidential booking information hacked off the reservation system, run by BA, that other airlines fed into. BA used the data to try and poach customers away from rivals. As a middle manager she became enmeshed in the BA–Virgin Atlantic dirty tricks affair in the early 1990s in a minor way.) 'The statistics were being gained completely illegally, yes, completely, but I had no idea at the time they were being collected. If I had known that they were being collected illegally I would have stopped the activity immediately. You do the best you can and when you find out that something is being done improperly you just stop it.'

Gender issues

Despite her title, CEO, she sees herself as 'one of the people'. She doesn't make a point of championing women in business; but she is annoyed by the British press's ambivalence towards successful women managers. 'There is a moral judgement underlining some of the press commentary which I find distasteful, because I have spent my whole life accepting people as they come and not being prescriptive about the way other people lead their lives.

'I don't remember experiencing gender barriers. If there were any, I didn't recognize them. I haven't ever encountered anything I would count as a gender barrier. I have always worked hard to be judged by my results. I have never given excuses, trying to manipulate people with my feminine wiles.

'I'm just a person trying to achieve things that I said I'd do. I try to be a very honourable businessperson, and fortunately that has met with success. Some women look for barriers, and if you look for them you'll find them. Others have been really and truly dealt with illegally and unfairly and that has to be addressed as well.

'But for your average woman, my advice would be to ignore it, just plough right over it. Whatever it is try to deal with the situation at hand as opposed to creating a geo-political issue around it.'

Winning the Veuve Clicquot Award

'I am thrilled to accept this award on behalf of everyone at Go. We have worked hard to build a European airline that blends professionalism and profits with friendliness. I also had the pleasure of meeting the other finalists of the awards and they impressed me tremendously. It is an even bigger honour having met them.'

Dianne Thompson

Dianne Thompson, CEO, Camelot

In March 2002 Dianne Thompson, CEO, announced a total revamp of Camelot's image. The £72 million re-launch of the national lottery saw a change to Camelot's logo and the introduction of new lotteries and games, as well as a special Golden Jubilee jackpot. It is the first big overhaul since the lottery began in 1994, and includes the replacement of all the terminals in Britain's retail outlets, bold new advertising campaigns and new directions in its marketing and promotion. Dianne Thompson was willing to change everything – the crossed-fingers logo, the slogan: 'It could be you!', the lottery game list – except the name of her organization, Camelot. 'There is a great deal of goodwill associated with the Camelot name', she said. 'We are seen as having integrity and being efficient.'

Camelot's crossed-fingered logo has been replaced with the stylized figure of a person reaching for a star, together with the tag line: 'Camelot – serving the nation's dreams.'

Typically of her leadership style, Dianne Thompson meets problems head on. 'The reason we want a new logo is ultimately to draw a line in the sand from the days of the fat cats', she said, referring to a period before she took over as chief executive, when high executive salaries were a matter of public criticism and ridicule. 'Everything about us has changed and the logo was the final brick. It is simple and unfussy, and signifies us striving to get better, reaching for the stars, which is what we are trying to do.'

Background and early education

Dianne Thompson is a northern woman with working-class roots. Her father was a butcher's delivery boy in Yorkshire who graduated from working with local shops to managing the region for the Co-op. His wife had a similar retail background and worked in a shoe shop as a fitting specialist. After serving in the Second World War, in the Wrens, her mother married her father in 1949. They had their first and only child – Dianne – in 1950. In answer to her own question of why she had no brothers or sisters, her mother said it was to give her something they hadn't had – opportunity. Those words stuck with the talented, but shy, 9-year-old.

'There was this weight on my slender shoulders. It meant that I had to make their sacrifice worth while. That's where this drive came from', she said. She went to grammar school and achieved O-levels and A-levels, which was further than her parents had gone. (Her father had to turn down a grammar school scholarship to work to support his own family.)

Typical of the northern families of that time, her mother did not drive a car and did the cooking and housework in addition to her job at the shoe shop. She travelled to London only twice. Her husband declined a much better job than the one he had because it was seven miles away from their home. 'Northerners in those days just didn't travel.'

Because they both worked in the retail trade, they took their time off – a half-day – on Tuesday. They spent the early part of Tuesday afternoon jointly doing household chores and then usually arrived at the school gates to collect Dianne for a ride in the country. She had a very happy childhood in a stable, old-fashioned family.

'My parents were very happy. We didn't have much, but we had a lot of love and a lot of encouragement', she remembered.

University education and early career

She went on to university to study French and English. 'I had no idea what I wanted to do except that I did not want to teach', she said. 'I fell into marketing by accident. In those days Manchester Business School and the University and what is now Manchester Metropolitan shared a career counselling service. My career adviser had been a product manager in marketing at CWS. She said she thought I'd be great in marketing, but I didn't have a clue about it.'

Dianne bought a handbook on marketing that also told the story of the Rochdale Pioneers and the history of the Co-op. She went for an interview with the Co-op. When they asked her about marketing she gave the definitions from the handbook, and when they questioned her about the Co-op she told them all she knew from the potted history she had read. She got the job.

Six weeks later she married a local lad whose father had also been a butcher, whose mother didn't drive a car and had never been to London. He mirrored her background perfectly and like her was on a four-year course at her university. She changed her maiden name, Wood, to her husband's name, Thompson. In her first job, she felt strange. 'To pick up the phone and say "Dianne Thompson" sounded so arrogant – fancy picking up the phone and saying your own name – I really could not do that at first – it took ages. My success has either brought out something that was latent deep inside me or I had to become what I am today to cope with it. I'm not sure', she admitted.

The Co-op was her first full-time job, but she had worked from an early age – 12 onwards – first in a local biscuit factory on Saturdays and during the summer months, and later in a pharmaceutical company called Lloyds that made Bonjela for gums and an adrenaline cream for strained muscles. The company also bottled and exported oxblood to African countries. 'By the end of the day you stood ankle deep in the oxblood spilt from filling up the bottles, and in the summer heat it went off and the stench was horrendous', she recalled.

While a student at the Manchester Metropolitan, she worked in the summers at a family hotel in Blackpool. The hotel could have taught the airlines all about overbooking. When the crunch came, the hotel staff had to give up their rooms to the overbooked guests. 'I slept in the back of a hatchback in the garage for two weeks', she remembered.

'My role models were my parents and it was just the normal thing that you worked.'

Were her parents proud of her achievements? Her father, at 75, is aware of her position and recently went to see her receive an honorary doctorate from Manchester Metropolitan. Her mother, who died of breast cancer at age 58, saw only glimmers of her daughter's success.

'She came to London from Batley for a day once when I had to run a stand at the Ideal Home Exhibition at Olympia for ICI – my second job. I was marketing a new product – a wallpaper – and we had a fashion show with models wearing the stuff . . . my mum was so proud of her daughter running this huge display stand telling these models what to do and she thought that I had made it big time.'

The big time was still years away. ICI wanted to fast track Dianne and other women managers to get more senior women managers and some women on their board. The plan developed by external consultants was for Dianne to leave marketing and to acquire line experience across ICI.

Academic career

They wanted to transfer her to ICI Organics. She wanted to stay marketing consumer products. Her husband was a research associate at Manchester University doing his third degree, an MA in econometrics. She jumped out of ICI to take on an academic job at Manchester Metropolitan as a lecturer in marketing. What started as a stop-gap job ended as a seven-year stint. 'You do learn by teaching', Dianne admitted. She learned volumes from what she had to read to bring herself up to speed, and from her sandwich-year students returning from jobs for their fourth and final year. She also learned from the consultancy assignments she undertook in her field and from joint ventures in developing a retail marketing degree programme with partners like the House of Fraser. 'Later in life when I came to Woolworths as Director of Marketing, two of the people I inherited in my team were people who had gone through my degree programme, so I got double benefit from the academic work I had done.'

She also started an ad agency while she was at Manchester Metropolitan called Thompson, Maud, Jones (TMJ), which is still trading today in Manchester. She correctly describes this period in her life as one of 'plate spinning'. In addition to being a full-time marketing lecturer with teaching and administration and research commitments, she was running the ad agency, doing other private consultancy assignments, working as an Open University tutor, helping as a consultant to a technology centre in Manchester designed to assist with business start-ups, and studying for the Institute of Marketing diploma. She liked the idea of having her life programmed very much in advance, and she shared the minding of their first child – a daughter – with her husband. 'It was the pressure of two commercial jobs that caused our marriage to fail – that and all the travelling I was doing. When I was MD of the UK part of a Swedish steel company, which involved a lot of travel, the marriage failed. Our daughter was 7 at the time.'

The ad business was so successful for her and her partners that a moment of truth came. As anticipated, it needed a full-time managing director, a post she had planned to take on when the time was right. But when that decision point arrived, she backed out and sold her interest in the business to her other partners. It was simply no longer challenging. She also decided to leave her academic job.

Real world marketing manager

While attending a DIY Week awards lunch, she met an ex-student of hers who said that Sterling Roncraft, makers of Ronseal, were looking for a marketing director based at their headquarters in Barnsley, Yorkshire – her home county. She phoned the MD and put her name forward for the job. She had to be vetted by a headhunter agency, but won the job. The previous marketing director had become MD of the company, but he still found time to interfere with her work, until she told him to let her get on with it or she would leave.

He stayed out of her way and she put together a new approach to marketing the existing line of products. She took the products away from the wood-care side of the business towards the high fashion side, re-branding them as decorative products rather than protective finishes. By also developing a line of light washes for wood – just when everyone was into restoring the wood in their houses and making it fresher and more beautiful – she captured massive market share from her competitor Cuprinol and created high visibility for herself. She went to America and sold her marketing ideas to her company's American owners.

The project was one of those solo activities that are becoming increasingly rare in organizations where team efforts prevail. She enjoyed the praise received for the resounding success of the work. She submitted the project to the Institute of Marketing, and it was accepted as the final piece of work she needed for her diploma.

After over two years with the company it became subject to a hostile takeover bid and under that duress was sold to Eastman Kodak. She was the last board member to leave the company, declining the offer to become MD. Instead she took up an MD position with Sandvik, the Swedish steel company, a fresh challenge as their first woman MD in an industry usually called a 'man's world'. It was a Swedish special steel company that manufactured steel to a British formula, but at mills in Sweden.

She stayed at the company for six years. She left it to limit the excessive travel she had been doing and, as her marriage collapsed, to focus on her 7-year-old daughter. The work/home balance had gone wrong with disastrous personal consequences. Her husband left her.

Helping Woolworths out of a crisis

Woolworths were in trouble and desperately needed an advertising and promotions controller. At first she felt that it was a step backwards in her career – to return to a functional job. But as Woolworths pointed out, she was leaving a company with only a few hundred UK employees to head up a function with over 40,000 employees. 'I took the job because there was no travelling. But also because I knew it was a job I could do; I had been doing that sort of marketing work nearly all my career. Although it was hard work with long hours and a lot to do, it was something I could handle. When we achieved great results it helped me regain my self-confidence as an individual. After I got back on track – a year to eighteen months later – Woolworths' directors gave me more things to do. They were very supportive. I became responsible for the Cultural Change Programme at Woolies, and the new store format development and all sorts of other things. I was promoted to Director of Marketing', she recalled.

Although Woolworths wanted to keep her, she needed to be back on a main board again, as she had been for five years previously. 'The chairman, Geoff Mulcahy, offered me two jobs – one as marketing director at Superdrug which would have had me reporting on the Superdrug Board, but the job was in Croydon', she explained. ' It was just too far to commute. I had promised my daughter when we moved south that we wouldn't move again until she finished her A-levels. I kept my promise. We are still in the house that we moved to in July '92, despite the fact that I have changed companies three times in that period.' The other job was marketing director of B&Q, which was based in Winchester – also too far for commuting and therefore impossible to take.

Crisis management in jewellery

Headhunters came along with other job offers: the MD job for Hilton National and the marketing director post at Signet, formerly Ratners, the global jewellers still in turmoil after Gerald Ratner's infamous speech.

She took the jewellery store challenge, but it proved impossible to salvage the Ratner brand. 'Out of 670 shops it was possible to save fewer than seventy. Part of the problem was the Signet Group's strategy of lining up their differently branded jewellery shops in a row: Ratners, H. Samuels, Ernest Jones and Leslie Davis', she explained. 'To convert the Ratner shop to one of the other names was nearly impossible, as it was already next door.'

Closing the shops was a brutal business she would rather forget. Staff were told in the morning and immediately escorted to collect their personal belongings and out of the door. With the staff gone, a hit squad arrived to clear the shop and close it. She is critical of Gerald Ratner for his millionaire lifestyle – a gym in his offices in Stratton Street, a personal helicopter at his beck and call – while working conditions at the company's factories in Birmingham were squalid. 'He may have been charismatic and very good at doing the talking,' she concluded, 'but he took too much cash out of the business and didn't reinvest enough.

'He also thought he was invincible when it came to the press. That's one lesson I have been careful to learn. It would have been very easy in the second half of last year to believe that I too was invincible, because the press were my friends. The day I came out of court after the judicial review victory it would have been easy to start believing that they will always be your friend. But if you look at the *Daily Mirror* four months later – four days after photos of me in the press as the winner of the Veuve Clicquot Business Woman of the Year Award – I'm pictured on the front page as "Miss Scrooge".'

The move to Camelot

After two and a half years at Signet, Dianne was ready to leave. She had done all she could there. As she puts it: 'I had new store formats for all the chains, closed Ratners, put in a new buying policy, installed a new product policy. All that was working well. I hired a new ad agency. The business was rebuilding itself. When I left six months later the company made profits of £27 million; last year [2000] profits were £40 million. The share price rose from 9 pence to 85 pence.' But it was not an easy three years. 'I don't think I laughed once in three years. There was no fun, it was sheer hard toil, so it was time to move on to something that was enjoyable as well as satisfying.'

She was headhunted for the Commercial Operations director's post at Camelot. At first she was doubtful. After all, the company was doing remarkably well without her. It had had a phenomenal start and she couldn't see how she'd make a difference. She met with Camelot's CEO Tim Holly and he took her though the lottery life cycle and told her of the challenges facing the group on the horizon – the marketing issues that would occur within four or five years. She was hooked on the future challenge and joined Camelot in February 1997. She was to run marketing sales, retail services and external affairs – anything that was outward facing. She walked straight into controversy. One of the popular papers obtained minutes from the flipchart of the top team on an away day to develop strategy. An innocent brainstorming session, based on an admission that if they lost the licence they would needed alternative things to do, was labelled 'Plottery' on the front page in the tabloid press. By summer she was dealing with the 'fat cats' pay accusations against Camelot's top managers. Then came the bribery allegations involving one of Camelot's shareholder directors and Richard Branson.

Of course, all these problems paled when compared with the massive public fight to renew Camelot's licence to continue to run the lottery. It was an issue that shook the organization to its roots. It gave Dianne the high profile she claims to have never sought. She rose to the challenge and won the battle in the most public of forums – the British national media and the courts. She had to take on Richard Branson and his rival bid to run the lottery as a non-profit organization (albeit with higher running costs) through a company called the People's Lottery. At two minutes past four on 19 December 2000 a fax arrived at Camelot's offices from the Commission announcing that they had won the licence to continue running the lottery. Her prize had been agreed in advance. She became CEO. She had actually been offered the job a full year earlier, but said she wasn't sure due to the high profile it required. Over the Christmas holidays she talked to her daughter, Jo, to her partner, Graham, and to her dad. By the first week in January she had accepted the promotion and was called Chief Executive Designate. The full confirmation of the title CEO was delayed until July 2000, by when the new licence was to have been secured. The plan was for her to take over from January. She put the bid in during February and ran the bid process. She interfaced with the Commission and the Department of Culture, Media and Sport (DCMS). Tim Holly kept in the background. No one expected the dramatic, public fight that followed.

Has it turned her head, this amazing rush of publicity and celebrity status? She became Business Woman of the Year, Marketer of the Year and received an honorary doctorate from her old college. She is now president of the Chartered Institute of Marketing. She is often recognized by the public. Does it go to her head? 'I am northern and working class and practical. It would be very hard for me not to have my feet firmly on the ground, that's the sort of person I am. A lot of good things have come to me because of the fight. It would be very easy to let it go to your head, but I'm the same person now that I was before all the publicity and all the nice things that have happened because of a screw-up by the Commission.'

Personal meaning of success

'I think that success is getting good results. For my daughter success in the future will be totally different. For me it is delivering in the job that I am holding, and the higher up the chain that you progress, the more you are responsible for keeping the business going by getting good results. I feel responsible for the livelihoods of over 800 people.'

Leadership style

'If there is one huge difference between men and women – and there are many – it is that women tend to be more open. From my experience throughout my career I know that women talk more openly about what they can do and what they can't do and the problems they have. It was very interesting that, when we were all at the Veuve Clicquot vineyards in France, each of the European award-winners talked about the worst moments – the trials and tribulations – in their careers with complete candour, except for the Japanese lady who through an interpreter said: "I have not had a bad moment in my career." And when we were discussing how we coped with stress, I said I coped by swimming because I go brain-dead when swimming and I count. We were all talking openly about what we did and again through an interpreter the Japanese lady said: "I do not have stress." Hers was a very male response.

'Last year I met Sir James Hann in Bristol by accident and we stayed in touch and I spoke to him two or three times when I needed help and motivation and encouragement and he was very good at that. So when we were having a board dinner to celebrate our success, I invited Sir James to the dinner as my escort. My partner Graham had moved to the United States. I told all our team who were at the dinner who he was and how much support he had given me. They said hello, nice to meet you and I've heard all about you and so forth, and he said to me, "I can't believe you told anyone." Yet his is a typical male response – to never admit needing help or support. Adrian Vickers from Abbot, Mead, Vickers, said that he started mentoring three months ago. One problem is that the men will not admit to having mentors – they are too macho to admit it; they feel: "I can do this on my own."

'My style of leadership has always been that I am only human; I will work incredibly hard – give of my all – I will do the best I can. In the end, you get what you see, and I think that in many ways that sort of open-ness has held me in good stead. But I'm sure there are people out there who think: "Good God, fancy her saying that!"'

Nikki Beckett

Nikki Beckett, CEO, NSB Retail Systems plc

'I'm not that patient', Nikki Beckett admits. 'I want what I want and I want it now, though I do usually remember to say please.' She flashes a dazzling smile that makes it hard for anyone to refuse her. What the engaging CEO of NSB Retail Systems wants is market leadership and financial dominance as a global software tycoon serving the retail trade. In 2001 her company grew to 1,400 employees with a turnover of £150 million and £15 million profits. She was not daunted by the obstacles in her way. She decided at an early age – 21 – that she would run her own public company by the time she was 35. 'I actually sat down on my twenty-first birthday and wrote a plan and I still pull it out and look at it', she said. She then set about using IBM for her own personal, in-house management education programme over the next decade and a half. It was premeditated.

Solid 'Big Blue' background

From the time she joined IBM as an 18-year-old fresh from her A-levels with just a summer job in mind (she thought she wanted to be a barrister) until she left fifteen years later, she studied all aspects of the business including finance, business, planning and systems. She paid particular attention to sales, acquisitions and deal-making. She enjoyed the excitement of being a management candidate in IBM – a big, vibrant company with 18,000 employees in Portsmouth alone, a third of a million worldwide. Because she was bright and on a fast track as a management trainee, under the 'Management Potential Scheme', she spent six months in every major department of the company, combined with an educational programme. 'The last department I went to in the seven-year-long training programme was sales and I loved it', she said. Later she benefited from being sent to IBM locations on foreign assignments. 'IBM was very good to me. They said to me, "Why do you want to go away to university?" and I said I wanted to have flexibility as I do not know what path I'm going to take – maybe law. But IBM persuaded me that the most flexible way forward for me was with them. They invested in me and for seven years I went to college whilst I was working with IBM and enjoying the management training.

'After those first seven years of formal education at IBM I went into the business development department, where I took on a variety of roles and a lot of them involved travel. I was based in White Plains, New York, for a period and then in Copenhagen and in Tel Aviv', she recounted. In Israel she looked at 'how we interacted with some of our international retail customers – how IBM interacted with third parties – from a business development perspective'. It was a marvellous opportunity for thinking about her own ambitious plans in the retail sector.

'I resigned from IBM in 1991, but was persuaded not to resign, but to stay on and run one of the businesses that we had taken an equity investment in. But at that stage I wanted to do my own thing. I lost faith that IBM was the right kind of company any more. It was not just what we were doing as a company or what we were not doing, we had lost some of the basic beliefs, some of the key values – respect for the individual, service to the customer, excellence in everything we do. The spiritual side of me felt that we had lost sight of that. I lost faith in IBM because of that, rather than because the business direction was something I did not agree with.

'But I stayed on to run one of the small companies IBM had taken an investment interest in. That gave me small company experience without the risk. It was something that IBM wanted me to do, but also something I wanted to do – running companies that IBM – very successfully – had taken an equity interest in and taking those companies to Initial Public Offering (IPO). I undertook roles like that for another four years. Then in early 1995, I thought, "OK, I am just going to do this for me now, rather than for IBM." I left very amicably. I went to IBM with my business plan and said, "I am going to sell on only IBM technology platforms for three years and deal exclusively with IBM for three years and I want you to help me." They did. They formed a partnership with me. As a start-up operation of only eighteen people in all, the link with IBM gave me a huge amount of credibility. I absolutely kept that commitment and I did not sell on anything other than IBM for three years.'

Fifteen years after her induction into the company she made a rather grand exit. She felt ready to launch her own niche IT service company to fill a gap in the market – 'There were good IT suppliers for manufacturing and for finance, but not for the retail trade', she said. Calling the new company NSB (the initials of her full name, Nicola Susan Beckett), she could hardly have prepared her launch more carefully. She created a sustainable business by aligning the technology to a strong knowledge of the retail industry to make a radical difference over time.

Her idea – to create a marketing firm to supply innovative IT solutions to retailers around the world – is now a public company in its seventh year. From offices in the UK, North America, France and Germany, NSB provides the systems to give retailers new methods for reaching out to their customers and keeping their loyalty. NSB systems support stores, kiosks, home shopping and Internet customers through one integrated process. NSB creates channels that can be used by customers to review products, check inventory levels, place orders and select the most appropriate means of delivery. Everything then is integrated with the supply chain. British clients include Harvey Nichols, House of Fraser, Selfridges, Bhs, Kingfisher, Arcadia, the shoe shops Stylo and Clarks, and fashion retailers Monsoon, Oasis and Matalan. American fashion clients include Tommy Hilfiger and DKNY.

With a little help from colleagues

To start up the new company, in February 1995, Nikki Beckett borrowed £200,000. The loan came from another software company, PRJ, whose founder was Australian entrepreneur Peter Johnson. She had met Johnson on a secondment from IBM to his US retail software company. He put up the loan on the basis that if it were repaid within a year he would receive a 25 per cent share in the business, but if it took five years to repay he would have a controlling interest in the company. She paid it off in one year.

'I had a clear belief that we could do it and be successful', she recalled. 'I am not a risk-taker. I run the business prudently and I conduct my life prudently. So I did all my homework and I understood the market I was going into. I looked very carefully at the competition. I looked at the dynamics affecting the market over a five-year period. I had a very detailed business plan. I minimized the risk.'

Geoff Beckett, her then husband, sixteen years older than Nikki, had himself enjoyed a successful career with IBM and had just been made redundant. He helped her start up the new company by taking responsibility for quality. As Nikki was pregnant with their younger son, Charlie, Geoff also agreed to spend more time running the home and looking after their first-born boy, James, only 2 years old then, allowing Nikki to concentrate on her new company. 'I formed the business with eighteen people and what I am really proud of is that sixteen of them are still with me', she said.

Meaning of success

If one defines success in terms of earned personal wealth she achieved success swiftly. She is still one of Britain's wealthiest women. 'I have already achieved about £25 million. It's more than I'll ever spend and I don't think I'm ever going to need any more.' The popular press is quick to point out that she drives an Aston Martin DB7 and likes designer fashion and expensive jewellery, but she is more interested in the challenge of growing the business than in increasing her personal wealth. 'I'm much more interested in how I'm going to make the next £100 million than in how I spend the £100 million I've already made', she said. 'I had a nice comfortable upbringing, so it is not as if I ever had to go without.' (Her father was a businessman in Portsmouth.) 'I see money as a scorecard, that is why I count it. It's important to me that the next level of people in my organization who have worked hard for success will personally benefit from it as I have done.'

Much of her wealth is in her shares. She had a 14.6 per cent stake in her software company worth about £60 million in spring 2000. She sold £6.1 million worth of her shares when they were at their height of £30.50, just before the high-tech shake-out that sent share prices plummeting. But she has now bought back many of the shares at a fraction of their earlier value. 'I'm aiming for the long term', she said. She argues that her shares are great value for anyone investing in the future.

Nikki Beckett feels that there is still a big difference between how the Americans and British view success. 'Our attitude toward entrepreneurs is not consistent, and it isn't as supportive as it needs to be', she said. 'Being an entrepreneur here is something you whisper about, whereas in North America wealth creation is highly prized. Our attitude to success ought to be more positive.' She sees the press as being at fault in their preoccupation with building up entrepreneurs just to knock them down. The same national newspapers that celebrated her Business Woman of the Year Award a few months earlier were quick to report that the champagne had gone flat as share prices plunged. She worries about the brain drain that sees talented entrepreneurs go to America with their ideas because raising money for them there is easier than in Britain.

'Our attitude to failure also has to change . . . People have to know that it is okay to fail', she said. 'Their [the Americans'] attitude is: "How do I know you are any good if you haven't screwed anything up yet" ', she said. Failure is valued for the experience it brings. It's how you recover from the inevitable failures that counts. She admits to making mistakes.

On 4 June 2001, NSB warned on profits for the second time in the year and shares tumbled to a low of 44½p. City analysts cut forecasts for the company's operating profits for the year to the end of December 2001 from £22 million to £15 million. Nikki Beckett said: 'Undoubtedly, things aren't going as well as last year. However, this company is still more profitable than other retail software companies and it has the leading market share. So it depends on how short-sighted people want to be about today's statement.' Not surprisingly she felt her shares at the low price were the 'bargain of the decade'.

'We are one of the three largest companies in our niche in the retail sector. Our competitors are very fragmented – the largest of them would be only a fifty-person company. If I go back to my 1995 business plan, I had identified all the prime competitors or potential competitors in the market in the UK and I either had an acquisition strategy for them or a kill plan. I executed it fairly ruthlessly.' She describes herself as fiercely competitive and joyful about winning.

'Everyone who joins your company is acknowledging that he or she believes in you personally, because they are placing their careers in your hands. I have always thought of that as a huge responsibility. I would not say that my actual need to shine is less, but I am happy to share the glory with more people. The key is getting people to aspire to greater things and to actually achieve more. To do so you have to be a constant example for the team. It is not just about the individual any more, rather about the things you want others to adopt. I always try my hardest to achieve a little beyond my comfort zone. I talk about taking on responsibility and I think it is my job to keep doing that, not to sit back. I am very much aware that I set the culture of my organization. I learned that from the senior people at IBM.' Honesty, integrity, teamwork, excellence, and customer service head the list of ten values she wants to permeate NSB in shaping its company culture, which is both its way of surviving in the marketplace and internally organizing itself.

Leadership style

Nikki Beckett is keen to grow the business and let others achieve personal wealth and the measure of satisfaction that she enjoys. A number of her staff have already become paper millionaires. Her leadership style is clearly bound up with her definition of success.

'I would distinguish leadership from management. What I was taught in IBM was that management is learning how to look after resources. Leadership is different. It involves inspiring people and causing them to do more than they think they can do. That to me is the greatest challenge and the greatest thrill of leading – making people far more successful than they think they can be. To do that you have to have an ambitious plan for the company – a big picture. She thinks in terms of growing the business and of financial targets. 'We've had a turnover this year [2001] of £150 million that generated £15 million profit', she said.

Much of her company's growth has been through acquisition. Between 1995 and its flotation on the Alternative Investment Market (AIM) in September 1997, NSB doubled in size. A year later, in 1998, it made its first acquisition, again doubling in size to about 200 employees. In 1999, Nikki Beckett merged her company with Unlimited Solutions, Inc., a North American company, bringing her workforce to 300 employees. In 2000 NSB acquired Real Time Control plc and STS Systems, giving it the global network it wanted and increasing its number of employees to 1,400.

She believed in her own business plans and put her money where her beliefs lay in two ways. Firstly, she invested in a large building in Birmingham near Aston University for the company's headquarters to enjoy the incentives Solihull Council gave to technology companies and to benefit from its geographical centrality in the country. Although the business required only two floors of the building, she wanted to have scope for expansion so rented out the rest of the premises. Secondly, she has already distributed 25 per cent of NSB's equity to the forty-five people who formed the company with her. The share-out was a 'thank you' for their contribution to the start-up, but, in keeping with her focus on expansion, she also saw it 'much more as golden handcuffs for our next stage of growth'.

She describes her management style as 'collaborative', inviting inputs from colleagues at the discussion stage. 'It's important to provide direction, clearly enunciated and broken down so that everyone knows his or her part in it.' Her vision is to be the global market leader and eventually to have a £10 billion company. Part of her vision for the future is 'one-to-one marketing', where computers help retailers make more profits by 'spying on' customers' personal shopping habits and then presenting them with a time-saving portfolio of products that fits their lifestyle. It has not been plain sailing for the NSB. During market jitters over tech stock she saw three-quarters of her company's paper value wiped out before the share prices rallied to reflect a more realistic value.

'I think having children – I've got two boys now, a 9-year-old and an 8-year-old – has caused me to manage differently. They have taught me how much more effective encouragement is than direction. The way to get a toddler or young child to do something is to make them think that it is their own idea and to be enthusiastic about it. To plant the seed and let them decide themselves. I have actually thought that behaviour in the organization is very much like behaviour in a group of toddlers. All kinds of egos are involved. It does not matter where an idea comes from. It is getting people to adopt it. When I first went to IBM it was just for a summer job and I was not very confident. I got pulled into a programme for management potential where 2,000 people from all over the country had applied for ten positions. I was given a place on the programme and had not even applied for it. So I thought of myself as lucky and was always trying to prove myself. When I was in my early twenties I was still not confident enough. I was always trying to prove how bright I was. It mattered to me much more then that an idea was identified as mine and acknowledged as such. But I have mellowed and have become much more confident in myself.'

The gender factor

'I never felt that there was any difference between what I was expected to achieve and what my brothers were expected to achieve. The expectations were absolutely gender-neutral – I was expected to do well.' She was a curious student who always wanted to know how things worked. 'I was always told "because it does" and I wanted to know *why* it did. My teachers would say because it does. I was never very happy or satisfied with that answer. I always wanted to know why and how.' She is reluctant to talk much about her family background, considering it a private matter.

Nikki Beckett feels that being a woman has not been a disadvantage, either at IBM or in building up her own business. 'There are probably times when I faced prejudice, and other people obviously do face prejudice', she admitted to journalist Dominic Rushe. 'It's just a matter of not accepting it. Most people, if they give much thought to it, will realize that their prejudice is irrational. If you face anything negative, just don't accept it. I can't think of anything in my career I have not done just because I am a woman.'

That is not to say that she applauds macho behaviour. 'I don't want to be sexist about this but there is one gender which tends to just shout louder if the message isn't getting through', she said. But she believes that behaviour breeds behaviour. 'I might have been tempted to use power more if I hadn't had children. If you deal with them like that they just show confusion and start to be aggressive back . . . What my boys, James and Charlie, have taught me is that you can't get anywhere by saying the same things louder.'

'The biggest barrier to success is the pressures we put on ourselves as women – all the things we think we have to be perfect at', she said. 'We have to be the perfect mother and wife, we have to look like Claudia Schiffer, and that constrains the amount [of time and energy and commitment] we put into our professional lives.'

She admitted that there have been times when she has used her gender as an advantage in business. 'Many people agree to see you out of curiosity and you can then exploit the opportunity.' But curiosity is not the only female advantage, she thinks.

She believes that women manage differently, giving them an edge in today's society. They are more nurturing and more intuitive, more in touch with people's feelings – all of which alters her approach to people. 'Men can be more direct, more confrontational. I have never been frightened to do things in a different way. This included working from home and taking weekends off work to be with the children and going on family holidays.' Improving work/life balance is something she strives for as part of looking after herself and fostering the pool of talent she needs to succeed in the software business.

About 80 per cent of her staff have taken up the share options on offer. She is straightforward in looking after her staff and wins their loyalty and commitment by her caring concern and charming manner. 'I'm quite intuitive about how people are feeling and I measure my approach in the light of that', she summed up. Yet she can also be demanding as she put it: 'I always expect the best from people, which is sometimes why people think I'm soft and naïve. I'm not at all naïve. If people know I expect the best from them, it is much harder for them to let me down.'

She recognizes that big business and technology are still dominated by men. She is living proof that talent matters and she takes seriously her role of recruiting and retaining talented software engineers. 'I knew right from the word go – at about 18 – that I was not very good at working for someone. I was much better at determining the way I wanted to go. By 21, I had a plan and it was clearly mapped out, down to wanting to run a public company by the time I was 35. It was a structured plan that must have emerged from one of my first roles in IBM in business planning. I felt strongly in a business context that if you do not know what you are trying to do, how will you know when you have achieved it? You have to have personal objectives and direction.'

She is impatient with the journalists who are concerned with how she spends money – on her car, clothes and jewellery, rather than on how she makes money through her company. 'I despair of the techno-babes head-lines', she said. The popular press nicknamed her 'Queen of the Cash Tills'.

She did not experience gender barriers to her advancement. 'It's hard work being a woman in business. You do actually give up other things to be successful in business and I think that many women say it is just not worth it. We must respect people who say: "I'm not prepared to prioritize to the extent to do this!" So my efforts are directed towards encouraging people who have the capability and desire but perhaps lack the networks or support structures.'

Her own company's employee gender profile is one-third women and two-thirds men, which is a very high ratio for women in IT. Yet she is the only woman on the main plc board. At the next level down from the plc board – the operating boards – there are a number of women and the ratio is two-thirds women to one-third men. She tries to make sure that there are no barriers to women advancing to the main plc board. 'But being on the main board involves acceptance in the City establishments. They like people they know', she admitted. 'When you are trying to appoint a plc director, you obviously have to consult the major shareholders of your company and they will say to you, we like people we know. Now, of course, I could be a plc director on other boards – you have to get to the point where you are known and accepted by the City institutions.'

The Veuve Clicquot Business Woman of the Year Award

Nicki Beckett was awarded the Veuve Clicquot Business Woman of the Year Award for 1999 and singled out by the committee for 'her charisma, inspirational management style and leadership qualities'.

'I was thrilled. I wasn't even aware I had been nominated until I was a finalist. It was exciting, especially when I saw who the other finalists were. That was when I felt particularly thrilled and honoured because it was such a strong group of other ladies.' Receiving the award from newscaster Sir Trevor McDonald at London's Claridges Hotel on 26 April 2000, she was quick to acknowledge the essential part played by her team. 'I am keen to do as much publicity about the award as possible, to encourage people to go out and start their own businesses by being a positive role model and just to increase the number of people trying. It is something I feel passionate about.'

She was also named Entrepreneur of the Year at the Alternative Investment Market awards the same year. Acknowledging the award, she said: 'It's recognition for me. It's hard work setting up a company. But it is also recognition for all the people who have made the success possible.'

North American focus

Her company continues to grow in a geographically dispersed pattern. In addition to the European offices, there are six offices in the United States. The office in Montreal employs 900 people. She was there on 11 September 2001 and was due in New York City to meet with customers when terrorists struck the World Trade Center, stopping North American air travel. 'Century 21, the big department store just across the road from the World Trade Center, is one of our customers and the store was badly damaged.'

She phoned some of her New York customers that day and offered to help in any way she could, and wrote to all customers. 'We took some of our New York customers and pulled all their processing into Montreal and did it for them', she said. 'That's all we could do. I could not get out of Montreal until the following Sunday.'

She thrives on face-to-face contact and needs to travel. She defines her company's success as 'every time one of our customers actually derives business benefit from what we do.' She adds, 'I still get a buzz every time the customer chooses us for the first time – that is a vindication of everything we have ever done.' She speaks those words with a passion that makes them totally believable.

Anne Wood CBE

Anne Wood CBE, founder and creative director, Ragdoll Productions

Anne Wood has done more for British creative exports than any other woman. Her TV programmes are screened in more than 120 countries. Her first *Teletubbies* series, which concluded with its 365th programme in October 2001, is still a worldwide sensation, watched by a billion children. The series has been translated into twenty foreign languages. It is unlikely that the Teletubbies themselves will ever disappear from television screens, or their many products – videos, dolls, lunch boxes, carousel lights, nursery resource packs, duvets, etc. – vanish from toy shops and supermarkets.

In a new series of fifty programmes for 2002, the *Teletubbies* characters will act as 'wraparound' TV presenters of 10–12 minute shorts, which will feature insert film (commentary-less film that plays on the Teletubbies' TV screen tummies) from around the globe. Anne Wood's original idea in the first *Teletubbies* series was to design the programmes for export, so that the foreign buyers could make their own, indigenous shorts to fill the slots. Now she will be buying the best of these shorts – re-importing those films – for a domestic audience. It is her form of the acceptable face of globalization. 'I think it's very relevant to today's society: that you should encourage an awareness of other cultures and other styles of living from an early age', she said.

The success of *Teletubbies* brought Anne Wood out of the anonymity of being a producer of British children's programmes into the dazzling fame of a globally celebrated film-maker. Before *Teletubbies* few people outside the world of children's films would have known her name, even though some of her earlier creations – like Roland Rat, and Rosie and Jim – had been household characters. Then suddenly, with *Teletubbies*, she and her small production company, Ragdoll, were the toast of children's TV around the globe. She made a fortune from her contract with the BBC for the programmes, from the American rights to the series, which she wisely and stubbornly kept for her own company, Ragdoll, and from her share in the profits from thousands of *Teletubbies* products that sold in the millions. *Broadcast* magazine listed Anne Wood and Ragdoll as the second richest broadcaster among the nations top 100 broadcasters, putting her worth at £150 million.

Although she never set out to be an entrepreneur, she won the Veuve Clicquot Business Woman of the Year Award for 1998. She received a CBE in 2000. She collected a BAFTA special award in November 2000. The *Teletubbies* series, in its own right, has captured a long list of awards, the latest in June 2001 from the Royal Television Society which honoured it with the Best Pre-School Education Award. The citation praised *Teletubbies* as 'a creative and exciting approach to concepts appropriate to the developmental level of a young child'. It continued: 'Not only is it stimulating without being overwhelming, it's also funny.'

In September 2001 she launched a new series based on an old favourite, Brum, a yellow vintage car with a mind of its own which has all sorts of adventures rescuing the crazy residents of the Big Town. The new series was designed to entertain children and to make them laugh. 'In today's world many children live in what they perceive as crazy urban environments', she said of the new series. 'Brum has fun with this idea. Brum is especially good at distinguishing between goodies and baddies in ways that make children laugh. Like Brum himself, the comedy is vintage.' Supporting merchandise for the new *Brum* series include a friction-powered model of the car and a Big Town Play Set, a beanie, plush and moving plush, stationery, craft sets and boardgames, and a coin-operated Brum ride-on. Brum has released his first single and album and has his own website. A leading video company, VCI, signed a seven-year deal with Ragdoll and Off-screen and launched its first video and DVD releases only four weeks after the first UK transmission.

At her home, in a village about a half-hour's drive from Stratford-upon-Avon, Anne Wood has permitted herself one luxury – a purpose-built workplace in the middle of her garden, where she and her creative colleagues can work. The 65-year-old former schoolteacher has no plans for retirement. 'Has retirement any meaning for someone like me?' she asked. 'The answer is: no, it hasn't. As in all times of cultural change – now with the technological revolution – you get childhood redefined. It's why I can't retire; it's so interesting. No I'm not going to retire. It's not an option for people like me. I will adjust to growing older.'

Intuition on an aeroplane

The idea for the *Teletubbies* came to her on a return flight from New York City, where she had been trying to sell some of Ragdoll's early productions to American television networks. She and her colleague Andrew Davenport watched a *Power Rangers* programme on the flight.

'*Power Rangers* used to incense me, because I knew it was seen by pre-schoolers who did not know what it was really about and so went round kicking each other in imitation', she recalled. 'Apparently a child in Norway was kicked to death in the playground from *Power Rangers* mimicking. They did not understand that such kicking hurts. What is it that the children like about this series? I think it is the fact that these characters are so clearly identifiable and tangible, and the theatre of it all. Andy and I agreed that we should be making Ragdoll's answer to *Power Rangers*, in which the characters all love instead of kick each other.

'Andy, who is very good at visualizing, started to doodle these little characters, who were kind of space men and he said this one has a laser and he does not know what it does. It made me laugh very much and we began to play with the idea. Andy has a great comic imagination. The creative process often involves humour as free lateral thinking links up things and ideas that were previously unrelated.'

Earlier Anne Wood had been invited by the BBC, as one of twelve children's production companies, to tender for a new series for pre-schoolers. It had taken her nearly a month to decide to put in a tender. 'The invitation sat on my desk for three weeks and I tried to pretend that it was not there', she explained. 'I had a little business plan. I had a sensible business that was turning over enough to make a profit.' She didn't feel a need to grow the business. She was comfortable with her creative team and with the clients she had – ITV and Channel 4. She knew that to undertake the tender and to win it would mean changing her business completely. The original requirement in the tender was to bid for 130 fifteen-minute programmes. (Later the scope was changed to 260 half-hour programmes and ultimately to 365 half-hour programmes.) 'I knew it would blow the scale of my business completely and I did not want to do it', she said from her new, modest offices in Stratford.

Fortunately, she was in regular contact with a businessman who, as part of a government scheme, used to visit her small company Ragdoll Productions to offer business advice as a consultant.

He soon realized that her business was different from the kind he normally helped and that he would have to raise the level of his intervention.

On each visit he would ask what was new. When she eventually told him about the invitation to tender from the BBC, he read it carefully and said, as Anne Wood recalled: '"You are going to tender for his, aren't you?" My hesitant response provoked him. "For heaven's sake, what is it you want to be? Haven't you always said to me that you've got to be the best pre-school producer? You can't ignore this." I knew he was right and he was only voicing what I knew deep down. So I said "Yes, we have got to respond to it."'

She had been using domestic video cameras to unobtrusively film children watching her own programmes. She knew, from these films, that she was not reaching the very young pre-school children. 'If you look at pre-school TV, you have four different audiences: 1-year-olds, 2-year-olds, 3-year-olds and 4-year-olds, and each audience is different. She engaged her staff at Ragdoll in discussing the differences between making a programme for 4-year-olds and one for 2-year-olds. Apparently, the 2-year-olds like hugs and repetitions.

First with a phone call and then with a face-to-face meeting, she clarified the tender's audience by talking to Anna Home, head of children's programmes at the BBC. Yes, the tender was for children's programmes for the very young – a 2-year-old audience. Anna had also come to the conclusion that there was a need for programmes for very young children that had not been met.

The idea of putting in the tender had been at the back of Anne Wood's mind when she and Andy Davenport playfully created on the flight back to Britain a rough sketch of the characters that would eventually become the globally cherished Teletubbies. She told him to go away and develop the characters. Independently, she started working on how to deliver 130 fifteen-minute programmes in a short time.

'I was thinking that there was no way I could take the characters out into the real world, which is what I normally do. I would have to have some real world stuff shot and some fictional stuff shot simultaneously and then bring them together. Rather than being spacemen, the characters Andy and I were playing with on the plane could be technological babies, but adopt the same kind of shape as the spacemen.

'If you look at the environment children are growing up in, there is ever-increasing technology. They are going to have to read a screen as well as a book. So I came up with this concept of their living in this sort of land which is a cross between where television comes from and nursery rhyme land with a windmill that drove them. The first primitive machine that a baby sees is often a little plastic windmill that the wind turns round. I thought they would recognize that, and also that they lived in a house over the hill and far away. It all linked with what Andy and I saw on that trip to the States in a space museum. Andy had said to me: "Isn't it funny that we've got all this technology and yet when they walk on the moon in those suits, they look just like toddlers with nappies on." '

She pulled her original ideas about the technological babies together and tested them on Andrew Davenport. 'One day I came into work and said to Andy, "Listen to this and see if you think it stands up!" I told him that we had to put children into the show, but that they could not come onto the set, because everything had to be shot separately. He said: "These are technological babies; you put the screen on their tummies." I said: "Brilliant – and you need to put antennas on their heads to get the pictures." That's how the full-blown idea came about. Then we had to work out how to do this. Actually we used a process called four-point tracking [special effects technology] which had never been done before. So first you dream the dream and then you ask "How can we make this work?" '

'The Teletubbies have to be four different sizes and four different fluorescent colours. You have to scale up from your smallest to your tallest. If your performer is six foot six and you put a Teletubby head on the top, you get a character the size of a Pickfords van. You can't have those walking about the street, they would terrify children', she spelled out.

She conceived *Teletubbies* and devised it, and Andy scripted the programmes. The series broke new ground with its dramas noted for their odd pacing, many pauses and repetitions, and verbal simplicity.

When the time came to submit Ragdoll's tender to the BBC, Anne Wood used a 'picture book' presentation of *Teletubbies* and captured their imaginations. She was shortlisted, and eventually won the tender in December 1995. 'By that time I had almost given up and I had already taken it to America and sold the idea to PSB [Public Service Broadcasting], who were at the time showing Tots TV.'

She kept that fact to herself, but it strengthened her in her negotiations with the BBC. But she was not prepared to meet the BBC's tight production schedule. Negotiations started in January and the BBC wanted the programmes in September. She argued for an extra year to do the production job properly but, in the end, settled for six months more and a March deadline. She did not budge from her position on the American rights to *Teletubbies* – they had to remain with her own company, Ragdoll. Her negotiating skills also secured a good deal for the company in the licensing of the official *Teletubbies* merchandise.

She was not the woman she once was in negotiating with the broadcasters. She was wiser and tougher. As Anne Wood put it: 'Everyone who works in the production game knows that the only way to survive is to hang on to as many rights as you can. Sometimes they will say: "If you do not give way on these rights, you will not get to make the show." You have to know what you are going to say if they say that to you. I was prepared to walk away with that show, if I did not get the date of transmission moved to give me time to do it properly and keep the American rights. Those were the two deal-breakers; everything else we could discuss. Many people inside the BBC asked why Ragdoll was allowed to keep the American rights and heads rolled because they felt their negotiators didn't put the right kind of pressure on me. But what they never accepted was that it did not matter what they said, I would not have given way.'

Freelance producer to reluctant entrepreneur

Entrepreneurs take risks. Anne Wood takes both creative risks and business risks. Her business proposition must have seemed outrageous at the time. She persuaded her colleagues at Ragdoll that they should invest £500,000 of the company's money in one creative project. The project was to produce a series of films about four alien creatures called Tinky-Winky, Dipsy, Laa-Laa and Po, who have television screens in their stomachs and live in a place called Teletubbieland. The Teletubbies would entertain 2-year-old children and help them learn. The project would sell worldwide.

Anne Wood still maintains that she is an entrepreneur by accident rather than design. She never set out to make vast amounts of money. At each step of the way in establishing her production company, Anne Wood was a reluctant entrepreneur. She was always more interested in the creative side of the work than in the business side. In fact, she gave up her freelance status to form a company because a broadcaster would no longer deal with her as a producer unless she became a company. She still has some hard feelings on the matter.

Anne Wood, as a freelance producer, was involved in the start-up of British breakfast television with TV AM in 1982. She remembers TV AM putting together its dream team to breakfast with the British public, and the chaos and changes the new station made to get more comfortable, viewer-friendly presenters to invade people's homes at such an early hour. Anne Wood was a vital part of the launch of TV AM, but in the background. As head of children's TV, she argued that an attractive programme for children would help TV AM create the first breakfast television programme for Britain. 'Children were the first audience to accept anything new,' she reasoned, 'whether it is breakfast television or new technology.' She discovered a puppeteer, David Claridge, with a portfolio of characters that included a rat. Her programmes featuring Roland Rat helped TV AM reach its target of a million viewers, as the character became a hit with children and adults alike. 'Greg Dyke was head of the programme', she recalled. 'He rang me up at home and said: "Anne, we've got the first million viewers and it is really down to your department."'

Although her contribution to boosting the ratings was recognized for the moment, a new management team took over at TV AM and the new director did not like what Anne Wood wanted to do. She wanted to establish an early Sunday morning programme for little children and to tie it in with a magazine for children published by one of the leading Sunday papers. 'He killed the idea stone dead in favour of showing cartoons, and that didn't interest me', she recalled. Shortly afterwards her contract with TV AM was not renewed, which for a freelance artist is the rough equivalent of being sacked. She left with no money. When the history of the station was written in a book called *Treachery*, Anne Wood's contribution was not even mentioned, she 'didn't even merit a footnote'.

She was hurt and troubled by the 'brutal' treatment. She was also out of work. She was living in Birmingham. She had one child at university at the time and one still in public school and a mortgage to pay off. But fortunately her husband was working and they managed the crisis. When she found work with Channel 4, she was told that TV stations could no longer deal with her as a freelance producer but only as a production company; she knew what she had to do. She spent 1983–84 'learning about how to set up a company, how to manage it and keep it all going'. It was not something she wanted to do – it was forced on her. Today she is philosophical about it all and quotes Bill Gates saying: 'Always welcome bad news because there is an opportunity in there.' 'That happened to me several times and I think everybody in business has that experience. I have learned every time the blow fell; I thought: "Right, now what am I going to do?" You pick yourself up and start again and you find a way. It's difficult and it doesn't get any easier.'

She set up her company in the front room of her house and called it after her daughter's favourite toy – a rag doll. She started reading pamphlets about management. She tried to pick up some knowledge of business practices. She feared that it was going to be a trial and error process, and she was right. She learned about intellectual property, contract negotiations and merchandising the hard way – by making mistakes and losing money she was entitled to.

At the time the custom in the television business was for the broadcaster to give production companies a further 10 per cent of their overall budget production fee at the end of the work. This provided money to tide them over to the next production project. In exchange for the cash – called a 'production fee' – the production company was not allowed to keep the copyright to its own work, which went to the broadcaster. 'So the broadcaster saw it as their divine right to have all the rights to our work', she explained. She learned at the start to let the broadcaster have the rights in the programme but not the 'character rights'. From day one her company made it a rule to retain the character rights, and that turned out to have been a master stroke.

She and Robin Stevens created *Pob's Programme* for Channel 4, and their first big hit, *Rosie and Jim*, told the story of two rag dolls and their secret life on a canal boat. It was watched by millions on TV and later on videocassette. Next came *Tots TV* as Andrew Davenport joined Ragdoll Productions. Trying to create a programme with more attention to children's language and feelings, they included a French-speaking character. It was an international hit and won five awards, including two BAFTA awards.

The video market changed the business radically. Until parents began buying videocassettes for their children, broadcasters gave children's TV low priority. The programmes were put on in early slots and were done because they were something the stations were required to do. 'Once the programmes became available on video, the broadcasters took a different view', Anne Wood explained. 'Central, for example, made a million pounds on video sales of Ragdoll's *Rosie and Jim* and didn't even tell me about it. I didn't get any money from the video. So I thought: "I'm not going to stand for this in the future", and did something about it.' By then Ragdoll had been in business for ten years. Although Ragdoll had the rights to the characters, the broadcaster had the rights to the programmes and was able to transfer them onto video and sell them without reference or payment to the authors of the programmes.

All of that was to change in the future as Anne Wood and Ragdoll learned to negotiate like 'business people' instead of producers grateful to go on working on the terms set by the broadcasters. Is it a ruthless business? 'You have no idea!' Ragdoll now receives a share of royalties of all merchandise sold worldwide to do with the Teletubbies, which the BBC administers, apart from the USA, where Ragdoll retained the rights and control the merchandising themselves.

By locating both its Ragdoll Shop and its new headquarters in Stratford-upon-Avon, Anne Wood was adding to the town's international reputation. 'People make the trip there specifically to see the Ragdoll Shop on Chapel Street', she said. 'Sometimes, once they've seen the Ragdoll Shop, they ask us, without tongue-in-cheek, is there anything else to see in Stratford?' Like Hamlet, Anne Wood feels that she holds 'the mirror up to nature' for children with her Ragdoll productions.

Unlike an ordinary shop, over half of the space is dedicated to play areas for children. They can watch videos on a replica of Rosie and Jim's *Ragdoll* boat, read books in the Little Book Room, ride in the magical Brum car, see themselves on TV in the Tots' cottage, talk to their favourite Ragdoll character on special telephone or post them letters or drawings in a dedicated post box, go 'online' to Ragdoll's websites to learn more about the company and its characters – for example, www.bbc.co.uk/teletubbies (Ragdoll has 1.5 million page impressions a week) – and operate the Teletubbies' control panels. They can also buy merchandise inspired by the characters. Sometimes, with parents' consent, Ragdoll films the children watching their programmes to check the impact they are having on different age groups. They also listen to what children and parents are saying to their staff, as the shop becomes a sounding board for ideas. Their findings are treated with the utmost confidentiality out of respect for their audience.

Northern roots

Anne Wood was born in Spennymoor, County Durham, a coal mining area, in 1937. Her father was a road worker who served in the Royal Marines during the war, and her mother worked in a munitions factory. She was looked after by her grandmother in her early years. Her own three brothers died before she was born, so she was cared for like an only child. She went to the village school at Tudhoe Colliery and experienced the close-knit, warm and loving mining community. The war bound them even closer together and little Anne had 'lots of funny memories of being in air raid shelters'. She credits her father with teaching her to think independently – to ask the question, 'why?'

'There was also that residual, Victorian claptrap from your mother: "Be a good, sweet maid, and let who will be clever"', so she was pulled in both directions. The rest of their family were coal miners. She felt comfortable among the Geordie women – strong and resilient. 'Kate Adie is a Geordie and comes from a similar background to me', she said of the BBC war correspondent.

She started her career as a teacher at Spennymoor Secondary Modern School where she stayed until marriage prompted her to move to the

South-East. She had two of her own children to raise – a boy, Christopher, who is now 32 and on the board of Ragdoll, and a girl, Katherine, who directs a gallery of contemporary art and acts as a trustee of the charity her mother established. (Her husband, Barrie, worked for Gallup Poll in his early career and later as a sociologist with a passion for films that led him to his taking a full-time job with the British Film Institute.)

Her first public projects for children were aimed at getting them to read more for pleasure, as she did. 'When I was teaching between 1960 and 1965 there were some tremendous children's books coming out and writers like Nina Bawden. She said to me that children live in the same world, but they perceive it differently. That had a tremendous effect on me and is something I always try to consider.'

She founded an independent magazine for parents named *Books For Your Children*. Soon her work was winning national awards. She received the Eleanor Farjeon Award for Services to Children's Books and the Roland Politzer Award for Book Promotion. Her magazine efforts led to publishing and television work with Tyne Tees and the creation for Yorkshire TV in 1979 of the *Book Tower* programme, which won two BAFTA awards and the Prix Jeunesse. She had found a new career as a producer of TV programmes for children.

Leadership style

Not surprisingly Anne Wood's leadership style tends to be collaborative. With a staff of about ninety at Ragdoll's headquarters in Stratford and at its London Pinewood Production studio, she expects people to be dedicated to producing the best-quality children's films possible. She leads by example, wearing her commitment on her sleeve.

She will collaborate with anyone who shares her high standards and commitment to children. For example, Ragdoll designed an eight-page section featuring Rosie and Jim and Brum in three issues of the parenting magazine *Right Start* in 2001.

Her leadership style is self-taught, as is her grasp of management tools and techniques. She is a charismatic leader and inspires people with her sense of fun and enthusiasm for what she is doing. Loyalty is what she expects of her staff and she makes it a point to keep them informed and empowered. People at Ragdoll – like her secretary, Carole Thompson – feel more like members of an extended family than employees of a global film production company.

A big part of her leadership role is to search for new talent. 'There are very few people who can do what we want in our area. It doesn't work to use traditional children's writers. [She has a great love for books by Roald Dahl and J.K. Rowling.] It is a different kind of writing. I am on the lookout all the time. I try people out. We do something that is very particular and we are looking for skills that people sometimes do not know they have. It costs this company a great deal of money to continue the search for talent; the right people are very hard to find.

'All the creators participate in the profits of what they do, and always have', she said. 'Keeping talent is very important.'

How did she react to winning the Veuve Clicquot Business Woman of the Year Award?

'I was invited to submit to the award panel three times and I had refused twice before. I have never felt that I was a businesswoman in the sense that I set up a business to be a successful business. I set up a business so I could go on doing the work that I loved to do. So I still feel a bit of a fraud when it comes to that. You see, people can be quite scathing. They say: "For someone who never intended to make money, you've made quite a lot." I say, yes, but it's all going back into the company and it does not have any reality for me.'

There are no yachts and helicopters in her lifestyle. She has a trust to support charities and her own personal charities, and an arrangement with Save the Children to investigate child labour and other issues of exploitation. When companies in other countries bid to make toys and other merchandise connected with Ragdoll characters, she has Save the Children check on them. 'The reason I go to people within Save the Children is that I feel I get an objective view from them of what really is going on rather than from the people who are running the factories.'

Her well-defined sense of social responsibility, however, cannot put right all the ills in the world. As she said: 'What I do is run this company to the best of my ability for the good of those who work in it and those who watch the programmes. More than that I cannot do, and I cannot be held responsible for the plight of children everywhere in the world.'

Barriers for women

'I am lucky that my work is with children. I have been patronized a great deal over the years, but you just come to accept it. I think my generation of women tend to let that sort of thing wash over them, perhaps more than the younger generation of women who quite rightly object to it. If you grew up in the 1950s, as I did, you just thought, well, that is how you are treated and did not let it get in the way at all.

'It did, of course, and there were times when people thought they would invest in Ragdoll or would get Ragdoll to do something for them, but did not. Then it would get back to me that their reason for inaction was that I was "uncontrollable", a maverick.'

In those circumstances she acknowledges that it probably wouldn't have worked out. 'I suppose there is still a feeling on the part of men that women need to be controlled. It comes from fear. If I had been working as a scientist, I might have had a different experience. But because I was working only with children – very young children at that – nobody thought it was serious.

'What is so interesting and why people are so fascinated with Ragdoll is that (1) the company was built without capital, and (2) the business is in an area previously perceived to be of no importance that is, in fact, acutely important.'

Despite phenomenal success, Anne Wood and Ragdoll do not have an easy life today. Apart from success giving her 'more thinking time' and more survival time ('if you had to fund the company from its own profits'), their track record does not of itself generate new business. Their success has not created a situation where broadcasters beat a path to their door. As she puts it: 'It does not give you more choice or any more options. That has been very disappointing. You would have thought that a broadcaster somewhere would have approached us to make some work for them, but no, not one. You are still in there pitching exactly as you were in the beginning.'

Dame Marjorie Scardino

Dame Marjorie Scardino, CEO, Pearson

On 11 September 2001, while the civilized world reeled from the terrorist attacks in New York City and Washington DC, Dame Marjorie Scardino, chief executive of Pearson plc, responded swiftly in the interest of the employees. Sixty-five of them worked for Pearson's New York Institute of Finance on the 17th floor of the north tower of the World Trade Center and all got out safely. The next day she sent an e-mail to each of Pearson's 28,000 employees. It said: 'Dear everyone, I want to make sure you know that our priority is that you are safe and sound in body and mind. Be guided by what you and your families need right now. There is no meeting you have to go to and no plane you have to get on if you don't feel comfortable doing it. For now look to yourselves and to your families, and to Pearson to help you any way we can.'

Most other CEOs were communicating different messages to their employees – about the likely economic consequences to their businesses in terms of diminished revenues, about strategies they should develop to limit the damage, or concerning the downsizing they would deem necessary to cope with the crisis.

Reflecting on her action three months later, Marjorie Scardino, 54, the only woman CEO of a FTSE 100 company, dismissed it as the only correct way to behave in dealing with the Pearson 'family'. She claimed to not be able to remember exactly what she said in the letter, and was surprised to find that other companies had obtained the full text of her now famous e-mail to use as an example of corporate caring.

Her 'family' is actually a global media empire that encompasses the *Financial Times* and other business newspapers, *The Economist*, Penguin Books, Prentice-Hall and other educational publishing and testing companies. It includes high-tech ventures, among them an educational portal, Learning Network, that reaches 12 million people a month, and the FT online site FT.com, an Internet financial news service with over 2 million subscribers. FT.com is now charging for its premium services – research, career services, and archives.

When she was appointed CEO in 1997, she sent an e-mail to everyone in the company. 'I described the kind of company I would like to work for and I got a fair number of responses. I began to use e-mail every time we had an important announcement. I realized that as we added more Americans I got a lot more e-mails back. Then it caught on. That was the best thing I did, because it gave me intimacy with 28,000 people. That has been helpful in changing the culture.'

The City responded by sending Pearson's share price into orbit. Experts estimated that perhaps a quarter of the multi-billion pound company's value was due to her. They called it the 'Marj factor'. She believes that it had little to do with her being a woman, but all to do with her delivering on objectives. Despite her satisfaction with creating shareholder value, she knew share price was only one indicator of success. She had the TV screen with its financial data from *Bloomberg News* taken out of her office within her first year, because she 'didn't want to keep looking at the share price, although it was rising at the time. If looking at the share price makes you afraid to take the kind of business risks you need to take, or to make some decisions that don't look good today but will pay back tomorrow, then I don't think you should look at your share price. Once it was beginning to scare me I stopped looking at it. I think we are here for the shareholders of tomorrow as well as today.'

The people side of her business is very important to her. She appointed David Bell as 'Director for People' (a title he chose), and applauded his knack of caring for and developing individuals and helping them to excel. She insisted the success she has experienced at Pearson so far is a team effort. When the company results are announced, she always demands that her Finance Director, John Makinson, is with her. She tries to put an arm round him in any photo call to make sure he is included in the newspaper photos. She complains when the press still continues to cut him out of the photographs and credits her with success as if it were something solo. 'It's annoying. It makes me look as if I think I am the only one who is doing all the work, and it is completely untrue. I get all the attention because I am the chief executive and partly because I am a woman – sort of a novelty, you know, like the only blonde-haired person in the whole of the FTSE. But I completely rely on the people who run the different businesses within Pearson.'

She is still fondly called 'The First Lady of the Footsie'. 'To a certain extent the chief executive is the embodiment of the company and there was a euphoria about Pearson and the team here, but it was never about me. I am just the same person as I was before.' Employees call her Marjorie or, fondly, 'Marj in charge'.

However, since the fourth quarter of 2001 she has been under growing pressure to improve Pearson's depressed share price. The falling share price is largely due to the world economic downturn since 11 September, registering the biggest collapse in advertising revenue since the recession of the early 1990s. 'Even with the downturn we are still doing quite well; our shares are worth 50 per cent more than they were a few years ago.'

The *Financial Times* makes much of its editorial independence. James Harding, the *FT*'s media editor, wrote that 'the Marj factor' was fading. Other newspapers began to ask 'will Marj stay in charge?' Marjorie Scardino told reporters that: 'The combination of our businesses will protect us.' Only about 30 per cent of Pearson's business was being affected by 'the worst turndown in advertising in a decade'. A full 70 per cent of the company's operating profits come from its education and publishing business. Her belief in lifetime learning is part of her vision for the company's long-term future and her reason for funding the Learning Network. Identifying new talent and promoting new authors is the essence of publishing. Her company Penguin, for example, has sold 2.6 million copies of Jamie Oliver's first two 'Naked Chef' cookbooks and is publishing a third.

Her own commitment to Pearson is clear. She is in it for the long haul. She became a British citizen last year, and in February 2002 the Queen created her a Dame of the British Empire.

Sorting out Pearson

Her work as CEO at Pearson so far has had four distinctive phases. The first involved reshaping the company from an old-style, unclear company to a more dynamic, focused, strategic one. When she took over leadership of the company, according to her the disposals were obvious. She sold off the bits of the company that were not part of its core competencies – a total of $3.6 billion worth of assets. Madame Tussaud's was sold. Alton Towers, being a part of The Tussauds Group, went. The investment bank Lazard was also sold. She got rid of a loss-making, US CD-ROM maker, Mindscape. She decided that Pearson TV was too small to stand alone and so merged it with the broadcasting assets of Bertelsmann (Germany) and Albert Frère (Belgium) to form a separately quoted European TV company, RTL.

Phase two was to examine what Pearson was particularly good at doing – 'things that appeal to the intellect: business information, education and publishing', as she put it. Acquisitions worth $8.5 billion came in this phase. She bought Simon & Schuster's educational business from Viacom in November 1998. Then she purchased the British illustrated publisher Dorling Kindersley in March 2000. Four months later she bought National Computer Systems (NCS) for £1.7 billion.

'Not many people understand this company', she said. 'NCS tests children and collects data that should enable us to create customized educational programmes. This is a revolution, and it crosses national boundaries. It allows us to offer education online, it allows us to free teachers from trying to figure out what is wrong with a child, why he/she isn't learning and how to help him/her.' With President George W. Bush planning to introduce compulsory testing, NCS, already a profitable company, is well positioned to make its contribution to Pearson's revenue stream. A bill which includes more national testing has just been passed by the US Congress and signed by President Bush. It could allocate at least $400 million to school testing, doubling that market by 2004–05.

Whilst engaging in deal-making, she led the company into phase-three activities – developing its news-media assets, both in educational publishing and in the Financial Times Group. She carried a fight for greater circulation of the *FT* to the door of her competitor, the *Wall Street Journal*, in the United States. By investing $60 million in the campaign, she was able to increase the US circulation from 30,000 to 140,000 in four years (and pay for the investment). Worldwide, the *FT*'s circulation shot up from 300,000 in 1997 to over 500,000 in the autumn of 2001. She also launched a new daily business paper in Germany with Bertelsmann, and in Russia with Dow-Jones. By March 2000 Pearson shares peaked at £23 at the height of the Internet boom.

The fourth phase, begun late in 2001, reveals an element of retrenchment in news media in reaction to unsettled financial markets and doubts about the soundness of Internet investments in terms of the revenues they will generate. Increasing shareholder value has always been one of her aims. When she was named head of Pearson, she said the doubling of share price within five years was a goal. She achieved it in half that time and went on to triple the share price.

She won the Veuve Clicquot Business Woman of the Year Award for 1997. The same year she won the Maria and Sidney E. Rolfe Award from the Women's Economic Roundtable and the New York City Partnership's International Commerce and Leadership Award. And she was the first ever woman to win the European Business Person of the Year for 2000 in the award's fifteen-year history.

Texas-American roots

Marjorie Scardino was born in Flagstaff, Arizona, on 25 January 1947, and was raised in a small town in Texas, Texarkana. Her father was an engineer in a local defence plant. He and his wife had two children – first-born Marjorie and five years later a son. She was a bright student, the kind whom people reminded 'could do anything in life she wanted to do'.

'I did not have a particular expectation. If I did have one, it was to be a journalist or a writer. Then at some point I decided that I would be in politics and I worked for a Congressman for a time.' That was in a Texas dominated by the Democratic Party and the machinery of politics as set in place by Lyndon Johnson, who became President after John Kennedy's assassination. She was a high school student at the time. 'My family was always interested in politics and my grandfather was a big supporter of Lyndon Johnson.'

Her love of education ran deep. 'My grandfather was a school principal in Texas, and I did completely adore him. It sounds corny, but he showed me that what we do matters. I think that the best companies are companies that have a genuine purpose, that offer their employees a chance to feel that when they get up in the morning they really are making a difference in somebody's life.'

When she had to choose her majors at university she chose psychology and French, not English literature. 'When you are 18, as I was then, if you are at all curious, it's hard to focus on what you want to study. I was interested in science and then I thought that I would be an experimental psychologist. But for that I would have had to run experiments with rats, and I did not like rats. I had no career plan.'

She obtained her first degree – a BA in French and psychology – from Baylor University in Waco, Texas.

She worked as a journalist and editor for the Associated Press, where she met her husband. She married Albert James Scardino, a journalist, in 1974. They have two sons, William, 20, and Hal, 16, and one daughter, Adelaide, 22. Albert stayed in journalism and Marjorie returned to law school.

She earned a law degree from the University of San Francisco. She practised law, specializing in business law, but doing whatever came up in a small town, in Savannah, Georgia, as a partner of the Brannen, Wessels & Searcy law firm from 1976–85.

The newspaper business

Together she and her husband started the *Georgia Gazette* in 1978. He won the Pulitzer prize in 1984 for the quality of his editorials in the paper, but the paper collapsed the following year. 'It was a great political success and a huge economic failure. It was a weekly newspaper in a town with a strong daily newspaper. It lasted eight years and it was very educational. I was doing a lot of writing, but I was also practising law. I would come in to the paper in the morning and in the evening and we would put out the paper at weekends.'

She had no formal business training or education and there was a time when she felt a need to fill that gap in her background. 'When we were doing the newspaper, that was the first budget I had ever known. We had a friend who was a dean of the Harvard Business School. I said to him "I think I will do that course that you offer at Harvard for thirteen weeks." He said "Do not go near it, because you are learning so much more having your own business than you could ever learn there at Harvard. You would just be bored." So I never thought of business school again.'

Her sceptical attitude toward formal business education has stayed with her. 'We try to find people at Pearson for our graduate trainee programme or for the strategy department who have had unusual careers and haven't just got out of university or business school. Business schools tend to teach people conformity in the way they think and we want just the opposite – creativity and asymmetrical ways of approaching problems.'

The *Georgia Gazette* collapsed in 1985, leaving them with debt. 'It took us almost until we moved to London to pay it all off.'

New York City: fresh start in the Big Apple

When their newspaper collapsed in 1985 Marjorie Scardino and her husband Albert moved the family to New York City, where he had a journalist job with the *New York Times* and she was headhunted to take a job with the US edition of *The Economist* magazine, a company in which Pearson has a stake. She became chief executive of The Economist Group.

'Running *The Economist* was great for me. It was very brave of them to hire somebody who had run just a little newspaper in Georgia. But their aim at that time was to grow and to make some transformations and I said "I know how to do that!" And the guy who was the CEO of *The Economist* in London at that point said, "Why not?"

'I had been an *Economist* reader and had a feel for it. Yes, it was a big opportunity for me, but it was not too big – only seventy-five people. My job was to think strategically: Where do we take it? What does the brand mean? I vaguely knew what to do because those things were what we had done for our own newspaper. I am reasonably good at thinking of possibilities. One thing that having a business that completely failed gives you is the lack of the fear of failure.'

At *The Economist* in New York the circulation trebled under her leadership. 'The circulation did grow a lot and everybody attributes that to me. But it was due to a team of people who knew what they were doing. The only smart thing I did was to keep them on. They were the ones who did it, and I made sure they had food and water. Then we acquired a few businesses and made *The Economist* a lot larger in America and much larger in the UK and that helped. We sort of raised its visibility!'

Move to London

The decision to come to London, England, was a difficult one. 'It was a big decision for me. My husband thought it was a great idea and my children thought it was a horrible idea. That was ten years ago and they are now 16, 20 and 22.

'So they went to school here, and one still goes to school here, and it worked out very well. London is a city and at that point they had spent more of their lives in New York City than anywhere else, so it was an easy transition. It would have been more wrenching to move to a small town.'

Business-wise the move to London was ideal for her. It also gave her a chance to know Pearson. 'I had been trying to convince Pearson for years to let *The Economist* run the *Financial Times* in America because we thought we could do it so much better. The managing director in Pearson was on *The Economist* board and I knew Dennis Stevenson from various research projects. I knew the other members of what I considered to be a fantastic team of people – I knew both David Bell (who is now Director for People) and John Makinson (who is the Finance Director).'

Move to the top

Looking back on her first five years as CEO of Pearson, Dame Marjorie Scardino feels that she has not changed her way of managing despite the increase in employees from 17,000 in 1997 to 28,000. With characteristic modesty she said: 'I probably should have changed style, but I have done pretty much as I had done at *The Economist*.'

She tries to go out into the businesses and with sales people. She backs her own Director for People, David Bell, in all his developmental activities for her employees. For two years now she and David Bell have been thinking about simplifying how they choose people to hire. 'We've tried to think of some criteria. One of them should be "Be able to suffer fools gladly, because we are all inherently foolish". Simple things like the things your mother taught you.'

She doesn't like rules and procedures. 'I always try to boil down a policy into a sentence. If I get a book of company rules I immediately try to figure out how I can break them, because they so irritate me.'

Leadership style

Sharing the credit for her achievements comes naturally. She makes sure she has the right people in place to run Pearson's companies. Her biggest acquisition to date – Simon & Schuster for $4.6 billion in November 1998 – was made with the help of Peter Jovanovich, a former president of education for McGraw-Hill. He now runs Pearson Education, which includes Simon & Schuster's former businesses as well as Pearson's own Addison-Wesley and Longman.

Share options for employees are as much part of her commitment to her staff as sharing credit. Under her leadership the percentage of Pearson employees owning stock has moved from only 20 per cent in 1996 to 96 per cent in 2001. 'Many people are in a share option scheme, and all are in a share bonus scheme. They may only have a 100 shares, but that makes them a shareholder and it changes their attitude.'

Even her critics admit that she has assembled a formidable management team that enjoys working together. 'When I became CEO, my biggest problem was the culture of the place. It was an old-style patriarchal company, where there were wonderful businesses like fine wine and china, a bank, a wax museum, an amusement park, newspapers and a book publishing business. I took away all the consultants' papers written about the business for Christmas (1996) and I read them. The path was pretty clear. Education, books and business information have a close relationship with each other and require similar skills. They would make a cohesive business. So we set about trying to achieve that.

'Changing the culture was a big challenge. People had been working in their own little part of Pearson and did not know what each other did. They did not take advantage of the fact that they were part of a larger company. They were also not too oriented toward performance. Sure they cared about what they did – and that's important – but they were not attuned to the financial measures. They also did not have a sense of being a company that had the ability and power to change their lives and make more of them. I wanted to change that!

'This is a company full of well-educated and creative people and it matters what they do. I don't think this group of 28,000 people would be good at manufacturing bricks. But as a group it matters to them to help children read.'

When we visited her she wore a baseball cap. It seemed out-of-sync with her title, chief executive, and the posh office she had occupied in the building on the Strand with commanding views of the Thames and the London Eye. But it also had a sense of fun about it, which is one thing she has tried to inject into the company.

Women on the board

Lacking a sense of fun is also, in her view, a barrier to women advancing to boardroom positions. In interviews for boardroom posts, women tend to take themselves too seriously. 'We've tried very hard and Dennis [Lord Stevenson] has worked hard to get more women on our board and more Europeans as well. What you need out of a board is people with a range of experience who can help you make good decisions.'

She agreed that companies with women as their customer base should reflect this at board level and should be scrutinized until they do so. She was happy to hear that a light was being shone on the forty-three companies in the FTSE 100 who have no women at all on their boards, including Sainsbury's, by a coalition of organizations comprising the Cranfield School of Management's Centre for Developing Women Business Leaders, Harriet Harman, the Solicitor-General, the Fawcett Society and the Industrial Society.

In her experience, however, women could do more to make themselves compatible with boardroom behaviours and environment. 'Many of the decisions about who goes on are determined by the chemistry of the new prospective member of the board and the board itself. I have been involved in interviews in which the women felt that they had to be serious and they intellectualized too many things that are not really intellectual. They just did not let themselves be who they were. It led the chief executive to fear that this person was going to be a bore on the board – too serious, and in a way too aggressive. At least twice I have seen a person rejected because of that fear. Women need to work hard at not taking themselves too seriously.'

The Veuve Clicquot Business Woman of the Year Award

Marjorie Scardino welcomed the Veuve Clicquot Business Woman of the Year Award because it was important for other women to see that women could become CEOs of top companies. 'The Veuve Clicquot Award is very important in Britain. It heightens the awareness of young women about their possibilities. I was fortunate enough to have parents who did not think that there were any limits to what you could do. No one told me that girls didn't do this, that or the other. Not all women have that sort of past and it is always good to see someone else succeed and to say "Gosh, that person looks ordinary. Maybe I can do that too." I guess I see myself that way too, as ordinary. The award has allowed me to transmit this message.

'When I was awarded the prize, I shared champagne around with every-body – the sort of head office crowd, the people on my floor. People here always like to see other people get on. Any time anything happens to me, the staff are incredibly nice.'

No gender obstacles to her career progress

When asked about any gender obstacles to her career, Marjorie Scardino said: 'I have been asked this question many times in my career and I do not think so. Things happened to me that happen to all women. When I was a lawyer they sent me home when I appeared in trousers. Ridiculous things like that. For most of us, our obstacles are in our own minds.'

She is wary of artificial constructs that are often created to explain lack of success in management careers. She hates interviews that probe into her background. 'People always ask women these questions because they are trying to find out how they got where they are. It is not ordinary. I do not think that people ever ask men these questions.'

Having children has not been a barrier to her success. 'I have three children, and I've always worked and didn't take much time off to have them. In a small town I could run home for lunchtime. It was easy to do so.'

That she strives for a better work/life balance was illustrated much later one day in London. She attended a business lunch with someone she did not know very well and cut the lunch short, saying, 'I have to go to an urgent meeting.' Actually she dashed off to see her son play in a football match. Across the pitch she noticed the only other parent attending the game, and cheering the other side on, was her chairman, Lord Stevenson, who had also left a meeting to see his son play.

'I hate talking about myself or pontificating. One of the things I do not like about some businessmen is that they appear to know all the answers. They know how to do things. They have been terribly successful in their jobs because they are so clever. They then go on and tell the rest of the world how they should behave in business. I think that is ridiculous. Everyone does it differently. Some of us succeed and some of us fail and some of us do both.'

Patricia Vaz

Patricia Vaz, executive director, BT Retail

In BT's newly restructured organization, with four distinct lines of business, Patricia Vaz sits on the board of Retail as an executive director. She is in charge of the whole of BT's Customer Service in the UK. She controls a budget of £1.4 billion a year and has 40,000 people working for her. She has spent the last twenty-five years working her way up from a clerical job to virtually the top of the company.

Today she is one of the most respected of the telecommunications giant's senior managers and a role model both inside and outside BT for women in management. Speaking at a conference, 'A Voice on the Board', in London in November 2001, she said: 'BT has two female directors on the plc board and they are both non-executive directors. So we have not got it right yet – the issue is how do you get executive directors from the female community on the boards of major companies. I am the nearest you have to it at the moment in BT.' How she got there is an astonishing story.

Family background and early education

Patricia Vaz is from Herne Bay, Kent. Her father was a bank clerk. Her mother was a deputy head of a junior convent school. Her mother was from 'quite a hard-up family where the boys quit school at 14 to put her through college'. Patricia's family consisted of three children – two girls and a younger boy. Naturally the mother had high educational expectations for her daughter Patricia, an energetic middle child. They were not met.

Patricia Vaz made an unpromising start that in no way foreshadowed her success in the management world. She left Canterbury Grammar School at age 17 in 1964 with only one A-level in Maths and the words of her headmistress ringing in her ears: 'Patricia, you'd better learn how to type!'

'It was the sixties and I was laid-back and lazy at school. I did well with my O-levels and then played too much netball and tennis. I had a laissez-faire approach to life. One A-level seemed okay to me', she explained. 'My mother was hugely disappointed in me.'

But she took the headmistress's advice and went to a technical college. In 1965 she became articled to a London chartered accountant. She married the same year at only 18, became a mother at 19, and was living with her husband and her son, Donovan, first at the YMCA and later in a one-bedroom flat in Tooting, south London.

Things looked rather bleak in her own self-assessment. 'My husband and I were determined not to allow our son to grow up in poverty. It was the move to that tiny flat and the realization that we were hard up that was the turning point in my life.'

Secretary to the print trade unions

She used her secretarial skills to obtain a job as bookkeeper at the Printing Federation in 1968, a group of print trade unions. In her six years there she advanced to head of administration. She expanded her role to include general administration and taking minutes at wage negotiations. She claims to have learned invaluable lessons witnessing the male posturing that went on. 'It was amazing how union officials' behaviour changed when they got to the negotiating table. I could see when people's egos needed to be stroked.' (She used the experience later as a senior manager in BT during the 1987 engineers' strike.)

But the print unions fell out with one another, the Federation broke up and she was made redundant. She had a brief spell as a legal secretary and, in 1975, she took an administration job in British Telecom. She was 28. Her husband also worked at BT as an engineer. BT employees, at that time of the old psychological contract of employment, talked about jobs for life with the telecommunications monopoly. It was a career move that would make all the difference to her life.

Inauspicious beginnings at BT

Her first job at BT was in personnel, allocating Arctic underwear for staff on Atlantic cable-laying ships. It told her immediately that personnel was not where she wanted to be; she needed to find a way out.

Patricia showed ambition and moved from clerical jobs to junior management jobs. 'When I joined BT as a clerical officer I moved up the organization by having a vision of where I wanted to be. There were twenty-nine males between me and the top. So I set a goal which was roughly five years ahead and I worked back from that goal to see what I had to do to get there in the five years. At first the goal was to secure a better position and to earn the most money. As I progressed up the organization my goals changed. Later on, I wanted more power and then I wanted to be the first woman to break through the barriers to a new post. At each stage I would reinvent my dream, if you like, and recalibrate it back to where I was to see what was necessary to move on.'

In her short stay in personnel she realized that it would take twenty years for a promotion to a senior position. In one of her low-level personnel jobs she became aware that the salaries of managers outside personnel were much greater. It focused her mind on moving out of support service roles into the technical heart of the business. But to do so she had to persuade her boss to transfer her from personnel to the network side of the business, which deals with the telephone system.

Switching from personnel to networks was something that was never done. 'I remember very clearly the first time that I made one of my big moves from personnel into network planning. My manager at the time, a woman, called me in and said: "This is a big mistake. You do realize that the only place where women will get on in this company is Personnel." I am pleased to say that she is still there at the same level!' Patricia Vaz threatened to leave the company and then rejoin on the technical side. Her resignation from BT would have forced her boss to write a long, tedious report on her exit. She got the transfer she wanted.

She knew that to make headway she would have to break a few moulds. 'I would have to break through into parts of the organization where women had never intruded before.' She did a few marketing jobs on the network side, but wanted to move into engineering. This was the male core of the now privatized company. Without ever studying engineering she applied for a job managing engineers in the field and got it. Her husband, himself a BT engineer, taught her a few technical terms and some set questions to try out on the men she managed in the field. They were impressed. Eventually she won the trust and respect of the men and did so well that she became district engineering manager for Kent and East Sussex. She began developing a disarming management style that won respect and fierce loyalty from her staff. She liked to surround herself with strong people who challenged her. 'I want them to want my job', she said.

'I do not think that there is anything wrong with using charm. I find that men rather like being charmed and they will often listen to you more effectively if you stretch their ego a bit. I do not like the parody of women having to claim to behave like a man, to be able to mix with the men and to get on with the men. I never went in much for drinking with the boys. I had a house to go to and meals to cook. I often wonder what would have happened if I had involved myself more in relationship-building and networking.'

She certainly did her homework and crunched the numbers on every project. She enjoyed being analytical and asking the tough questions at meetings. One colleague summed up her nonchalant style during a meeting in her office. 'I sat there being very attentive. Patricia seemed relaxed to the point where she didn't look as if she was paying any attention. Then the steel trap shut. She asked a question I couldn't answer.'

Payphone turnround

Her most challenging promotion came in 1990 when she was put in charge of BT's payphone operations. It could have been a poisoned chalice. The payphones – 130,000 of them – were a great source of embarrassment to BT as well as losing £70 million a year. The press reflected the cynicism and public dissatisfaction with the service. She welcomed the opportunity to modernize the payphone business and built a team to turn it round.

She decided to create BT payphones as a separate business within the company, with its own profit and loss accounts and its own assets. She had 4,000 people helping her redesign the business. Where they were going, how to cut costs and how to improve and grow the business were the main questions they worked on. One invented a new design for the coin chute that saved them £8 for each phone. Someone else had the idea of introducing BT smart cards. Which phones needed to be cash-based and which could be converted to the BT card posed a huge problem. She set about tearing out the old, red telephone boxes and replacing them with shiny new modern fixtures. This effort met opposition from conservationists, who obtained preservation orders on over a thousand old red telephone boxes in towns and villages and at historical landmarks across Britain. She increased the number of sites, introduced phone cards and stepped up maintenance.

Ideas from the workforce were reinforced by management initiatives. New technology, new systems and new ways of running the service, with more accountability, emerged until the phone boxes stopped losing money. Within four years payphones were generating an annual profit of £60 million and the business had doubled in size. She reduced faults from an average of thirty per phone a year to sixteen, then drove them down still further. She was credited with winning back big accounts like the Post Office and Forte. She had created a smooth running operation that served the communities at a time when few people had cell phones and the poor and older people especially depended on the BT phone box on the corner. A good press justifiably followed.

It was a great challenge with high risk. It involved reaching out to the community and building support from groups as diverse as the police force, senior citizen organizations, judges and church groups. She developed flying squads of BT's own crime stoppers to protect the new payphones against robbery and vandalism. Her men once uncovered a school for thieves being run near a prison. She had other teams work on making the phones as burglar-proof as possible. She helped target the vandals and in the courts gave a real picture of the total cost of vandalism. The damage done to the phone and phone box was only part of it – there was also the lost revenue and the time spent by a number of BT engineers to repair the service. Courts responded by handing down tougher punishments for the vandalism.

Just as progress was being made, a new threat emerged with the advent of cheap, battery-powered electric drills during Christmas 1992. Armed with this new weapon thieves broke into 55,000 phone boxes in one year. The damage was put at £30 million. This new threat was met head on by task forces working out strategies to deal with it, including building in a super-tough, reinforced money box. By the spring of 1993, in a fight-back typical of the woman, she convinced the company that the battle could be won and obtained a budget of £10 million to secure BT's coin-based payphones against theft and vandalism.

Veuve Clicquot Business Woman of the Year Award

Patricia Vaz won the Veuve Clicquot Business Woman of the Year Award for 1994 on the crest of her payphone success for turning the loss-making 'Cinderella' division into an independent and profitable entity within BT. She said of the honour: 'I thoroughly enjoyed myself. The public expo-sure it gave me was enormous and through it I was offered many opportunities to meet different sections of the business community. I learned a great deal about a great many subjects – including, I have to say, myself.'

She won the award for her 'intrapreneurship' – acting like an entrepre-neur within a large corporation rather than starting up her own business. She was in fact the first corporate ladder-climber to receive the award.

But this accolade did not mean as much to her as becoming a Level Two manager at BT after entering the company as a clerical worker. 'It was the first time I'd reached a graduate grade', she reflected. 'Luckily, my mother lived to see it, but she knew I could have been there more than ten years earlier if I'd gone to university as I was supposed to. My mother said women could do anything a man could do and I was determined to prove she was right.'

BT was very proud of her award and made much of it through in-house publicity. 'What we were doing could be benchmarked against other outside organizations.' She was asked to lecture across the world to a wide variety of audiences. The press coverage of the company was very favourable for months after the presentation of the award.

Upward mobility

BT was quick to recognize her powerful management style and personal charisma. She was put in charge of a company-wide change programme called 'Breakout', which aimed to re-engineer every aspect of BT's busi-ness, involving every one of its then 260,000 employees in trying to map the future as a world player in telecommunications. The focus was on a continuous review of procedures and practices. As a member of the group's quality control team, she reported directly to Dr Alan Rudge, who was then deputy group managing director.

Next she was appointed director of Procurement and Logistics with a brief to look after all purchasing worldwide and manage warehousing and distribution. The assignment came at a time when technology and deregulation were revolutionizing the telecommunications industry world-wide. It was a tough assignment. She had to transform the supply chain of the business, closing down lots of warehouses and introducing new technology into both procurement and logistics. Yet despite the unpopularity of the closures, as a manager she received a phenomenal 98 per cent approval rating on the internal 'Care Survey'. (The Care Survey is an employee satisfaction survey used on a regular basis by BT across the company, and containing nearly three hundred items.) Mainly this was because of the way she supported her people during the change – helping them to find alternative jobs, retraining them where necessary and giving them the confidence to treat change as an opportunity.

Handbag management style

The handbag is quite a different symbol for Patricia Vaz from what it was for former Prime Minister Margaret Thatcher. To be 'handbagged' by Margaret Thatcher was to be brought in line with the Iron Lady's political will on issues. For Patricia Vaz the handbag was her own benign management technique in data reduction, as she explained. 'Whether it is running a business unit or developing your people, I've found that there are two or three things that you have to watch out for and be very, very vigilant about. I invented what I call a handbag report that keeps track of these key indicators. Each month I ask my people to provide me with a handbag report. I want only enough indicators to give me a hold over my business that I can fit into my handbag. I don't want great stacks of statistics, because they do not always tell you what is really going on. I would rather be vigilant about these few critical success factors – the ones I carry around with me in my handbag.'

Over the years Patricia Vaz has developed her own style of management that is as effective as it is distinctive.

'I am passionate about equality of opportunity based on a meritocracy. I look every single year at all the performance indicators of all my people. I strip out the females and the people from ethnic minorities to see if their performance rankings are in any way out of line with the males or the majority of the workforce. I do the same with salaries. I watch every year when the salary reviews take place to make sure that we are not allowing people to be disadvantaged because of where they come from or who they are; and because my people know that I do this – that I am vigilant about these things – that in itself has reduced discrepancies.

'I have also produced a set of personal values over the years – these value statements are a sort of scaffolding around the way you expect the people in your unit to work and the way you expect your people to behave. For example, my values around harassment call for zero tolerance. The people in my unit know that. If you disregard this value, you'll be fired. It is difficult to fire someone and you have to prove the harassment, but it can be done. But you have to create an environment where people are treated positively and not undermined.

'When I first joined the company it was made clear to me that this was a male company. I would go round the exchanges that we operated and I would find girlie pictures everywhere. There were no ladies' toilets, nothing at all for women. So I decided to set my values and to tell people what they were and that it was not acceptable to me to go into an environment where I felt insulted. I simply said to the men: "Would you want your wife or daughter to be in this environment? If the answer is no – and it always is – why do you expect me or anyone else like me to put up with it?"'

Clarity of thought is another key variable in her management style. 'This is something that we are quite good at as women, although many men have the attribute as well. It's being able to define the desired state, understand the gap and break it down into manageable chunks. You know how you get to the first stage of the goal and then the second stage of the goal – that's clarity of thought. Having it has stood me in very good stead. It does not seem to matter what particular part of the organization I am involved in or how big the challenges facing me – you need to define the desired state, understand the gap and then break it down to get from where you are to the goal.

'As you progress you develop more confidence in your own abilities, you participate more effectively and start to draw most of your colleagues in the same direction. Managing relationships is critical – that is one I am still working on. You have to constantly keep on top of it. Because you know that other people's goals can conflict with yours. You have to be able to create somehow a win–win situation.'

Part of managing relationships is managing competition between people. 'Men are very competitive and women sometimes shrink from being competitive. You have to acknowledge that it is there and that you have a choice as to whether you want to compete in certain situations or back away. A number of women have said to me that they didn't want to be in the game at all. When you explore why not it is because they don't want the competition and the fight. To compete you must put your head above the parapet and you often get bruised. You have to understand that competition is a fact of life – and then choose to step up to the competition with a willing heart.'

Integrity is another of her key values. 'This is one of my hot buttons. I cannot abide people who are not honest and open enough to acknowledge the real situation. Sometimes I really strain on this one. I go to all the meetings and listen. I've found that I do not actually need to voice my opinion – just being there with them is enough. But it frustrates me when I see people not acknowledging the reality of the situation. It takes guts to say "stop!" but unless we accept the reality of where we are now it is unlikely that we will be able to take the steps to where we want to be – the desired state.'

Leadership style

Tenacity is one of her dominant leadership qualities. 'To achieve a leadership position in any organization you need tenacity – you must keep going and keep trying and you have to be brave. I remember the first time I sat on the board – I was the only woman – the experience overwhelmed me. I was overpowered by the very fact that they had asked me to be there, I sat silent for the first three meetings as if I had been struck dumb. They were all so eloquent in putting their views forward that I was awestruck. But as I listened I realized that they were all making the same point. They were just reproducing it in a different way to make their voices heard.

'The realization hit me right between the eyes. I thought "maybe it's time for me to stop fluffing around". So I plucked up courage and said: "look, isn't there a simpler way of looking at this? Isn't it just this, this and this." And the CEO at the time turned to me and said, "I wondered when you were going to speak." The truth is he could have made it easier for me and drawn me out earlier on some of the topics, if he had been listening not just to words but aware of the body language.

'I've never forgotten that and I try to listen to people and note their body language and where they are uncomfortable and draw them into conversations at meetings before problems arise. It's a form of empathy and empathy is something women are particularly good at. Empathy involves listening and checking for understanding. It's something women do well. I met a scuba diver once on holiday in the West Indies and he persuaded me to try the sport. He said to me that he preferred to train a woman rather than a man in scuba diving. He said, because a man will go to death's door, he will see it in front of him and swim up to it – the macho thing is: "I can do this!" Whereas a woman will always say, "Can we avoid the danger, what if, can we find a way of overcoming this, can we be safe?" Checking for understanding enables you to expose the weaknesses and the risks in what you are trying to do. If you can expose them, then you can devise a strategy that mitigates those risks.'

Conflict resolution is another contribution she makes to her organization as part of her leadership style. 'I do inject an element of conflict resolution among the people I lead. It's the same sort of thing I've been doing at home in the family – it comes naturally to me. I've done it all my life. I find it easy to say, "well you are being hurtful here" or "someone has a problem here, let's address it". Women often have a different perspective on conflict resolution because our level of experience is different and our lives are different.

'I am terribly impatient with organizational politics. I can't stand people speaking simply because they need to be heard. I usually say, "Let's stop the nonsense and get this straight."'

Gender barriers to career success

'The long-hours culture in BT is something I've had to fight against from the beginning of my career. It was very prevalent at the start and probably is still there to an extent, but at least there is a little more recognition of it now. In the early days the long-hours culture was such that men would bring a second jacket to work and hang it over the back of their chair so it looked as though they were still there, even if they weren't. Your commitment to work was measured by the hours you put in and your chance of promotion was measured by this perceived commitment, not what you delivered.

'I had a difficult time when I joined BT. I had a son to look after and a house to run. I had a childminder to look after my son only to a certain time. I needed to catch a 5.30 train every night. So I had to use my negotiating skills. I'd go to my manager and say: "Look, I'll do a deal with you. If you do not hold meetings at 4.30 in the afternoon when you know I can't stay and cannot participate effectively long enough, I'll take work home and do these specific things in my own time." And I would list all the things I was prepared to offer if they did not make my life impossible. That idea was completely new to my manager. He said: "No one has ever done this before, what do you mean?"

'I don't think these managers made things difficult for working mothers deliberately. They just didn't think things through – for instance, when they would plan to have a workshop they would often ask people to attend the night before they needed to so that they could have a team-building event in the hotel bar. To do that to a woman who has to pay a childminder to look after her child overnight or who has to depend on her husband for child care (if she has one), is not very considerate. I would say to my managers and I do it even now, I will not come the night before just to have a good team meeting in the bar, but I will come in the morning. If you are going to give me some meaningful work the night before I will have to make arrangements. But do not do this unnecessarily and do not do it if you have other women on your staff. You have to raise the level of awareness repeatedly. Otherwise it never stops and this band of brothers does stick together, especially in the pub.

'I remember at one stage in my career I had a building to refurbish. I recall how a senior manager argued for the radical open plan where no one had offices, and he was delighted with the benefits of the idea whereby he could meet up with all his colleagues easily and often. He said that he would be able to make decisions with his colleagues on the board in the gym. Or in the corridor or even in the men's toilets. He forgot I was on his board and that I didn't plan to put a microphone in the gents to participate in decision-making. He was so used to an all-male environment that he didn't realize what he was saying, but that one thoughtless comment was enough to immediately make some of us worried about being able to stay involved in the business.

'Institutional prejudice is something we have to be very vigilant about because it is so easy to choose people in your own image. We all do it to an extent. If I look at what happens to graduates who join our company and how many achieve promotions, why is it that when you reach a certain level the number of women selected is so very low? I have come to the conclusion that, since we do choose people in our own image, we must inject a change in the critical mass and produce more women at all levels to do the choosing as well as to be chosen from.

'You have to face up to conflict and I understand why some women feel the fight is just not worth the winning. I can respect that and I believe that is why so many women leave the corporate environment to set up their own companies.'

Another barrier she encountered was guilt. 'The final self-imposed barrier is guilt. I can remember being racked with guilt in the early days of my career. First it was guilt about leaving my son with the childminder. I was surrounded by neighbours who said this was terrible, and did I realize that he could become a criminal when he grows up because he is a latch-key child. I am talking about thirty years ago – people are more enlightened nowadays. But there is still guilt associated with the fact that you may not be giving the quality attention you should to all the components in your particular work/life balancing act.

'I had a conversation with some female senior management colleagues in which one of them said: "I feel I am a mother by the skin of my teeth." Another said, "Why is it I feel guilty if I am working from home and I hang out the washing? It takes me only ten minutes to do so, but I feel guilty about doing something not work-related, when I'm supposed to be working from home for BT." It doesn't matter that when the men come into work on a Monday morning they spend at least twenty minutes talking about football and women do not want that. Self-imposed guilt feelings seem to be more characteristic of women than of men.'

She sums it up with a quote from Shirley Brunnel: 'Do women want to fight the battle? Is the want to go through the fight greater than the want to be safe where you are?'

'We have identified getting the work/life balance right as a key retention tool.' It is particularly difficult in her part of the telecommunications business – customer service. Because customers demand round-the-clock service, she needs to find engineers who do not mind working unsociable hours like 'after eight o'clock at night or all through the night'. But it is also difficult to manage performance in a more flexible environment.

One of her biggest challenges is changing the reward structure for her engineers, accustomed to a standard rate of pay plus overtime, to a bonus scheme based on performance. 'The managers are going to have to manage by output rather than input. They are going to have to stop cracking the whip and saying, "Work faster, I want another job from you today." Their people will decide how many jobs they want to do because they know what they want to earn. There is going to be an enormous pull from the people who want to earn more money and therefore get the flaws in the systems and processes put right. Most of my managers in the engineering field are regrettably still men. There are some women, but they are dominated by men. Neither men nor women have ever managed in this way and they don't know what to do. So I'm having to develop training programmes for them on how to manage and lead from the middle – that is, in a supportive, troubleshooting way – still providing the clarity of direction but then being able to achieve through releasing the talents and harnessing the enthusiasm and commitment of their people.'

There are solid business reasons for getting the work/life balance right for BT's employees. 'There are 4,000 registered homeworkers in BT at the moment. But we have another 10,000 people – like me – who have no offices, but just wander around and sometimes work from home, but most often travel from one location to another. Having just that small number of homeworkers and non-office bound workers has saved BT £22 million in accommodation costs. Imagine the savings if we step that up as we intend to do. The technology available to us all now enables us to work in a different way. With new technology I can organize conference calls and I can hold a meeting while I am still in my pyjamas.'

Raising her voice

Patricia Vaz believes fiercely in being heard. 'As a senior manager I have a big voice in the organization and I use it. I make a lot of noise – in fact, too much noise for some of my colleagues. But I have a duty to raise my voice – I've got there and I'm making a difference.

'I talked with one of our senior women managers who was considering leaving. "Why are you going to leave? You're great", I said to her. It was nothing to do with the pay, nor was it to do with the organization – which she loves. It was to do with an environment in which she felt she was not listened to. Her worries about her clients were not being taken seriously and she was not being heard. She wrote to her manager about it and he, not knowing how to handle her issue, simply ran away from it. Men often run away from the softer bits because they are harder to cope with than the tough technical or financial problems. It's up to us women to put forward coping strategies for the men on these softer matters. It's no good just expecting them to change, because they do not know how to. As I did in negotiating with my own manager on long-working hours, we have to open negotiations on changing the environment. Put a proposition to a man and say this is having this effect on women – if you could do this, it would help me and all my female colleagues. Nine out of ten times it's simple stuff and they are happy to sort it out. But first you have to help them understand the situation and then to learn how to cope with it.

'We have not succeeded yet in creating a company culture that celebrates gender diversity. We have not quite got there when it comes to the necessary cultural changes, and that is where my big voice is still needed. The number of women managers should rise and that is right, but unless you change the culture women will not want to fight. You do need to fight even today.'

Patsy Bloom

Patsy Bloom, founder and former chief executive, Pet Plan Group

'I had a dog, Jamie, that was very sick, with a history of illness. One night I went out to dinner with an old boyfriend. We were talking about the dog and about the high cost of vet fees and he said, "Isn't there a BUPA or PPP for animals?" and I said, "No." He said, "Why don't you start one?" and I said, "Don't be so silly." It was the only idea I've had that seemed better the morning after the night before.

'The next day I started to research the idea and the deeper I got into it the more potential I discovered it had. I had no intention of giving up my job. I thought the animal health insurance plan was something I could do part-time and possibly earn myself £25 a week extra. At the Central British Fund for Jewish Refugees (CBF) I was earning £4,000 a year – that was in 1976–77. I went to CBF and told them that I had this idea and asked them if I could go part-time to develop it. I guaranteed them that I would bring in the same results at work, but that I needed time to follow up on this idea. They were very decent and let me do it.'

She channelled her considerable energy into testing out the idea. She went to a neighbour, Annie Dickins, and asked her if she would spend £10 a year to insure her pets. The neighbour, a professed animal-lover, said: 'Yes, of course', and ended up deputy head of one of the four divisions of the new business start-up.

Patsy Bloom, who described herself as '*not* a scatty animal-lover' but a businesswoman, went in search of a business partner. She found David Simpson and they invested £250 each into the new venture. She had to borrow the money from her father. She then made two key decisions: (1) to never insure the animals themselves, but to turn instead to established companies – at first a small company, Dog Breeders Insurance, then later one of the insurance giants, Lloyds of London, and finally Cornhill Insurance – for the underwriting, and (2) to commit herself full-time to running the business.

Once she was full-time she enlisted the help of vets across the country and persuaded them to hand out her leaflets explaining Pet Plan. The year was 1977. Some of these vets at first threw cold water on the idea, saying insuring pets had failed before; most, however, co-operated. She explained

Pet Plan as a classic win–win situation for everyone. Owners of the pets received better, cost-effective treatment for the pets through the scheme. Vets were able to provide the best affordable medical care for the domestic animals and leisure horses. Her company, in exchange for a welcomed product and quality service, would grow and become powerful and profitable.

Sixteen years later, as a stunningly successful entrepreneur, aged 52, she collected the Veuve Clicquot Business Woman of the Year Award for 1992. She had defined a new service industry – health care insurance for domestic animals. She had created a profitable and expanding business, the Pet Plan Group of Companies, that still leads the market and has given rise to other companies, imitating their approach. At the time of the award in March 1993 the Pet Plan Group of Companies was operating 350,000 policies, controlled 51 per cent of the market for small domestic animals and a large slice of the leisure horse market. Turnover was running at £20 million.

Having founded and led the Pet Plan Group of Companies as chief executive for twenty years, Patsy Bloom sold the Group for £32.5 million to Cornhill Insurance in May 1996. By then Pet Plan had 400,000 policy-holders and had reached £40 million turnover. It had only made a dent in the potential market of Britain's 7 million dogs, of which just 12 per cent are insured, and 7.2 million cats, of which just 3 per cent have cover. Pet Plan had 30 per cent of the insurance market for the UK's 450,000 horses. It had launched a special credit card aimed at animal lovers.

Patsy Bloom received half of the sale price – £16 million – making her by far the highest woman earner in Britain that year; her business partner, David Simpson, took the other half. Together they made a spectacular 64,900 fold return on their joint £500 investment in the business. They both stayed with the new owners as board members. Then she retired to enjoy life from her flat in Central London, to administer Pet Plan Charities and to invest the money she made in property.

Family background and early education

Patsy Bloom grew up in a small family – just herself and one brother, Roy, her father Len Bloom and her mother Freda. 'I was brought up in a North London Jewish family where everybody worked in that culture then and now. My parents had three sweet shops called Tommy Frost's and were working seven days a week to run them. I worked in the shops as a kid. Small talk in our house was conversations about other people's businesses. At age 11, I decided that I wanted to work for myself.'

She described her mother, who is still alive, as kind, pragmatic and full of common sense. She herself was more like her father – driven, full of rigid principles and passionately devoted to work. 'Black and white, no compromise' was how she put it.

'My father was part businessman and part professional punter, which made me very much not a gambler. He contracted angina when he was 43 and was advised by his doctor to get fresh air, so he began going to the races.' How good the betting was for his heart is debatable. As a consequence, any instinct to gamble with money was removed for both her and her brother at an early age. 'My attitude to money is fairly cautious. Later in life when I hired my first chauffeur, I had an image of my dead father saying: "Who do you think you are, Patsy Bloom?"' Her grandmother took her to every film of every Broadway musical there was. It gave her a life-long love of musical theatre. She developed her own taste for New Orleans jazz.

'I never wanted to be told what to do. That's why I didn't marry till three years ago because I was never going to get married to anyone who told me what to do.' (She married Robert Blausten in London in December 1999, three years after she sold her share in the business.)

'It is part of the Jewish culture to want to work for yourself or to want to work at the top. I wanted to be independent. I remember my first pay packet. I was so excited because I no longer had to ask my father for pocket money.

'I went to a convent school from ages 4–8 and hated it. Then I went to a local school where we lived and then attended the local grammar school, Paddington and Maida Vale. I don't think I completed one single day of my entire education inside a classroom. I was hauled out of the classroom for one reason or another. I always rebelled. I left school at 15.' She didn't have a single O-level. She went to secretarial college, 'which is what good girls did'. Her first secretarial job was working for trumpeter Eddie Calvert.

First jobs in advertising

'I went to work in advertising. In the late fifties, early sixties, it was full of Hooray Henries and a fun thing to do. I think I probably was not bad at it. Looking back, I realize that I worked for some very famous names – Alexander Butterfield [where she looked after the Oxfam account – "I refused to touch a typewriter after that"], Mary Quant Cosmetics, *Queen* magazine, Anthony Cheetham, and the charity Central British Fund for Jewish Refugees (CBF).

'While at Oxfam I worked for a man who had a profound influence on the charity side of my life. In those early jobs, I was either promoted or fired. I was never one to be just left in a corner quietly doing my work. I liked doing outrageous things.

'When I was about 30, I went to work full-time for the Charity. I had already decided that I was not going to make my mark on the world in advertising. It's funny now – but I thought I was too old to achieve anything then. I went to work for World Jewish Relief, a large, reputable charitable organization. I was there on and off for about eight or nine years. I had a fabulous job and a fabulous social life. They were fantastic to me. On the side I always did some public relations or marketing jobs, which was in the open – they knew about the freelance work. At the Charity, I just did not earn enough to live on. My story is very much a woman's story, because no man would have done what I did – no man would have worked for the Charity in the first place.'

Starting up Pet Plan

Having researched the idea of a medical health plan for domestic animals and found it full of potential, Patsy Bloom felt the need for a partner. 'I wanted a man as a partner, not a woman. I looked at the business plan and at first thought I'd do it myself. Then I remembered that I was a marketing person – that was my trade. I looked at my gaps and decided this thing needed a man.' She points out that few bank managers took women seriously in 1977. 'I also wanted someone who was not Jewish – someone from a different culture, someone who was more "country". I was "town", a Londoner. I needed someone exactly opposite to me, someone to make up what I lacked. If I had wanted someone to tell me I was wonderful, I would have put my mother on the board.

'I started this thing like a hobby and it began to grow. I was doing it part-time. So I was photocopying Pet Plan orders on the Chief Rabbi's photocopier.' She is also a self-confessed workaholic, so not having a marriage or children to worry about suited the high-energy approach and long hours she invested in the business.

'My aunt Sadie came to work for me and my parents worked for me free, and every boyfriend I had ended up giving me the best financial advice in the City for nothing except wonderful dinner dates. The biggest decision – if you talk about this as we do in bridge [she's a fanatical bridge player] – the key card decision – was that we were never the insurer. We found this little old insurance company, Dog Breeders Insurance, to do that and that was easy. It soon became apparent that the little company could not handle the volume of business we created. Fortunately, we were headhunted to take the business to Lloyds. It was like grown-up status to have Lloyds as our underwriter. We were now something. In those days – twenty-five years ago – to be underwritten by Lloyds was the ultimate. It was rock-solid security – a real cachet for us.'

During the nearly twenty years she did business with Lloyds from year three of Pet Plan until virtually when she sold the business to Cornhill Insurance, she worked closely with Lloyds. She enjoyed the rough and tumble of the Lloyds dealers, who reminded her more of market traders than conventional insurance men.

'The second key card decision was my decision to go full-time. This moment of decision-making is very clear for me. I remember being on my own one Sunday. I was pacing the floor at home and thinking that I really did have to decide whether to go full-time or not and it was probably the bravest decision. I was quite well protected in that I knew that the Charity would take me back. But I had a flat and a mortgage to pay for. I decided that weekend to bite the bullet. If I did not go full-time the business was never doing to progress. On that Sunday evening I phoned the manager of Dog Breeders Insurance and asked him if he was satisfied with the business. Isn't that a typical woman asking someone else if they were all right? He said he was, so I drew strength from that fact and I gave in my notice at the Charity. But for years afterwards I had the same dream, that I wanted my old job back and they wouldn't give it to me. As we became more successful, the dream faded away.

'I went full-time and David Simpson, who had his own property and finance business and was only a "sleeping partner" in Pet Plan, was happy to keep things that way.' She did the legwork setting up the company. 'It was like inventing Kleenex. I had to sell the concept before I could sell the product', she recalled. She travelled around, accompanied by Annie Dickins, to dog shows and veterinary surgeries promoting the new product of domestic animal insurance. She would sponsor local meetings of the British Small Animal Veterinary Association. But only on condition that they would allow her to give a short talk. 'They must have thought I was mad', she recalled. But today she is an honorary member of the Association.

Coming from a marketing background rather than an insurance one proved to be an advantage. She looked at the product and service she was offering from a pet owner's point of view, not an insurer's. 'The policies that did exist would only provide cover for animals under 8 years old, and would not pay up if the sicknesses were hereditary or congenital. What was the use of that to the owner?' she asked.

Pet Plan decided against insuring industrial animals like pigs, chickens, cows and sheep. The company listed a few other animals on their exclusion list, such as pet parrots. Rabbits eventually became a rapidly increasing part of the business. Coverage for domestic pets under Pet Plan policies rival the medical care given to humans. Broken legs are set for cats and dogs, cataracts are removed from dogs' eyes and pacemakers fitted to dogs' hearts.

At the time Patsy Bloom received the Veuve Clicquot Award claims on the company were relatively modest. A chinchilla cat that kept getting mouth ulcers from eating frogs was treated three times under the Pet Plan policy. A poodle that swallowed a Rod Stewart cassette got a £167 claim paid. A St Bernard that fell off a cliff in Devon had a claim for £1,300 paid, despite the suspicion that it might have been attempted suicide rather than an attacking swarm of wasps, as the owner insisted.

Today the rise in claims being paid to clients reflects both the increase in the cost of living and the more sophisticated treatment afforded animals. A record £10,000 claim was paid to a client in January 2002 to cover veterinary treatment for a Labrador that enabled it to walk again. As Patsy

Bloom predicted, Pet Plan continues to grow. Today it has over half a million clients – a 42 per cent market share. It receives 1,300 claims per day and pays out approximately £850,000 each week.

Pet Plan was quick to respond to the special needs of pit bull owners in the early 1990s. The Dangerous Dog Act required that they have their dogs muzzled and insured. They were the only company to offer insurance specifically for dangerous dogs, thereby gaining a monopoly position.

It was a challenge to make allies of the veterinarians in building the business. She relied on vets, 'the most honest professionals in the country'. She worked first from her flat in London's Maida Vale and then from a small, windowless office above the old Wood Lane Underground Station in Shepherd's Bush, before moving to a spacious Georgian-style house in an affluent London suburb. She also targeted breeders and included visits to them as she travelled the country. She did not mind doing the lion's share of the work for Pet Plan. 'But after two years or so, I said to David that we had to sit down and talk about the business. We had about eleven staff at the time and I told David that, if we wanted to go further, either he had to go full-time or we had to hire someone to take on his role. So he came on full-time. Yet it was not full-time the way I was doing. He had other business interests to look after as well, but he ran them from Pet Plan, which became his first business.

'David and I had an extremely volatile relationship. But now I will say what I thought for many, many years and it's something I still believe today. To be really successful you need a man and a woman in the business. I would not have been able to achieve all that I did without him or without a man as a partner. I have always said that without me as a partner he would have achieved nothing at all!'

Maturing the business

'For the first five years I ran the business single-handedly. For the next ten years David and I ran it together, and for the last five years David ran it and I started to step back.'

Including horses among the recipients of Pet Plan insurance in 1988 was a strategic move for the company. Patsy Bloom took personal charge of the Equine Division. 'I wasn't conscious of it at the time, but I suppose I was becoming stale. It was fun to have my hands on something that was small again.' The effort was bolstered by Pet Plan's purchase of Norwich Union's equine book, making it the largest leisure horse insurer. Suddenly – with the expansion into horses – the City began taking Pet Plan seriously. There were pressures to go public, but she was set against it. 'First, if we go public, they will come to me and ask me all those questions. They'll ask me about all the figures for today's business and the projected figures for tomorrow's business, and I won't have a clue about the numbers they want for their investment forecasts because I am concerned about what is happening with the vet down the road and why we are not getting more support from him.'

Expanding abroad is always a danger for young companies. 'When the company was about ten years old we had two non-executive directors. We also had an outside financial adviser, a long-term friend of mine. There would be six of us sat round the boardroom table – all men except me. All the men would start pontificating about what they were going to do. "I think now that we should go into America", one would say. "Yes, go into America!" they would agree. And another would say: "I think we should go into South Africa – and what about Europe?" And they would chatter away saying we definitely should be doing this and that. I would bang the bloody table and scream, and say: "Excuse me, we have not got into Birmingham yet. We have not resolved the problems with the carbon sheets on the application forms for cover, so before you guys go running off round the world, we had better establish the business that we have here." When I brought these men into the boardroom it was to help plan the business professionally – to be fair – but I hadn't realized that they would be all global and no details.'

A flirtation with taking the idea to America nearly caused the company's collapse. 'My biggest mistake was an ill-fated venture into the United States in the early 1980s when, although I was convinced we were going to be a success, we were a very small company. It started at the Cruft's dog show, where we had a stand. A New York dog breeder who had seen us there phoned and said she'd like to take the idea to the States. She had worked in public relations and her husband was vice-president of an insurance company. I met them in a flat they had in London. The situation seemed ideal; they had the right credentials. She was not an insurance broker but said she would sit the exams. I liked America very much and was very excited.

'I called David Simpson and told him we could go into America and it wouldn't cost us anything. He came over in a cab to join the discussion. We didn't ask for references because of her husband's job. In the end, we left to draw up plans. Because a number of pet insurance schemes had failed in the US, we decided to offer a scheme aimed specifically at breeders. The woman said she had the contacts. It was decided I would go to New York to set things up. I was there for three weeks. I should have been home minding the shop.

'The contracts were being set up when I got the first signs that all was not well. She said she got involved with dogs after seeing one left in a car with the window opened only a fraction: she smashed the window with a brick and took the dog out. And the husband was never available to give insurance advice, which was what he was going to bring to the arrangement. She had taken her exams and wanted to open an office but had no money. So we advanced her funds against her customers for an office and equipment. Some months later all we had done was spend money.

'In about eight months she had sold ten policies, including those for her own dogs, for a gross premium of $5,000. We faced one claim for $10,000 on a show dog that had a heart attack and about $15,000 in other claims. The deal cost us about £30,000 at a time when we could ill afford it. It almost cost us our international underwriter and nearly cost us our partnership. We've not been back to the US since . . . I'm not saying we won't go back – but getting carried away by the glamour of wanting to do something was nearly catastrophic.

'Some months later a competitor was able to set up in our UK market and I'm sure it was because my eye was not on the ball. In some ways, though, it may have been the best money we ever lost – because it may have saved us making the same mistake years later, with a few extra noughts.'

Among her hardest decisions was to let go of the people who started the business with her. 'Eventually we let go of everybody. As we let go of old cronies, the business did expand and we prepared for the next stage of development. It could not breathe unless it had new people in it. But once I had let all the old people go, I no longer liked the company. But we had doubled and trebled our sales and operations. Then I decided to get rid of me. Once we went to Cornhill Insurance and benefited from their financial management, I could see it played to David's strengths. He came back into his own. I looked at this and thought to myself, if I wrote out my self-assessment on a piece of paper against the requirements of my job in this new set up, I think I would fire myself. I no longer had any desire to be President and to go to the office every day.'

Selling up shop

'I think timing in life is everything. I was hungry when I started and unhappy when I finished. By this time I was earning loads of money and I could do what I liked. I either do something because I'm passionate about it or I do not do it at all. I am not a person to sit on the sidelines. Just before Tony Blair came to power in 1997 I went to lunch at the Savoy with one of our famous non-executive directors. That's what City people do – lunch at the Savoy – and all of their key business decisions are made at the Savoy. He was a good friend of David's and a good business friend of mine, and he spoke kindly in my interest. He said that it was likely that Tony Blair would win the election and that there was a very good chance that Capital Gains Tax (CGT) would go up, because that's what they thought in those days. He said that I may find that the £10 million I was worth, or whatever it was then, was going to be halved because of tax and that it would take me another five years to get it back.

'I finished the lunch. I took a cab all the way to Chiswick. I walked into the office and told David I wanted to sell the business. He nearly fainted. We put the business into play that day.

'We employed Rothschilds, the famous merchant bankers, to create an auction for Pet Plan. Five companies expressed serious interest, culminating in Cornhill putting in the best offer.'

Cornhill Insurance plc had been underwriting Pet Plan's policies for the previous two years and knew the company's potential. Under the new owners, Pet Plan's staff of 200 remained at their headquarters in Brentford, Essex. As a unit of Germany's Allianz AG Holding, Cornhill Insurance had the resources to take the business further and faster. Patsy Bloom went on the board of Cornhill's new subsidiary Pet Plan, with responsibilities for marketing and promotion. David Simpson became chief executive.

Her comments on the sale were characteristically upbeat. 'The company is so enormous now it couldn't possibly continue to expand without substantial investment, particularly in technology. We've taken it a long way from £500 between a couple of people.

'Tony Blair did win the election, but he did not put the tax up. We sold the business and I was absolutely delighted. And the business has doubled and trebled since then and is worth hundreds of thousands more, but that makes not the slightest difference to me. I had a good time whilst I was there – not so good those last two or three years – and a wonderful time afterwards.'

Pet Plan Charitable Trust

'One thing that we kept was the Pet Plan Charitable Trust. David and I still sit on the board. I was chairman for two years and I stepped back from that and handed the chairmanship to David. I am still a life-time trustee, and that is now my main involvement. In fact they just phoned me to remind me that it is Pet Plan's 25th anniversary. The Trust gives grants for veterinary research and equipment.'

Looking back on personal success

'Timing is everything and luck is important too, but I have to say that it is much more than that. Pet Plan was based on a solid foundation – all those things that I had learned in my marketing trade. The product had to be good and the service as well. Today people talk about spin-doctors. None of that matters if the product is no good. You might sell it the first year but the customers will not come back.'

What did it feel like to sell her brainchild after twenty years of nourishing it? 'People asked if I felt like I was losing a baby, but I told them quite the reverse. It was like trying to kick a reluctant teenager out of the house.'

Veuve Clicquot Business Woman of the Year Award

Patsy Bloom received the Veuve Clicquot Business Woman of the Year Award (1992) from Health Secretary Virginia Bottomley, a long-term champion of women's advancement in management, at Claridges in London at a lunch celebration. 'It's incredibly exciting to win', she said.

'When I started I thought I had a good idea. The veterinary profession said it had never worked in the past, but I made it work. When I first took my idea to an insurance company they laughed at it. They couldn't believe that anyone could make money out of cats and dogs. But I hung on in there and proved them wrong', she said to the audience gathered for the ceremony.

She predicted a bright future for her company. 'Pet Plan is not a fashion business, built on the latest trend of the day. It will do just as well in a recession as in a boom.' After receiving the award, she said she would be back in the office, if not later in the afternoon then in the morning for sure. 'I will be celebrating with my Yorkie, Champers!' she said on receiving the case of special vintage La Grande Dame champagne.

Her final words to the women and men gathered to celebrate her achievement were from the heart. 'If I hadn't looked for a male partner, when I started, I wouldn't have been taken seriously in the City. There is still a lack of understanding today, but things are immeasurably better. There is no doubt that these women [other winners of the award] and others like them have pushed the barriers back for women. But the main change is that today men under 40 seem to treat women as equals. I don't think women are ever going to be the same as men, they are different. But they can play equally important roles.'

Looking back on the award, Patsy Bloom said that it had a great impact both on her company and on herself personally. 'It put us into a much broader market, since people like Anita Roddick had won the award in the past.'

She also credited the award with bringing her out of her shell, changing her life. 'I married the business. For more than fifteen years I worked every day of the week, 100 hours a week.' That is, until she won the award. 'It brought me out of the closet. I started meeting new people and realized just how stuck I had become in that little animal world.' She began giving interviews to newspapers, going out to lunch without a business agenda, and publicizing the work of the Pet Plan Charitable Trust. She displayed the Award prominently on a coffee table in her flat to remind herself of the recognition and the symbol of personal change.

Gender barriers to success

Men behaving badly in the boardroom is one of her frustrations. She observed it when the company was growing and the men on the board were more concerned with global expansion than with the details of running the business.

'If you sit at a board meeting of most companies you'll find that they are run by men who say things like, "Absolutely right! You are absolutely right, old chap!" Then they leave the boardroom and say something totally different and go off and do their own thing. But they never let the team down – they are all bloody cricket players. I find that entrepreneurial people, particularly women, are different. I was quite a good leader of the team, but I am not a team player.'

She was not strategic by nature, but learned to be strategic for the good of the business. 'I have absolute tunnel vision, and I will not go to the second step until the first step is secure. We ploughed every single penny that we made back into the business. We didn't allow ourselves to be side-tracked.' Her business partner David Simpson agreed about her focus on the job at hand, and indicated one of their individual differences that made the partnership thrive. 'She has absolute determination and drive. While I tend to look forward and conceptualize, she is great at pushing things through.'

She does not see herself as a role model. But she does have advice to those starting out in business, particularly entrepreneurs:

- You need dedication, energy, a strong element of good luck and of course a good product.
- Surround yourself with a strong team with skills complementary to your own and do not be afraid to delegate.
- You must have a talent to inspire.
- Go for venture capital.

'Venture capital was not available when I began. It's a different ball game now. You could not start up a company the way we did with private money.'

Phyllis Cunningham CBE

Phyllis Cunningham CBE, former chief executive, The Royal Marsden Hospital

Although Phyllis Cunningham is by nature introverted and reserved, she was never shy when it came to fulfilling her role as chief executive. 'When I have a cloak on that says "Chief Executive" or "Chairman", I can walk into a room and start talking with people I do not know, or give a speech to thousands at a conference. If it is planned and part of my role, I can do it. Although I would not normally stand up with a mike and ask questions at a meeting, if there is something to do connected with my role – like spontaneously giving a vote of thanks – I can do it. I am not intimidated.'

In her last full-time job as chief executive of the Royal Marsden NHS Hospital, Phyllis Cunningham managed 2,000, employees and was responsible for the welfare of thousands of patients. She worked with skilled surgeons and other doctors and technicians, medical researchers and scientists on her team at the Royal Marsden Hospital. She also raised funds in the millions for her hospital. She dealt with doctors and medical researchers from around the world who came to see their state-of-the-art treatment for cancer sufferers. She negotiated with entrenched trade unions. She engaged in complex political processes with ministers of government, shadow ministers and other politicians, who placed the National Health Service high on their agendas.

She was Veuve Clicquot's Business Woman of the Year for 1991. In 1994 she was a finalist for a European Women of Achievement Award. She received a CBE from the Queen in 1997 for her contributions to health care.

Friend to Princess Diana

As chief executive of the NHS's Royal Marsden Hospital, Phyllis Cunningham became a friend of Princess Diana. She travelled to a conference in Chicago with the Princess. They both gave talks to the conference and flew back to London together. It was one of their many shared experiences, which ranged from visits to patients to public speeches and fund-raising for Britain's leading specialist cancer hospital.

'I went to the sale of her dresses with her as well. The Princess of Wales was President of the Royal Marsden Hospital, so we did many things together. She came to Marsden on her first solo visit after she was married. I had never seen a young person with such empathy with people. It was amazing that first time, and it was amazing all the other times over the years that I knew her. She was a wonderful person who really did care for people. It was not a duty and certainly not an act. When we were visiting hospitals in New York she would not allow her lady-in-waiting or the police into the room. Only she and I would go in to see patients.'

Phyllis Cunningham was at her town house in Brentford Dock in Brentford, Middlesex when she learned of Princess Diana's death. 'They phoned me at 6 a.m. and by 8 a.m. I was whizzed off to the BBC and was there most of the day commenting on it. I suppose that helped my grieving for her. But it was the same for me as it was for many people – it just didn't sink in – you just did not think it had happened. Even at the funeral it did not sink in. It was only afterwards when everything became quiet that I deeply felt the loss.'

Early retirement

After twenty-four years' service at the Royal Marsden, Phyllis Cunningham retired as chief executive in May 1998. She chose her moment unselfishly and purposely. 'I had been involved in the consultation for the new NHS and I knew that it was going to take ten years to put in place. I had another three years to go on my contract. I felt that it would be wrong for me to put in place the foundation stones of that ten-year development.' Rather than burden her successors with her freshly laid 'foundation' for the new era, she opted out early. In doing so she knew that the board that she had worked so well with would be in a position to choose a new chief executive who, like her, would be totally committed to Marsden.

The Marsden staff marked her retirement as 'the end of an era'. She arrived at the famous hospital in November 1974 to take up the post of deputy house governor and made headlines six years later as the second woman to be appointed to a senior health position in the United Kingdom, when she became chief executive.

She steered the Royal Marsden through numerous reviews of London teaching hospitals, threats of merger and closure. She also saw it through to Trust status in 1994. 'When I went to the Royal Marsden, friends suggested that it might be a depressing place to work, but I found the atmosphere to be welcoming, friendly and helpful. The staff have a great sense of loyalty and commitment which has carried the hospital through all the upheavals of change.'

She had just turned 61 and with her record could have expected a worthwhile appointment from the new Labour government. She had tremendous experience in the campaign to save the Royal Marsden from closure.

'I spent a whole year talking to politicians and being in the House of Lords and the House of Commons lobbying in the hospital's interest. To help raise the £25 million we needed, I was in the City a lot, meeting businessmen and women trying to win their support for our work.' These were not the normal activities of a chief executive of a NHS hospital. She was 'not party political in any way', but her name was on the appointments register at Number 10. 'Things I thought might come my way, I think, ended up as political appointments for other people who suited the new government better', was how she framed her disappointment. It was a worrying time for her. 'When I was going through this first and second year of doing nothing, I kept on having to say to myself, "You may not get anything else again."'

She lives alone, age 64, in Brentford, Middlesex in a town house on the Thames. But for her, retirement eventually did not mean excessive leisure time. She serves on the Ministerial Advisory Board Medical Devices Agency. ('An agency that looks after the standards of everything from a syringe to a piece of radiotherapy equipment.') She is also a board member and trustee of Headley Court. She is a trustee and member of council of St Christopher's Hospice, Sydenham, Kent. ('It was founded by Dame Cecily Sanders.') She is active in her parish, St Anne's Church, Kew, as a member of the Parochial Church Council, the Finance Committee and the Restoration Committee. She was governor of Christ's School, Richmond, Surrey from 1995 to 1999.

Family background and early education

Phyllis Cunningham is a policeman's daughter from Manchester, the eldest child of two. Her brother is six years younger. Her mother looked after the family full-time until her own mother came to live with them and she could go out to work as a shop assistant in the local shops. Her mother today still lives in the same house in Chorlton-cum-Hardy, about seven miles from the centre of Manchester, that she shared with her husband and the two children.

'My parents gave us all they could. My father was a police constable all his life. Those were hard times during the war years when he was always out dealing with the blitz and we never knew if he would come back again. He was a very compassionate man and he was a much loved man in central Manchester', she recalled. When he retired, Constable Andrew Cunningham received full centre-spreads in all the Manchester newspapers. Everyone knew and respected this quiet policeman who kept his strong Scottish accent all his life.

The Cunningham house was a friendly place. Phyllis Cunningham recalled: 'Our house was a very open house. Regardless of what time you arrived, you sat for a meal and the food just had to spread. To my irritation very often my brother would have people over working on his car and I'd have to make toast for them, sometimes using an entire loaf.'

She passed her eleven-plus and went to Central Grammar School. There she thought about studying medicine, but she was not sure she was bright enough and there was no career counselling as there is for children today. 'I tried on one occasion to talk to our head but he was a very difficult man who was trying to make his way in politics and really wasn't interested', she said.

Her brother later went to the same school and she felt that their parents 'went without' to give them education. 'I then thought of nursing, but my father put his foot down. He saw a lot of traffic accidents and casualties and he didn't want me mopping up.

'I had always had a bent for business and organization. I handled money well and I organized well. I always ended up as secretary at the church groups or tennis clubs that I belonged to. So I got a Business Studies Diploma and sought out a hospital environment straight from college.'

Entering the medical world

With her Business Studies Diploma in hand, from Lorebum College, Manchester, Phyllis Cunningham went to Withington Hospital in Manchester for her first job and was hired immediately as a secretary. Her head was full of management, but she had to start out as a secretary. 'It wasn't easy. I went in as a secretary with a view to getting on the regional training programme for administration.' She bumped straight into her first gender barrier. 'The very few places on the programme were given to men. After talking with what used to be called the group secretary, I could see that I was never going to achieve a place on the administrative training programme. In the end I decided that there was no way to advance, so I left the hospital service and took a job at Geigy Pharmaceuticals.

'I worked there for the medical director in a sort of secretarial research assistant capacity. But he did give me all sorts of developmental things to do, like running the double blind trials on new drugs. I had to work with medical people in a number of hospitals to set up the trials. I was about 23 at the time and he was a super man to work for. He mentored me – although we never called it that in those days. He was half-time with Geigy and half-time in clinical practice at Manchester Royal Hospital. When he told me he had decided to go back into clinical practice full-time, his role as mentor came to the fore. He said "Well, you have a future here, but you must think about what you really want to do." The company offered me a job in Basle, but I was not interested. When I said that I was thinking about going back into the health service, he suggested that I should try working abroad to experience another health environment and then come back to Britain to see if I still wanted to work in the health service.'

An American approach to medical care

She joined her friend Wendy from Geigy Pharmaceuticals who had already decided to work in America. They went to New York City where she took a post at the Roosevelt Hospital near the Lincoln Centre. Her first job there in 1962 was as an assistant administrator in the Psychiatric Unit. 'I was very fortunate with the post; it gave me a lot of responsibility and an insight into a different health system. I was on the ward – at the administrative area at the end of the ward so I was very involved with the patients. I had to interview them about their health insurance and other things. I had to read their social history to decide whether or not they could pay for the treatment – there were some quite tragic situations. But the really dangerous patients went to Bellevue Hospital.

'There were many women in senior positions in the New York hospitals. The deputy vice-president of my hospital was a woman – a very formidable woman who had been there a while. Other assistants in that office were also women, and the male managers were very good with women and willing to talk to them and listen. This struck me as a huge difference from current practice at that time in the UK. My immediate boss was the psychiatric medical director, and he was a man.'

Both young women had promised their parents back in Manchester that they would return to them after two years and they kept their word, although they found an exciting way of returning to the UK. 'Living our English lifestyle in New York City – we got on the bus or the subway, not into taxis, even in the rain – we went to the theatre and did all sorts of things, but on American salaries we managed to amass some money. You then either brought it home with you and sank it all into a mortgage or you blew it. We decided to blow it.

'First we sent all our stuff across to San Francisco and then took a Greyhound bus with one case each and set off on our journey. Although it was a 3,000-mile trip from New York to San Francisco, we zigzagged backwards and forwards for 11,000 miles in search of America for about four weeks, staying at bed and breakfast places and motels. And then we stayed in San Francisco for three or four days with friends, before setting off round the world on a cruise liner. It took us to Hawaii, the Philippines, the Far East (Hong Kong and the New Territories of China), and then through the Suez Canal, around the Mediterranean, Italy and Spain and back to England. The ship was used as a transit ship and the whole journey took four and a half months.'

The first officer also took a special interest in them. 'I went up the gang plank in San Francisco and the first officer at the top shouted, "Good God, hello Phyllis!" He turned out to be the cousin of a friend of mine from home. As a result, although we were not first-class passengers, we got invited to all of the officers' parties. When we got to ports of call, we went out with whichever of the officers who were not on duty and were taken to the real places not the tourist traps.' She had a female doctor friend in the Philippines and was treated royally there.

She arrived at home in Manchester in the summer of 1964. Back in New York City the medical director of her department, with the approval of the president of the hospital, held her position open for six months, so sure was he that she would come back.

'I loved the States and had a wonderful experience there, but I just felt that it wasn't where I wanted to live and work for the rest of my life, and I was conscious of my family. Having said that, having left the bosom of my family, I felt that I could not settle again in Manchester. So after talking with Tom, my previous mentor at Geigy Pharmaceuticals, I decided to go back into the NHS and go to London.'

A promising career in the NHS

Phyllis Cunningham made a great start in London. She won a job in the planning department of the Royal Free Hospital with her first interview. It could not have been better, as the department was planning an entirely new Royal Free Hospital.

'It was all under the auspices of a section of the house governor's office. At the point I arrived no one knew whether the project would ever come to fruition. It was still just talk between the Department of Health and the hospital. At the start, I became planning co-ordinator and then planning officer for the new Royal Free.

'Throughout my career things have never been straightforward. I've never held just a normal administrative job. Nothing was ever routine. There always has been an added dimension. In planning the new Royal Free, for example, I had to do things I had never dreamed of doing. I met with architects, engineers, designers, management consultants and all sorts of experts. I became a liaison between the medical people and the architects and builders, telling the medical people what they could have and what they could not have. I travelled with the architects and engineers to look at other hospitals in other places. As a result of those visits I did some work in developing countries, which was outside my job description so I did that in my holidays. Algeria was one of the countries.

'This new hospital project was a very big one for the late 1960s and cost over £10 million then, which in today's money would be ten times that figure.'

Phyllis Cunningham had only a very basic career plan. 'I have never said I am here now and I want to be there in five years and there in ten years. I have always just done a job until there was no longer any challenge or I had completed what I was doing and therefore it was time for me to move on. The new Royal Free took me ten years. Having started it with lines on a piece of paper, I saw it through to my first patient in a bed. It was a very satisfying job and I met many wonderful, diverse people.

'When my work setting up the new hospital was finished I wanted to go back into pure management, as I called it. Both the district administrator and indeed the Department of Health said to me, "Look you have had a vast experience in this line and we would like you to stay on capital works and so on." They offered me an enormous salary to go and work in the Department of Health. But working in that environment was far from my ideal. My own district manager said, "I don't think that you will get into management – not because you couldn't do it but because the competition will be too great and you have been on the sidelines with your new hospital project." He was wrong.'

From deputy to the top at the Royal Marsden

'I got the first job I applied for and became deputy to the House of Governors of the Royal Marsden. [At the time, house governors were what the chief executives of all the big London teaching hospitals were called.] I was thrilled and very surprised to obtain the post.' It was especially sweet to have won the post against the odds and the lower expectations of her boss.

'I have never been frightened to tackle things, but I'm not someone who starts off confident and brash. I generally buckle down and I will find out. I am not frightened; if I don't know things I'll ask people.

'I went there in 1974 and was there for twenty-four years. I became chief executive in 1981. Royal Marsden was the first cancer hospital in the world. It has just celebrated its 150th anniversary. William Marsden founded it. The hospital had many "firsts" in radium and other treatments for cancer. As a postgraduate teaching hospital it has many great people. It also teaches consultants who want to specialize in cancer. It is a big research organization and the home of the Institute of Cancer Research, which emanated from its clinical research department. It is very much on the international circuit in terms of research and education all over the world. Many nurses and medical personnel who come to Marsden for their training then go off to places around the globe. The heads of most the majority of cancer units up and down the country have passed through Marsden.'

Management style

'My management style – to be honest – did not change over the twenty-four years I was at the Royal Marsden. I've always had a very open policy. I like to talk with people to get their views. But I'm very careful not to usurp the authority of my directors or managers. Part of my management style was to be always approachable, to make it clear to others that there were channels there for them to use, but that did not mean that I would not listen to what they had to say. I did recognize that the buck stopped with me. There were many hard times during my stay at Marsden. As everyone knows, it is lonely at the top. But I never abused my status or stood on ceremony.'

She did not have to deal with the trade unions often, but when she did she met face to face with the top trade union people. 'We always had what they called "full and frank discussions".

'I never went to conferences for the sake of going, to seek the limelight or centre stage. I only went to those events that I thought were important to the staff or patients at Marsden. Their interests dictated where I went and why I went there.

'Because we did not run our hospital through a district authority, I had direct relationships with under-secretaries and permanent secretaries. I developed a political nous due to these contacts and was able to analyse political currents in the Health Service.'

Veuve Clicquot Business Woman of the Year Award

Phyllis Cunningham won the Veuve Clicquot Business Woman of the Year Award for 1991 for her leadership of Britain's premier specialist cancer hospital. She was the first person from the public sector to win the award and to date remains the only winner from the public sector. 'I was stunned to be nominated for the award and to be among the shortlist of five. When I saw the powerful, talkative and confident women on the shortlist, I came back to Marsden and said that I hadn't a hope of winning. I was astounded when they told me I had won. We had our photograph taken against the background of Tower Bridge.

'The impact it had at the hospital was enormous and lovely. The award had an even greater impact at the Department of Health, which was very interesting.' The press coverage was the best of all the awards to date. 'Four doctors were prepared to stand out in the cold at seven in the morning to have their pictures taken with me, as Marsden rallied round the award.'

She realizes that her award was unique for many reasons. 'The other winners were very much within their channels of business, however prominent. When I think back, none of the other winners would have had the wide experience I've had or met the people that I did.'

Few gender barriers to her career

Apart from those barriers she found at the very start of her career in the NHS in Manchester upon entering the secretarial job after college – where only men were put forward for the administrative training schemes – Phyllis Cunningham has not encountered many gender barriers to her advancement. 'When I came to be deputy of the Marsden, there were two applications from women and four from men. Later, when I applied for chief executive, although I was the in-house candidate, there were a large number of applicants for the post and I was not guaranteed the job by any means. I was the only woman candidate. I suppose that it was not until 1974 that there were a few women in management roles. Now there are many women in managerial positions in the NHS.

'I have never been a feminist *per se*. But I have encouraged many of my women staff members to seek goals that they may not have thought they were able to achieve. I have never believed in the token woman and I still believe fervently in the best person for the job.'

Prue Leith OBE

Prue Leith OBE, founder, Leith School of Food and Wine

Today her name is synonymous with fine food everywhere. She has been a telly-cook and broadcaster. She has published twelve cookbooks. She founded a famous cookery school that still carries her name: Leith's School of Food and Wine, although she no longer owns it. Her restaurant, Leith's Restaurant, is among London's finest and won the Michelin star for its culinary achievements in January 1994. She has held cookery editor or food columnist jobs for the *Daily Mail*, the *Sunday Express*, the *Guardian* and the *Mirror*. And notwithstanding a deep-seated corporate sexism, she has served as a board member for a dozen companies, including British Rail, Safeway, Whitbread, Woolworths, Halifax and TriVen, a venture capital initiative of Matrix Securities.

She served for two years (1995–97) as chairman of the Royal Society for the Encouragement of Arts, Manufactures and Commerce (RSA) and remains a vice-president. She became the chairman of its Education Advisory Group in January 2001. She is quick to help charities and initiate community service projects, particularly to do with schools. She was awarded an OBE in 1989 for services to food.

A cookery charity she initiated with Delia Smith, Jane Asher and Lloyd Grossman formed a joint venture with a property company (St Modwen plc) in March 2001 to develop a Grade II listed hospital at Stafford into a mecca for food lovers. Plans include a newly built shopping centre dedicated to kitchen and food retail, including a British Food Showcase. An 'Eating History' visitors' attraction is designed for the hospital building. The complex will include a 100-room hotel, a Food in Art gallery and the British Hospitality College.

At the time of life when many people retire, she began a new career as a successful novelist, published by Penguin.

Yet her arrival in London in the 1960s was distinctly unpromising. Prue Leith came to London as a directionless young South African dropout student. She and a girlfriend had wanted a break from their studies in Paris and persuaded their parents back in South Africa to fund their study of cordon bleu cooking at a renowned French school. Later the girls found out that what they had thought was an exorbitant tuition fee for the entire course had been merely the 10 per cent deposit. The cost of the course was beyond their means, so they took the summer off and Prue Leith came to London instead. Although she had never cooked before, not even in her own family kitchen, she took a cooking course and stayed.

Growing up in Johannesburg

Prue Leith was born a middle child to well-off parents in Johannesburg. She has one older brother and one younger one. Although the country at the time was blighted by apartheid, her parents were liberal and numbered 'people mainstream South Africa didn't care for' among their friends. Her mother, Margaret Inglis, was 'South Africa's leading actress, hugely successful – the country's equivalent to Peggy Ashcroft'. She owes her interest in the arts and her artistic flare and sense of experimentation to her mother. Perhaps her business acumen came from her father, Sam Leith, who was a director at a large subsidiary of ICI. He was a chemist and had been in the same chemical company 'man and boy', as was the custom then. She remembers him as: 'Hardworking and extremely balanced at a time when one didn't have to work 16-hour days to prove oneself.' Sadly he died when she was only 21.

'If you look at people who have done well, nearly all of them have been encouraged as kids. It might have been by a teacher or their parents', she said. 'I grew up happy!' Recently, on a film script-writing course, she took issue with the tutor who maintained that you had to have an unhappy childhood to be a writer. 'When I said to him that I had a happy childhood and had published two novels so far, he said: "You just think you had a happy childhood, you had a miserable childhood", but he was wrong and silly as well.

'We had a marvellous childhood. My parents were hugely loving.'

But food was something the servants took care of. Neither of her parents cooked and 'it was just never considered as a career'.

Young Prue had her own horse. As a girl, riding was all she ever wanted to do. She tried to persuade her father to let her leave school (which she never liked) at 15 to be a riding teacher. But he insisted that she stay in school and get educated in something – whatever she chose. Left to her own designs she would have spent her life riding.

'All my young life, before my father died, I was undecided about what I wanted to do. Actually, I wanted to do everything. First I went to drama school, and then I went to art school, and then I went to do a BA in French, and then changed my mind and decided to do a French Civilization course at the Sorbonne in Paris. Then I decided I wanted to be a cook. All of this dithering must have driven him to despair, wondering if I would ever get my act together. But he supported me all the way through it. Always when I achieved something, even today, if anything good happens, I would like him to be there to know that I did do it and that I'm not just unstable.

'He would say things like, "Anybody can start a novel and anybody can start weeding a garden, and anybody can start a baby; but the novel gets more difficult after Chapter 3, the lawn seems endless, and babies grow up and become a complete pain." It's his doggedness and his belief that it is the carrying through with something that is the difficult thing. He was very, very good at "stickability". I'm sure that 90 per cent of my success has been due to my being, like him, very dogged. I am only 10 per cent imagination, innovation and all those other things. Success is due to my staying with things.'

She had to learn 'stickability'. Her first attempt at finding a career – drama school in Cape Town – ended in tears. 'Because my mother was an actress and because I had been in every school play and was keen on acting, I wanted to be a professional actress. I can remember father filling in this form with me and him saying: "It says here *hobbies*; I wish I could put *reading* here!" I loved plays and the rehearsals and studying the plays, but I did not like the acting bit.'

She moved on to stage design and enrolled in art school. 'One day this famous old sculptor, who taught there, came to the life class and he stood behind me and asked what I was doing in his life class. I said I wanted to be a stage designer and he said he did not think I would be up to it. In those days you were allowed to tell a student you thought their work was hopeless. I went on to study French.'

At university studying French, Prue Leith neglected her studies in favour of the beach, and paid the price of being unprepared for her second-year exams. She took three exams and felt she had done so badly in them that she dropped out of university rather than take the other three exams. It was a miscalculation she would regret for the rest of her life, starting with the day she received pass marks for the first three exams. But she had already begun her studies in France. She interrupted the course to come home for her father's death from cancer and then returned to her course in Paris.

Getting into food

You cannot live in France, as Prue Leith did for two years, without becoming interested in food. She traces the start of her keen interest to one summer when she worked as an *au pair* for a Belgian couple. They went on holiday as a family and stayed near Bayonne. 'The woman did all the cooking for her two little children of 6 months and 18 months and her husband and me. She would go to three different bakers and took great care about everything. She would not let me cook the children's supper because she knew from the fact that I spoke English that I would crucify the food. If we were having steak and salad for supper, a single tiny steak would get seared and be blue in the middle, and be perfectly made with tiny chopped shallots, the salad beautifully dressed for the 18-month-old.

The baby got exactly the same thing, but liquidized so that the mother and I could spoon-feed her. One day we were discussing English food and I said: "I am not English but South African so stop blaming me for terrible food." And they asked me what the national dish of South Africa was. When I said: "corn on the cob" they roared with laughter and said they gave that only to their cattle.'

To prove her point that corn on the cob could be delicious, Prue Leith picked some ripe yellow maize, then boiled it until it was done; but it seemed tough, so she boiled it more and it was 'disgusting'. She lost her case for the corn and it made her angry.

'That holiday was the catalyst. I went back to Paris and told my father of my further career change. I now wanted to be a cook.' She remembers hearing her father 'suck in his breath'. A girlfriend was also studying in Paris and the two of them went along to a cordon bleu school in Paris to sign up for a summer course.

'Neither of us spoke very good French and so we went along to this school and could just manage a few words. We asked the cost of tuition in our poor French and they wrote down a huge amount of money that made my father rock at the cost.' But both sets of parents agreed to pay the fees for the school for the girls and they bought their little caps and aprons. 'But when we arrived at the school to start the classes, they asked us for some more money. We said we had paid it the previous week. They said that was just the 10 per cent deposit. So we couldn't go there and what we thought we could just afford to pay was lost in the deposit.' The girls took the summer off.

Prue Leith then enrolled in a cordon bleu school in London, bluffing her way onto the course. It was an advanced course and she knew nothing. It required work experience as a cook and she had none. Cheekily she gave them the menu to a restaurant, where she had worked as a waitress and done washing up, and the school thought that she had been a cook there. On the course she was lucky to be paired up with a woman who owned her own coffee shop and made cakes and teas. The woman sailed through the baking parts of the course and made them both look good.

Personal meaning of success: spotting talent

Is that when she realized that she had a wonderful talent for food? 'I don't think that I am particularly talented. I just love food and I care enough about it to try hard. I think my real talent is that I can spot talent and I am very willing. If someone else can do something better than I can, I think it's crazy not to hire them. I swear that most of my success has involved having chefs in the business who can cook better than I can, and accountants in the business who can add up better than I can. The main problem with entrepreneurs is that they think that they have to do it all themselves, or they think they know how to do it all themselves. I know very well that I am not the best. But I am good enough to see who can do it. I have never been the best chef in the world, but I am a pretty good cook.'

Starting up in the cookery business

After the three-month course Prue Leith, armed with an 1,100-page cordon bleu cookery book, took her first job working as a cook for a firm of solicitors, McKenna, that now has about 300 partners. But then they had only three partners, and a few years later when she left them they had nine partners. 'I cooked for the partners and their guests, about six people, for three days a week for £8.' That gave her £4 to pay her rent and £4 to spend. She cooked for the solicitors for over two years. 'I just started from page one and worked my way through this book. They were remarkably tolerant, because when I got to the chicken chapter, it went on for a long time. I presume I occasionally put something else in, but I was not into balanced meals, I was into teaching myself to cook.'

She remembers the first time she was asked to have lunch with them. She felt very grown-up until someone poked around in her salad and pulled out a long chain with a rubber sink plug attached to the end. 'At least it proves I wash the lettuce', she quipped, while dying inside.

Through the people she met at the law firm she obtained private work catering their parties and dinners. It was a great business in that it did not require capital. All it required was her cookery talent and personality, the clients paying for all the ingredients. Sometimes they would send her to Harrods and she'd put the price of the food on their accounts and have it delivered.

She also had the nous for the catering business, as she explained. 'I realized that the secret, if I wanted to make a business out of this, was to do more. It also meant that to do quality work you had to charge more for the washing up than for the cooking. Most of the clients would want you to cook the dinner and then stay and wash up and perhaps wait on tables as well. You cannot do a very good job in the kitchen if you have to wait on tables too. It limits the menu you can offer. For instance, you couldn't cook a soufflé or anything last-minute because you would be needed in the dining room. You simply cannot do your best. I would charge them three shillings an hour for cooking and three or four shillings an hour if they wanted me to stay on to do the washing up. That would concentrate their minds on getting a waitress who would also wash up. If I could leave for home when the pudding went, and didn't have to wait for coffee, I could do a hell of a lot more work.'

She was making pâté and terrines for pubs. 'For the Balls Brothers pub chain I made pork liver terrine, and still can't eat the stuff because I used to make that wonderful real pork terrine that is wrapped in bacon with chunky lumps of pork. It is made with minced pig liver, minced onions and lots of seasoning. I used to mix it in an enormous fish kettle and it was *freezing* cold. The minced liver from the butcher came straight out of his chiller, bitterly cold. I was my own mixing machine; I would mix it by hand – up past my elbows in the freezing stuff.' Then she realized that she could hire a 14-year-old boy to do the mixing for her. He was living in Paddington in Craven Road and he was the son of a tradesman. 'I paid him quite well and he loved the work and the idea that he was earning money, unlike his mates. I think we make a mistake with children, if we never let them work. We regard childhood as some sacred thing and children do not even make their own beds or wash the family car or rake the gravel driveway or anything. It's a rotten training for life.'

Networking her way to success

Prue Leith has always been a great networker. It stems from her belief that everyone is important whatever his or her social status. 'I don't think companies are made by great chefs and great managers; they are made by everybody, and that includes the kitchen porter and the waiter and the bottle washer and everyone else.' Her networking also comes naturally to her warm, outgoing personality. She is easy to talk with and easier to like, and it paid off right from the start. 'I met this butler when I was going round doing people's dinner parties. He worked for a firm of stockbrokers in the City and he said: "Would you like to do the food for the stockbrokers?" I said "Yes" and he explained the unique circumstances.' The stockbrokers' lease disallowed food prepared in their premises because there was already a restaurant in the basement. Doing food for the stockbrokers and delivering the food to them was perfect for her operations. It meant that she could produce food simultaneously for more than one customer. The butler found her other clients and the waitresses she hired to serve food also found her clients. The customers would ask them, 'Do you know a good cook?' and they would recommend her. Her reputation grew among the lawyers and stockbrokers with ambitious wives who gave balls and big parties.

Prue Leith tells a story that illustrates the importance of being on good terms with the domestic help, in this case the butler of a wealthy woman whose dinner party she was catering in her grand house. She arrived at the kitchens to find that someone had let the Aga go out. She stoked the stove with anthracite and got it going again, but by six o'clock it was hardly warm, certainly not hot enough for the Beef Wellington she was trying to prepare. She 'curled up in a foetal position, praying and wanting to die'. The butler came to the rescue. He took his time with the pre-dinner drinks. He then served wine at a snail's pace, followed by water, then napkins laid on laps very slowly. Then came rolls, butter and fish plates. As she described it: 'The butler ensured that the guests took an hour to eat the salmon, and the Beef Wellington was perfect!'

Her catering success set her up to fulfil a dream she'd had since living in Paris.

The restaurant

'Ever since my Paris days I had had this idea of opening my own restaurant. There was no question of being able to afford a restaurant. Every caterer wants to be a restaurateur. In my catering business I was very successful. I was no longer a cook in a bed-sit with a wooden spoon in one hand and a frying pan in the other. I was now living in a little mews cottage that I had bought in Paddington. The garage was my storage room and the kitchen was the kitchen and the sitting room was the office and I lived in the bedroom upstairs. I knew I had to get premises for a proper catering company and stop using the mews house as a base without planning permission, but I wanted a restaurant. So I decided to do both. I would open a restaurant and use the kitchen for both the catering business that was making money and the restaurant. I borrowed some money from the bank and a lot more money from my mother. The whole venture cost £30,000, probably more than ten times that in today's money. A City whiz kid invested £3,000 and got 10 per cent of the company, but I bought him out for £6,000 a year later because I knew he would always have his 10 per cent as a sleeping partner if I didn't act quickly. He thought doubling his money in a year was a fair return and he went off happy.' She opened her first restaurant in Kensington Park Road.

She was nervous about the restaurant. Her first attempt at a new business had failed. She tried to capitalize on her knowledge and love of theatre and provide food for actors in between the matinee and the evening show. It never got off the ground due to her poor market research. 'My idea was to provide wonderful trays of food for actors on Wednesdays and Saturdays between the matinees and the evening shows, but it was a bad idea. First of all you have to get past the doorman, who takes all your profits; secondly, half the actors do not eat between shows and the other half want to have a walk in the park or a drink in the pub or something other than food. Very few order from them, then when you go back the next week the play has closed. I also hadn't reckoned on matinees being on different days.'

Rayne Kruger, a South African writer and family friend from theatre days in Johannesburg, who had moved to England with his first wife before her father died, taught Prue Leith to do double-entry bookkeeping. He taught her how to use a 36-column analysis book to record money in and money out, which she found so effective for herself and her managers that they continued to keep to the same system even when they were turning over £11 million. Eventually they put that system on the computer in preference to the day ledgers traditionally used in catering. Her idea was that if she, not gifted in maths, could learn the system then she could require its mastery from her other employees. 'We had managers who had never been to business school and managers who had been chefs and they all learned how to do this system', she explained. There is a tendency for cooks to find figures a bore. But Prue Leith grew to like them. 'After a while you realize that there is as much satisfaction about a good profit and loss account as there is in producing a beautiful buffet. It's the same thing – all the bits coming together. To this day a couple of my managers, who now work for huge multinationals, still use our system of accounts secretly on their own because they do not believe the figures in the more sophisticated accounts that are sent from head office.'

Rayne Kruger had become chairman of Prue Leith's businesses. Kruger's first wife and Prue Leith's mother had been partners in a theatre company in South Africa and Prue and their daughter were close friends. As Rayne Kruger continued as chairman in Prue Leith's catering and restaurant businesses, their relationship changed. Despite the earlier family history and the daughters' friendship and the age gap of eighteen years, they fell in love and eventually married when she was 34. They raised two children. They remain married today.

'It was very difficult for the families for a year or so. My mother always claims that the reason that Rayne and I fell in love was that my father had died and I was looking for a replacement. I suppose there is something in that if you go for an older man that has also been your chairman,' she wondered.

The female advantage

Kensington Park Gardens turned out to be not the best place to open a restaurant. Prue Leith now knows that the best place to open a new restaurant is between two other successful restaurants and that a restaurant area like Fulham would have been better. 'It was a question of fools rushing in and we were lucky. I knew nothing about the restaurant business and I should have first gone and worked in one, but never did. I suddenly realized that I was losing money hand over fist since the opening. Other restaurateurs helped me. I think that is one of the advantages of being a woman.'

Her habit of networking proved decisive. 'I joined the Restaurateurs Association, which was just starting, and I went to a cocktail party at the House of Commons, where I meet Albert Roux and Joseph Berkman, who used to own the Geneva Group. They said: "Your place is packed, you must be minting it." I said well it is packed, but I am losing money. And they said "you can't be." So I said come and tell me why.'

The famous Albert Roux visited her restaurant and offered his advice. 'He stood by the dustbins in the kitchen and he plunged his great arm in and fished out an apple. "What's the matter with this apple?" he asked. I turned it over and said: "It's bad." He said, "No, no, only one side is bad, one side is good." He asked why we were throwing away the watercress stalks. I said, "Albert, it's the leaves that you eat", and he said there was more flavour in the stalks which should be used for soup. He asked why we were buying cream in giant jars. I said because you get a discount if you buy it in big tubs and that we used a lot of it. He said that if you buy it in small pots the chef will take the trouble to scrape every last bit out, whereas if you buy it in big gallons you will use much more. He noticed as he stood by the dustbins that there was a lot of food coming out of the restaurant and going into the bins. He came to my office, where I was working away at the bills, and said: "Either you are serving revolting food, or you're giving too much." That made me chop down the portions. He was amazing on all these little details.'

Joseph Berkman also visited her restaurant. 'Joseph was completely different. He went straight to the books and did not go near the kitchen. He said: "Your chef is robbing you blind, anyone can see that." I owned the restaurant and I did not know what the percentages should be. When the chef went on holiday, I watched the whole thing very carefully and discovered that Joseph was right.'

Quality first

Most restaurants pay their chefs a bonus if they meet certain gross margins. But that system tempts them to cheat the customers to ensure that they achieve their bonus. They would use inferior cuts of meat and too small portions. 'To avoid this happening, we developed a different system. First we would work out carefully what the gross margins should be and agree that with the chef. If he achieved his target he got the bonus. But if he did too well on his gross margins, he lost his bonus.

'When we opened the Queen Elizabeth Conference Centre, a very big contract for us, one we "bet the farm" on as it doubled the number of staff we employed and doubled our turnover, I hired a new chef for the place. I had spent the week with him talking about quality and showing him pictures of our food and giving him my cookbooks and asking him the kind of food he liked, trying to drum into him that quality is what matters most. Our first buffet there was a very cheap one, where the customers were paying a "fiver" for a plate of food, pudding, or cheese and a glass of wine.

'I went in the kitchen to find that the chef had made a trifle with tinned pears, Bird's custard and synthetic cream and the cheese was great slabs of rubbery, cheddar that looked horrible. And the second chef was carving chrysanthemums out of turnips and dyeing them with fancy colours. I went ballistic and threw the turnips into the bin and told them I could not serve any of that food. I made them change their menu within an hour. Afterwards I sat down with this new head chef and asked him what he thought he was doing. He said in his own defence that he had heard the quality lecture from every boss he had worked for, but that in the end the only thing they cared about was the gross profit and he felt that he couldn't risk it. "You would say yes to quality, but in the end accuse me of not making my margins", was how he put it.'

Actions for quality always speak louder than words. The chef became converted to her brand of quality and stayed with her for nine years. As executive head chef for the whole group, he went round the company preaching quality and telling the story of his first encounter with her commitment to quality. 'You decide on what the menu is going to be when you have listened to what the customer wants and then you price it. If they do not like it, you just find another menu. You do not change the one you have agreed on. You must start with what you want. Even today most banquets start with the customer saying "I have £15 to spend per plate", the caterer then says "Good, they have given us a price, make sure we get three or four quid out of it", and that's much more than they should. Then they work to £10 per plate including service, which does nothing for the quality of food for the customer.

'The most important thing about running a big business is keeping the philosophy pure and intact', she said.

'Leith's stands for quality and simplicity. Quality is what you have to think about all the time. I truly believe that if you are selling a sandwich or a sea bream, it should be the best of its kind or the closest you can get to the best.' She lists her best moment in management as: 'Leith's Restaurant receiving a Michelin star.'

Leith's School of Food and Wine

'In 1974 I was talking with Caroline Waldegrave, head chef of our catering company, and I said to her: "This is ridiculous. We hire these young cooks and you spend all your time teaching them our way of doing things." We called it simple (not sophisticated) country house cooking. It's the sort of cooking that a good cook does, quite fashionable, but not extreme, not some sort of chef's fancy dancing.'

Caroline Waldegrave had to help the young chefs unlearn a lot of what they were taught in cookery school. 'We did not go in for making radishes into roses, which is very old-fashioned now but at the time was what they were taught. My image of Caroline is of her with her arm round some poor girl who is weeping on her first or second day with us and Caroline is explaining to her that we do not cut carrots like that. She was comforting but firm and would never abandon the message. One of the problems of our industry is that very few people in managerial positions are like Caroline, nobody is nice to the new people who arrive.

'I said to Caroline: "We should open a cookery school. Then we could teach the young chefs and hire them when they are finished with the course. All the time they are learning, they will be paying us instead of us paying them."' By the time Prue Leith was ready to act on the idea, Caroline was off working in America. Prue Leith invited her back to run the cookery school. 'She was 23 at the time and I was about ten years older and neither of us thought we were too young to do it.'

In the beginning they took in the overflow from the cordon bleu school, where both women had trained. At their request, the cordon bleu school generously referred their surplus students to Prue Leith's school. Leith's School of Food and Wine had thirty students the first term, then a capacity sixty students the next term. Then they moved to their present premises at 21 St Alban's Grove, London W8, where they could handle ninety-six students. If the potential students came alone, Caroline, who looked about the same age as the students (or younger), interviewed them. If they came with their mothers, a sense of *gravitas* was called for and Prue Leith, trying to look older than her 35 years, did the interviewing.

Today the School has an international reputation and attracts chefs for professional training. It offers diploma, advanced, intermediate and beginner's courses. For the amateur there are cookery evening classes, holiday courses, special interest and wine courses.

The School's founders have used the teachers and students to develop many recipes, which took five years to compile into a cookbook and a further five years to refine in a revised edition of the work. Co-authored by Prue Leith and Caroline Waldegrave, *Leith's Cookery Bible* is a 700-page *magnum opus* with 1,500 recipes, which demonstrates the synergies she likes to develop between people who share her passion for promoting good food. It has sold over 250,000 copies and is in its fifth edition.

Multi-tasked and mellowing out

Prue Leith was careful to grow the business gradually – each ring of the business expanding outward slowly. Unlike Terence Conran, who was her contemporary in the restaurant business, she did not risk it all on one toss of the dice. 'Terence had the entrepreneur's risk-taking attitude, which I never had. He would go for broke and have to sell the business and then buy it back. He would make fortunes and lose fortunes. Now of course he only makes fortunes!'

Meanwhile Prue Leith enjoyed her interest in other things. She brought up two children, her son, Daniel and her adopted daughter, Li-Da. Eventually both children went to Scotland for their university studies – Daniel to study history at Edinburgh University and Li-Da to European studies and marketing at Strathclyde.

She had met her fellow entrepreneurs in the business through attending the first meeting of the Restaurateurs Association and, as a founding member, stayed active with the association. She kept involved in the wider community through the RSA and other charity groups. Many of them had to do with schools. She chairs 3Es the first commercial company to run state schools under contract, turning round failing schools, writing e-learning packages for the Internet, running nursery schools and delivering adult education.

The first board of directors that she joined was Traveller's Fare, a subsidiary of British Rail, at the request of Sir Peter Parker, who used to frequent her restaurant. She later moved up to the main board of British Rail. She considered him to be a genuine mentor and role model. 'He's not a guru, but Sir Peter Parker combines sense and sensibility, the pursuit of profit and the pursuit of justice.' It was the first of over a dozen places on the boards of companies from food and retail business.

Leadership style

'My management style was always conciliatory, non-confrontational. I wanted to encourage people to do their best and enjoy what they were doing. It's the teacher in me. Caroline had a similar style.

'I don't think women are as driven as men fuelled by testosterone, to seek excitement and glory and ego-gratification in business. I set up the company with separate divisions and made divisional directors. So there was Leith Restaurant and Leith Cookery School and the Catering Company. We also had the personnel department which was the service organization and the buying bit.'

She feels that empowerment is often bogus, 'a con'. Her best advice for young managers would be to realize that 'trust is more important than contracts and that you should only hire people you like'.

Executive pay is one of the management issues she feels strongly about. 'I'd like remuneration committees to have to make a connection between top pay and bottom pay', she said. 'In the US between 1990 and 1995, chief executives' pay grew 92 per cent, profits grew 75 per cent, employees' pay grew 16 per cent and job losses went up 39 per cent. If we go on rewarding the bosses with pay rises eight times the rate of those at the bottom, it does not take a genius to see that way revolution lies.'

The Veuve Clicquot Business Woman of the Year Award

In April 1991 she received the Veuve Clicquot Business Woman of the Year Award for 1990. Coming when it did, the award had tremendous publicity and a powerful effect on staff morale. 'It was a marvellous feeling to win it, as I had been nominated ten times for the award. The nomination that won came from Peter Parker of British Rail, where I had worked with Traveller's Fare and on the Board of Directors.'

Selling up

'When I was 51 I thought that I would like to sell the business for three reasons. One was that my husband, Rayne, is nearly eighteen years older than I. He'd soon be 70 and if we were to have time together, we had to do it now. The second reason was that we had had a very successful few years and I thought that I would get some decent money for the business now. The third reason, maybe the most important, was the bad experience I had in Hyde Park and Kensington Gardens. We had taken on a contract to do the catering in both those parks with a missionary zeal. I had the New York Tavern On The Green in mind. I thought we would be able to persuade the world that the British would eat decent food, if they were offered it.' She read the park situation wrong, not reckoning on the fact that the park authorities would not allow taxi-drops, that there would be nowhere to park, and that the infrastructure was so poor there were no lights in the park during the night and the drains and loos were blocked much of the time. Moreover, she misjudged the public's commitment to good food. If the weather was slightly overcast they would not walk to the restaurants, and if it was sunny they wanted hot dogs and chips. Her vision of Chardonnay and smoked salmon under the trees was not shared by the park-goers, who still wanted 'slimy burgers', which of course she would not serve. The venture cost her company £300,000 by the time the contract ran out. When asked to renew their contract for another three years, she said 'No'!

She thought about going public, but decided against it. In 1993 she sold her catering enterprise, with an annual turnover of £17 million, to the French company Eurest International, part of the French Accor group and the biggest contract caterer in Europe, but was retained by the firm to remain in charge. In May 1994 her husband Rayne Kruger had his final board meeting after thirty years as chairman of Leith's and retired at the age of 72.

Separately she sold Leith's School of Food and Wine in a management buy-out deal to her long-term manager and friend Caroline Waldegrave, who had helped found the School.

She was still in charge of catering, if no longer the owner, and relished winning a £2.5 million catering contract for the Edinburgh International Conference Centre in September 1994. At age 54, she achieved her target of downshifting. She was secure in her personal wealth and still had the challenge of running the catering contracts. In thirty years she had come full circle. As she put it: 'I went into the kitchen because I didn't want to sit in an office all day, now I sit in an office most days and enjoy it.' She was still on the boards of the Argyll Group and Leeds Building Society. She was also chairman of the Restaurateurs Association of Great Britain.

Novelist

At university the young Prue Leith loved reading plays and interpreting roles in plays. It is perhaps not surprising that she would return to that interest late in life and begin to mine her own rich experiences as a novelist. Her first two novels *Leaving Patrick* and *Sisters*, published by Penguin, sold well and she has now delivered her third novel using the context of landscape gardening. She always knew she could write and had thousands of column inches of journalism over the years to prove her talent. But writing fiction was a new challenge and a chance to draw from the deep wells of memory and imagination.

So far the reviews of her novels have been promising. The *Daily Mail* said: 'Prue Leith was not just born to cook . . . she was also born to write . . . perfect entertainment for that summer holiday.'

The Big Bowl and The Great British Kitchen

Two projects take up most of Prue Leith's time these days – The Big Bowl and The Great British Kitchen.

The Big Bowl is due to open in London's Shoreditch late in 2002. It is an initiative of training for life, a charity dedicated to helping disadvantaged young people into work. 'The programme provides support, mentoring and training to improve their lifestyles and attitudes, rather that just giving them a technical skill', Prue Leith explained.

'In addition to the usual training-charity work, we have developed "social enterprises" that make money for the charity, at the same time as providing "job rehearsal" for our trainees. One is a commercial gym in which they can work out alongside ordinary members, and in which they are also trained to be fitness instructors, aerobics teachers, etc. We also run a web design company, staffed by our trainees, with profitable contracts with several agencies and government departments.

'It works like this. When the trainees have developed sufficient confidence, communication skills and the right attitudes, they are given jobs in the gym or web design company. They are paid, and the work is real, but they still receive help from their mentors and they will be working towards a Certificate of Employability, which they can take to our partner organizations and other prospective employers to provide confidence that the candidate will turn up on time, in the right clothes, with the right attitude.

'The initiative has been well received by the industry, and Compass was one of the first to support us with the secondee, John Kettle, to help us with concept and design. In addition, money and in-kind support is coming from the Learning and Skills Council, government and local government, Pret a Manger, Marriott, Whitbread and Places for People who will, we hope, be our joint venture partner, to expand the model countrywide', she said.

She initiated the idea and set up the project. It is chaired by Simon Ward, ex-director of Whitbread, a trustee of Training for Life.

The Great British Kitchen will be the National Centre for the Culinary Arts, a £40 million project on a 28-acre site in Stafford, devoted to the promotion of good food to the public. It is scheduled to open in 2004.

A listed Georgian hospital building will be restored to house the cultural and charitable initiatives which will be run by the British Food Trust, promoters of the scheme.

'The idea is to try to counter centuries of slander against the British and their relationship with food', Prue Leith said, something she has spent most of adult her life doing notably well.

Ann Gloag

Ann Gloag, founder, Stagecoach

Ann Gloag has created one of the most amazing success stories in modern business. She is a global player in transport in buses and trains. Twenty years ago she left her job as a nursing sister in a Scottish hospital to start a small business, which grew into a bus company called Stagecoach. Stagecoach was started in partnership with her then husband, Robin Gloag, and kid brother Brian Souter, twelve years younger. The trio invested her bus-driver father's £12,000 redundancy money in the business based in Perth. 'We were very nervous about using his money. It was all he had and he showed absolute trust in us.' It was a family affair. On the first routes, Robin Gloag drove the bus, her brother Brian, an accountant by training, kept the books and schedules. She made the sandwiches and did the marketing with another brother David Souter, only three years her junior, who thought up the name 'Stagecoach'. It was a much better name than Brian's suggestion – 'Blunderbus'.

Today her company, Stagecoach Group plc, still based in Perth but specializing in bus and train transport, is worth £5 billion. It employs 40,000 people across 115 subsidiaries worldwide. Its turnover in 2001 was £2,083.5 million.

Ann Gloag has become Scotland's wealthiest woman, and Britain's second wealthiest woman after Queen Elizabeth. Her annual salary does not indicate her true wealth. On 17 December 1996, Ann Gloag decided to sell 400,000 of her own shares in Stagecoach Group plc. Her brother Brian sold 400,000 of his shares. The brother–sister team made £5.6 million from the sale. She retained a stake in the company worth at the time £195 million, while his holding was £234 million.

She admits that she enjoys her wealth, and how much she spends is carefully chronicled in the popular press. She bought the 24-bedroom Beaufort Castle with all of its furniture and 800 acres of land for £3.5 million, to use only occasionally. She purchased a former hilltop hotel, now called Balcraig House, outside of Scone for her normal home, where she resides with her second husband David McCleary, his three children, an adopted son Peter, now 17, and the three children of her deceased son Jonathan.

'Of course, I can afford material possessions and I do enjoy them. I can't deny that it's lovely to know that if you want something you can have it, that you don't need to save up. I buy a lot of clothes and jewellery because I need them for business functions and I have a passion for fast cars – my Mercedes 560 is a real joy – however, it doesn't make me ecstatic and it's not what happiness is about. There are far more important things in life. I still see all my old neighbours, school friends and nursing colleagues. I'm not aware of treating people differently or them me. Perth is a small city and if you got too big for your boots then people would let you know.' Were she a man, the press might concentrate their reports on what she accomplishes rather than what she buys.

Mercy ships for Africa

Yet her works of charity are much more sustained, extravagant and staggeringly generous than any urge for luxury items for herself. She recently bought a Danish ferry for £4 million to donate to a medical organization called Mercy Ships to be used off the coast of Africa, and is currently raising the further £18 million needed to turn the ship into a floating hospital. ('We still have £12 million to raise. As a floating hospital, it has to be equipped to a very high standard. We expect the ship to last for twenty-five years.') The refitting is taking place in the Cammell Laird shipyard in Newcastle. In early 2001, she made a fund-raising trip to New York City for Mercy Ships and coincidentally spoke at a dinner the same night that Bill and Hillary Clinton were speaking at another dinner they hosted across town. She raised twice as much money as the Clintons did.

'You might well ask me why I don't give the remaining millions to finish the refit, which I could afford to do', she said. 'But I believe in partnership and want others to join in the project by making donations.' When finished, the ship, named *Africa Mercy*, will join three other medical ships already at work.

One of these ships, the *Anastasis*, was berthed in Benin's main port of Cotonou for six months during 2000–01. (Benin is a country sandwiched between Nigeria and Togo on the West Coast of Africa.) In April 2001 whilst working as a nurse on the ship, she complained that neither Mathieu Kerekou, the President of Benin, nor any member of his government had visited the ship during the six months they had been docked in Cotonou. Within 48 hours of her complaint, the President, with a retinue of fifty of his ministers and officials, came to pay a visit. It was the day before his inauguration to a second term in office.

'This is the lady I've been talking about', the President said to his ministers and the press. 'Look at her. When I was shown the picture of the ship [that she bought] I did not believe it. Now I have seen her and I still do not believe it. She is the lady who had bought a ship and named and designated it *Africa Mercy*. She did not name it after herself. She named it after

Africa. Now she is here visiting our country. It is one thing to write a cheque, it is quite another thing to come here and work here. Here is someone who puts her faith into action.' After spending more than an hour on board the ship, President Kerekou told his health minister to arrange for a car to collect Ann Gloag so she could attend his inauguration, along with the presidents of twelve African nations, which she did.

Ann Gloag visited the ship for two weeks at a time twice last year to do her bit to make the difference using her nursing skills. In addition to caring for patients, she also studied what worked well on the hospital ship and what was dysfunctional, with a view to making design improvements on the new hospital ship *Africa Mercy* in the Cammell Laird shipyard. 'I do not think my best contribution is my nursing skills, but I do it. Where the benefit comes is that it gives me a chance to work alongside the doctors and other nurses and that helps me to know what we need to do with the new ship. I get their opinions about what they like and do not like. They are not always right, but I want them to feel that they have an input – and they really do.'

There are 350 volunteer crew on the ship. Each one pays £250 per week to work aboard the medical charity ship. Their contributions cover its operating costs. In addition the crew are called upon to donate their blood when required by the patients, as there is no blood bank. 'A lot of the doctors and nurses would have come from a church background. When I was last on the ship there were thirty nationalities and every religion', Ann Gloag said.

Donald Stephens, the president of Mercy Ships, called Ann Gloag's £4 million donation to the cause the most significant in the charity's twenty-three-year history. Since he founded the organization the floating hospitals have served in more than seventy port areas around the world, providing medical and dental assistance, teaching agricultural skills and offering development services.

Ann Gloag's work with the hospital ships is far from her first charity venture in Africa. Shortly after going to Malawi to set up a bus company, she became appalled by the lack of medical facilities there. She used her own money to establish a burns clinic. She set up an orphanage in Kenya. She adopted a boy whom she found in a ditch in Kenya when he was a baby, Peter. At first the Kenyan authorities said that she could not take him out of the country. She challenged their decision and threatened to appeal to the President of Kenya. She made a donation of £500,000 to Save the Children and built and equipped a 120-bed general hospital.

She instituted the Balcraig Foundation to spend £1 million of her own money on good causes each year. Her definition of a good cause is as wide as the world. She organized a Christmas stay in Scotland in 1997 for thirty-two children from the nuclear disaster town of Chernobyl. Earlier that year she launched 'React Scotland', a charity to care for terminally-ill children. 'I am a trustee of the Princess Royal Trust for Carers, Princess Anne's charity. I have a big dinner on Thursday night with the Princess and an auction on Friday (during January 2002). She works very hard, you know; she has built centres for carers all over the country.'

Buses and trains

Ann Gloag was the Veuve Clicquot Business Woman of the Year for 1989. She maintains that the award raised her national profile and helped with the flotation of Stagecoach on the Stock Exchange in 1993. The share price was set at 112p and within three years had more than quadrupled to 517p, outperforming the market by more than 200 per cent. Together the sister and brother team owned nearly two-fifths of the company, making her shares in 1996 worth £140 million, and his worth £168 million. Today they still control of 25.1 per cent of shares with a value of approximately £235 million.

Stagecoach won its first British Rail franchise two years later. Since then its rail operations, South West Trains services in and out of London's Waterloo Station, and an £825 million purchase of a train-leasing company, Porterbrook Leasing, have contributed greatly to the company's revenues, earning £8 million profits in 1997. (Porterbrook Leasing is one of three train-leasing companies that has a guaranteed income stream ensured by the Labour government. The various train-operating companies must pay the rolling stock companies annual charges to lease the trains.) During the same period Stagecoach was also fined £1 million for causing disruption to commuters travelling to and from London by the cancellation of services after axing the number of train drivers to cut costs.

Going global was a great challenge. They have been successful in Malawi and Kenya in Africa. In Malawi they bought the Bus Company Malawi and the United Transport Bus Company. 'We became the whole bus transport system for the country and took buses from here. We set up long-distance bus routes between the country's two major cities and served the passengers coffee and sandwiches, as we did in Britain. The response to the bus service was so good that we nearly bankrupted the National Airline.' When she arranged the shipment of the buses to Malawi, she put used hospital equipment and other supplies in the containers with the buses and distributed it to medical facilities throughout the country. She set up a burns unit called the Stagecoach Burns Unit at Queen Elizabeth General Hospital in Blantyre, Malawi. She got medical staff from Scotland – 'the girls I used to work with there' and one doctor, plastic surgeon Howard Stevenson from Dundee, who designed the unit – to volunteer during their holidays to go to Malawi to help train nurses to run the burns unit. 'We ran the unit for ten years and took the worst burn cases from near and far, serving a population of 14 million people.'

Stagecoach opened operations gradually in Hong Kong, which have done very well. 'There is a lot of potential in China, although they have to get to know you before they will do business with you.' In New Zealand Stagecoach has great opportunities for growth. The company has also made a few small investments in buses in Australia. It is just a toehold in Australia at the school bus end of the market and they will have to decide whether to grow the business bigger or to pull out of the country.

'When you go into a country, if you cannot add to what you start with quickly enough, you end up spreading the management too thin.' After a few years of successful operating in Portugal, in June 2001, Stagecoach sold its business there because neither the location nor the scale of the operation fitted its strategy.

Results for 2001 included the first full-year contribution from Coach USA, which was below expectations yet full of potential.

'We've had a lot of setbacks and no way did we get everything right every time. As long as you get more right than you get wrong then you're OK. Timing has always been important to us.' Canada was a failure for a number of reasons. 'We went into Canada – fortunately we did not buy a big business there – at the time of the Gulf War. You know how Canadians stay at home during wars, so there was very little airport business. You can cope with a 10 per cent drop in revenue, but when you get a 30 per cent drop you're in trouble. We managed to sell up the business package and get out of it. It was a good lesson for us. It taught us that it is easier to buy than to sell.'

Although in the end they did not lose much money in the Canadian adventure, it was 'very, very hard work. Brian went to Canada and was there virtually 80 per cent of the time. I was doing the lot here. Fortunately, we had not "bet the farm" on the Canadian deal.'

What was it like working with her brother? 'It's great. We would never have been the size that we are today if we had not been a brother–sister team. It's a very good relationship and we balance each other out. When one of us was having a bad day, the other was having a good day. He is a very enthusiastic person; so am I. We are both real risk-takers.'

Not everything she touches turns to gold. Her company began buying up small airports, starting in Scotland with Prestwick. It was to be the start of Stagecoach Aviation. Skavsta Airport in Stockholm was next on their hit list of European airports. But they soon retreated from the venture and sold the Prestwick facility after finding the airport business too difficult to develop.

Growing up in a council house

Paul Young's popular song 'Living in the Love of the Common People' would have found meaning in Ann Gloag's close-knit, strict, Methodist family. She was the eldest of three children, born in Perth and raised in a council house. Her father was a bus driver and her mother worked at home raising the three children. The home was dominated by a strong Protestant work ethic. There was no alcohol, no television allowed. 'It was a very happy home and our parents were very loving', she recalled. 'Although we never starved we certainly didn't have any spare money for life's little luxuries. We were poor but blissfully happy. My parents were wonderful and ensured we had a marvellous upbringing. As a wee girl I can't remember ever dreaming that one day I would be a millionaire. My biggest ambition was to become a nurse, that was all I ever wanted to be.

'My mother was always focused on education and my father, in his own very small way, was a bit of an entrepreneur. When he was a bus driver he used to buy and sell cars. He would go to the car market and buy a car and bring it home and clean it up and sell it on. When we were small, he would go to the car market on a Wednesday – the day it was on. He would take us off school. We would go with him to Glasgow and look round at all the cars. If he had a good day and made a good deal, we would get a treat of fish and chips and ice cream. Very simple stuff; he always took us with him and it was very family-focused.

'As we got a little older, and he bought a car on the market, he occasionally would say: "You can have a share in the sale if you want; have you got any money?" We did have a bit of money from fruit picking and potato picking and we would take a share in a deal, maybe putting in a few pounds. He would give us a pro rata return on what we invested against the profit made.

'I always look back and think that I learned a lot about dealing and negotiations from those trips with my father from a very young age. It does not matter if it is a pound or a million pounds, the basic principles are the same. I always thought my father was very good in teaching me. He had no further education and left school when he was about 12.'

Ann Gloag and Brian Souter were very pleased to host two celebrations to mark their parents' 60th wedding anniversary in June 2001 – one at her Beaufort Castle and the other at her brother Brian's place at Ochtertyre, a rambling mansion and estate near Crieff where he lives with his wife and children. They spared no expense to make it an occasion to remember. 'We had lots of relatives from overseas and we made it a bit special, because they were pretty special!'

Ann did not do well at school, nor did she enjoy it. Her brother David was very academic and later became a minister in the Church of Scotland. 'David's very clever and my mother had great aspirations for him. She thought he would be a doctor. I was not great at school. I wanted to mess around. The only time I focused at school was when at secondary school I entered a course for girls who wanted to do nursing. I had always wanted to be a nurse, always. When I got into that course I did really well. I began to come into my own.' She stayed at her mixed secondary school until she was 17 to finish the nursing course. She left Perth comprehensive school without an O-level, but she was determined to become a nurse.

She worked hard during the training and attended to sick children in Glasgow before returning to Perth to do her general nursing. 'I loved it and got promoted to sister very young. That's nothing now but I was promoted to sister by the time I was 22 and that was young then. Actually I loved everything about nursing – the hospitals, which are social places where you know everybody including the cleaners. I liked that type of environment.'

She met her first husband, Robin Gloag, at the hospital where she worked. 'I always knew I would be the breadwinner right from the start when I met my first husband Robin when we were 18. I was a nurse at Perth Infirmary at the time, and he came in with a torn cartilage.' She married him just before she qualified as a sister. They had two children, a girl, Pamela, and four years later Jonathan. The marriage lasted twenty-two years. When they divorced in 1983 she decided to keep her married name for continuity. It was also an old Scottish name associated with a famous distillery.

Seven years later, in 1990, she married a local businessman, David McLeary, a widower with three children. Andrew was two years younger than Jonathan, and the twins, Peter and Sarah, were two years younger than their brother Andrew. Jonathan married his stepsister Sarah and had three children with her.

Today Ann Gloag cannot wait to take her five grandchildren, along with other members of her family, to Africa to see the hospital ship she works on and to experience the culture of service she is so dedicated to. After suffering the personal tragedy of her own 28-year-old son Jonathan's death in September 1999, she spent seven months in private. When she emerged into public life the following April she was pushing a pram with her daughter Pamela's children and leading a hundred women on a march opposing the repeal of Clause 28. Five days later she announced that she would step down from the executive board of Stagecoach and remain only as a non-executive director to be able to devote more time to her charities.

Small beginnings

Nursing is poorly paid. Her growing family was always short of money to make ends meet. In 1976 she founded a small, part-time, caravan rental business to supplement her nurse's salary. 'I loved my job, but I knew that I was never going to get that much money from it so I decided to start up a small business. At that time the rail network had a system whereby you could put your car on a trailer on the train and you would sit in a carriage. But it only went as far as Perth. So I had this crazy idea of setting up a caravan hire business. You could then get off the train with your car and pick up a caravan from me and tour the north of Scotland and come back to Perth and drop off your caravan and get back on the train with your car. I did it part-time.

'It worked well for a number of years. But it was very hectic for me, and my marriage at the time was pretty far gone. I had about fifteen caravans. The trouble was that all the changeovers were made on a Friday night or a Saturday. That was OK; I was able to do my nursing. But being a theatre nurse I had to be on call. So if there was an accident and it was my night on call, I'd be called out for duty. So I had to juggle the children, changing the caravans around and doing my theatre sister call duties all the time. Brian, who was twelve years younger than me, used to help me clean the caravans on a Friday night and he was an enormous help. Some of my friends at the hospital were also helpful and would swap call nights with me. I must have driven everyone crazy. Brian was great – he would clean the caravans and he would help me with the kids. Brian said: "Ann, you are going to be dead before you are 40. You're never going to hold all of this together."

'I went from doing the caravans to hiring out minibuses and I began to build up the business. My brother, David, who is now the minister, came back to Scotland with his two children after his marriage split up. We were both feeling a bit war-weary and so we decided that we should all go to China. We would buy a bus and just take all of the children to China with us. This was before the Iran–Iraq war and you could drive there. We allocated all the jobs for the journey and Brian was to write to the Chinese Embassy and get all the visas and what have you for the trip.

'Our father helped us find the bus and we bought it for £250. At the time there was a very large motorway bypass on the main A9 north of Perth. I was renting a lot of minibuses to Balfour Beatty and earning really good money from the business. One day I came in from work to find the phone ringing and a guy from Balfour Beatty on the phone wanting another six more minibuses to get more men onto the site.

'I said, Jimmy, why do you not have a big bus? Of course, this is the bus we had ready to go to China. So I threw the kids in the car and drove up the road to see Jimmy and struck a deal: £140 per week for the bus and he was to put the driver on and he was to insure it and put the fuel in the bus.

'I worried about how I was going to tell my two brothers what I had done. But they said it was brilliant – the best thing you could have done. We were careful with the money because we thought this contract was not going to last indefinitely. That bus ran for fourteen months. We bought another bus with the money we had stored up.

'At that time Brian had just started a job with Andersens and he said that he really didn't like it and that he didn't want to be an accountant all his life. He said that he was just reading in the papers that day that the government was changing all the rules. You used to need a licence to travel to have a bus service, and you could not get a licence because there was a monopoly. "I just read that we could buy a bus and run it from Scotland to London and that this is what we want to be doing", he said. That was the deregulation. You had to travel a distance of more that fifteen miles before you could pick up passengers.'

She gave up nursing and moved the minibus business, called Gloagtrotter, to the new business which her brother David named Stagecoach. They began with just one local bus route in Perth that undercut their main rival. They slowly built up a small network. With their Dundee–London via Glasgow service, run with two used buses, they decimated the competition. They were treated with derision by the established bus companies, the Scottish Bus Group and the National Bus Company. These companies would not permit Stagecoach to use any of their depots. 'At one time we thought of calling ourselves the Classical Bus Company, because we were using all the statues in the town centre as pick up points for our passengers.

'They did not treat us seriously and that did us a huge favour. They said things like: "It will not last", and "Their old man's a bus driver", and "They have not got any money." If these guys had treated us seriously and come out fighting they could have killed us off in a month. It was a David and Goliath thing and people actually liked that and supported us. We were the first over the parapet. There was a lot of criticism of Stagecoach and our aggressive behaviour. It was not aggressive at all. It was just that we were the first to do it and there is a price to pay for being first.'

Her father's health was bad by then. He had taken redundancy as a bus driver so he never drove for Stagecoach. 'But he invested every penny of it with our company – I think it was £12,000. We tried to give it back but he would not take it. Now of course he has had a great deal of pleasure for his investment. But at the time think of the faith that he had in us to give us £12,000 – all he had. That made it worse for us – imagine the responsibility we had. The only house we had was mine and that was up to the bank for security. We sold our cars and everything to raise the money we needed for the business.'

Ann Gloag cut her husband Robin Gloag out of the business in 1983, when their marriage hit the rocks, but she maintained that it was a 'business decision', not a personal vendetta. He was voted off the board and given two coaches, a car and £8,000, which was a third of the value of the business at that time. After the divorce, when he tried to set up a rival bus business called Highwayman, he ran into the same tactics Stagecoach employed on everyone. His fares were undercut repeatedly and he was driven out of that end of the bus business. He settled for a coach-hire niche in the market and a quiet life.

'Other bus companies could have done in 1985 what we did but they didn't.' Stagecoach started to buy up small bus companies across the whole of Scotland. They were accused of 'ruthless methods', fierce price-cutting and cherry-picking the best routes. Ann Gloag did not see their business practices as unethical. 'It's a tough business and competition was intense. But if it hadn't been us it would have been someone else. At the beginning we were struggling to survive, not thinking how much money we could make.

'As the company developed, for seven years we answered the phones every night, either Brian or I on alternate nights. Talk about sleep deprivation! On a good night you might get six calls; on a bad night you might get forty.

'You'd get all kinds of customer complaints, sometimes from passengers the worse for drink who had criticisms to make. With these complainers I'd say: "I'm only the night receptionist, please phone back in the morning to talk with management." Little did the caller realize that I was also top management. We took risks and they paid off.'

With the Conservative government's privatization of the National Bus Company (NBC) in 1986, hundreds of small operators sprang up to begin a hectic chase for passengers. A year later Stagecoach bought Hampshire Bus, thereby becoming the first independent bus operator to buy a National Bus Company subsidiary. It set off a chain reaction of mergers and acquisitions that resulted in the bus business being concentrated in the hands of just a few big private players. Stagecoach became one of the three biggest. Eventually they even took over their old rivals, the National Bus Company – the company that wouldn't let them use the depots. 'I don't think having Christian principles makes people soft', she said.

Their strategy was simple: acquire a struggling bus company and undercut the main operator. Sell off unneeded property. Before long they had acquired forty bus companies across Britain, capturing 17 per cent of the bus market. The Conservative government's policy of privatization had proved to be a bonanza for Ann Gloag and her brother Brian. Critics say that privatization and deregulation handed opportunities to them on a plate, allowing them to make huge profits from public assets they had bought at knockdown prices. Ann Gloag argued that they worked prodigiously hard to build the business and took the necessary risks to seize opportunities that were open to others. By 1998, Stagecoach was a plc worth £4.5 billion; by 2001 it was worth £5 billion. Anne Gloag and Brian Souter became the first Scots to break through the billion-pound barrier.

Personal meaning of success

Her personal meaning of success has changed over the past twenty years. At first it was earning more money through the caravan business to help ends meet on a nurse's salary with two children and a husband to worry about. Then it shifted to not losing the redundancy money that her father had invested in her bus business. Then it moved up a gear to protecting her own house. It next became beating the competition. And then going global with both the bus and train business. Finally, now that she is retired and just a non-executive, she is striving to raise the money to finish the hospital ship.

She cannot remember when she became a millionaire. 'I don't really know the moment. I can't remember a specific time or day when I knew I had become "the millionairess". So there was no instant elation or the urge to rush out and spend, spend, spend. It was some time in 1987. I was so exhausted running the business that I really didn't have time to find out. Anyway, it wasn't a target I had set myself. Making that first million happened gradually because of the business taking off, not through any desire to become a millionaire *per se*. When the government decided to privatize National Bus in 1987 we bought three companies, including Hampshire Bus. Four months later we sold one of its properties for more than we paid for the company. That was the big breakthrough. I knew then I had a million in the bank and my family was secure. For the first time in my life the worry of the bank possessing my house was gone and I could breathe easy. It was a feeling of quiet satisfaction, I suppose, rather than nerve-tingling excitement.

'In those early days, I used to say my definition of success was getting the Scottish Bus Group and the National Bus to acknowledge that we were a real threat to them – for them to actually recognize us.'

Being able to help others with both individual and collective acts of charity has been a growing part of her definition of success. For example, in April 1998 she flew Yana Czichevskaya 2,000 miles from the Ukraine for treatment by Howard Stevenson, a top plastic surgeon in Dundee. The 19-year-old had suffered 50 per cent burns to her body, including her face, when she was trapped in a blazing car crash. Her cousin wrote to people all over the world for help and Ann Gloag was the first to respond. Everything was paid for by Ann Gloag's Balcraig Foundation, set up to spend a million pounds of her fortune on good causes each year.

That trust is still in place and operating. 'But my definition of success right now is to find a way to raise the £12 million more to finish the ship. Writing the cheque myself wouldn't be a success. I only want to be in partnership. It is only successful when other independently wealthy people come along and share our vision and wish for the ship.'

Her idea of partnership is broad enough to include governments. 'I actually see what we are doing with Mercy Ships as a responsibility of governments. I look at EU money and my definition of success is to get the EU to say: "Wait a minute, you should not be doing one ship, you should be doing six and we will fund it."'

Her values are rooted in the caring profession and she tries to be proactive. She has given £300,000 to Robert Gordon University to set up a chair of nursing development.

Gender barriers on the road

The transport industry has never been known for providing career opportunities for women. Yet Ann Gloag didn't find many gender barriers in her successful career. 'I could count on one hand the times there have been a problem. I think it is difficult for women who are professionals, maybe it's the ownership that makes the difference.'

One incident reminded Ann Gloag how hostile the environment could be for a woman. She had gone to a transport golf dinner at the Connaught Rooms in London in 1990, where she was the only woman. 'I had been invited by the people that build our buses, and we were big business for them as we ordered a thousand buses a year. This guy walked up to me and said, "Excuse me, you have no right to be here."

'I was amazed and said, "Pardon?"

'He said again, "You have no right to be here, this is a men's only dinner."

'I said, "excuse me, do not take it up with me. I am on invitation from this man and we are his biggest customer. I was sent an invitation and I have come 500 miles to this dinner, so don't take it up with me."

'He got very rude and said, "Get out of here now!"

'I said, 'I have an invitation. I've travelled, and I'm staying. OK?"'

Her brother Brian came over to them and was engaged by the man. 'Is she with you?', he asked.

'She's here in her own right', Brian said. The man didn't accept Brian's word and again – more aggressively – told her to leave immediately or he would have her removed.

Finally, she drew herself up to her full height – 4 ft 10 in. – and warned him: 'There are at least thirty men in this room on my payroll and some pretty big ones at that. I promise you, if you lay a hand on me you'll be really, really sorry. That's the first thing! Secondly, I do promise you that you'll be reading about yourself in the press in the morning, because I won a fairly high profile award last year and I promise you, you'll be reading about this.' She did not leave.

Ann Gloag did not allow the issue of her being a woman to limit her career. She does admit that it was easier for her than it might have been for other women once she established an independent power base with her own company. Most of the people she dealt with in business had to cope with her calling the shots. 'I did all the purchasing for many years. I never felt that I struggled as a female in that world. I knew I was in a position of power because I was writing the cheques. So maybe I am not the right person to make judgements on gender discrimination. I can only speak from my experience and I did not find it difficult.'

In the early days of building the business she depended on her mother to help her with her two children. 'I was lucky because my mother was actually marvellous. She would be there when they came home from school and during the summer holidays. Sometimes she would take them and sometimes they would come to the bus garage. It was all a long time ago, but when I mentioned this fact to a women's group recently it created quite a stir. Some women shouted: "You abused your mother!" But we – neither she nor I – never saw it that way.

'Brian didn't marry until he was 36, so my grandchildren are nearer to Brian's children than to my own.'

The Veuve Clicquot Business Woman of the Year Award

The timing of the Veuve Clicquot Business Woman of the Year Award for 1989, presented in April 1990, could not have been better for Ann Gloag. It raised both her profile and her company's public image in the run up to flotation. 'I got the award for 1989 and the business was pretty hectic at the time. It was very nice to have the outside acknowledgement, but it was not life-changing. I had to prioritize the business demands. The award did raise the profile of the business and it helped us when we went public.'

Her mother did not mind that the award came from a company that deals in alcohol. Her brother Brian was not jealous. 'He is not a jealous person and he has won loads of awards. That is the great thing about brothers and sisters as a team. As he gets awards I am as pleased for him as he was for me.'

The honour was the first of many to follow that included one of three European Women of Achievement awards in 1992. She was the first woman to top the voting in the Corporate Elite Leadership Awards in 1994. That same year she won the top accolade in the service category award, whilst her brother Brian Souter was a runner up for the award.

The Elite Leadership Awards are organized jointly by the magazine *Scottish Business Insider* and financial advisers Ernst & Young and are based on nominations from more than 250 senior Scottish executives. The year she won the top award there were over 400 nominations covering 126 different individuals thought to have contributed most to the development of the Scottish economy in the previous year. The *Insider*'s editorial director Chris Baur said: 'It's clear from voters that Ann Gloag triumphed because her peers highly appreciate her quite single-minded exhibition of business flair, strategic clarity and downright opportunism, and in this part of the world such role models have been all too rare.'

Donald Turner, Ernst & Young's regional managing partner, added meaningfully: 'I'm convinced that Ann Gloag's success speaks volumes for the role women now play in Scottish business and the respect they command.'

Leadership and management style

Ann Gloag tries to involve her bus drivers in the business with a share in the equity in Stagecoach. Up to 3 per cent of the company's pre-tax profits are given to the drivers in shares every year. In 1996 over ten million shares were held in trust for the employees that were worth £12 million. Today the number of shares held in trust is over fifteen million. In addition some employees own shares in their own right.

Her negotiating skills have won her a mixed press. Financial journalists talk about her steely stare that intimidates even formidable City analysts. One said: 'In dealing with her, you don't see the bullet until it hits you.'

Some of the bad press is generated by envy, she believes. Of the forty complaints of unfair trading practices levelled against Stagecoach with the Office of Fair Trading, only two have been upheld. The Monopolies and Mergers Commission, focusing on the North-East, described the company's practices in putting Darlington Transport Company out of business as 'predatory, deplorable and against the public interest'. Stagecoach has been censured eight times by the Commission.

What does she say to this level of criticism? She argues that transport in general, and the bus business in particular, can be competitive and even brutal. There certainly is fierce competition among the market leaders in the bus business. In 1997 Stagecoach was pushed into third place among British bus operators by first-place FirstBus and second-place Cowie. These three companies controlled over 55 per cent of the market. They all receive large, disguised taxpayer subsidies from the government. Without government subsidies, Stagecoach rejoined, bus fares would be 12 per cent higher.

Her attitude towards business ethics in their work in developing countries is very clear. No bribes are ever given. Transparency is maintained. If she chooses to make a return for conducting successful business in a developing nation, the return is a public project that everyone can benefit from like a hospital or clinic, an orphanage or school, never a backhander to a politician.

'When you go to see presidents and ministers in developing countries they are always looking for bribes. They looked at us and said that we were very mean. We said that we will not give bribes; it is a company policy – absolutely no bribes, but we will do projects that will benefit the whole country. In Kenya, for example, we set up an orphanage. Our projects were a way of demonstrating to them that we do things to benefit everybody. But with all our projects, it was very difficult to keep up standards when we were not there. With the medical ships it is much easier. The ship sails out fully equipped for four or six months and everyone is a volunteer – not one person is paid.'

Helping other Scottish entrepreneurs

The most important lesson life has taught Ann Gloag is to keep learning
new things – 'anything to avoid ending up like a dinosaur', she said. She
has learned mostly the hard way by doing. But she is not arrogant about
what she has achieved and she is quite willing to help other entrepreneurs
benefit from her rich experience. She joined forces with another outstanding
Scottish entrepreneur, Tom Farmer, founder of Kwik-Fit, the exhaust
system and tyre service chain. The two Scots put cash into a £25 million
Scottish Equity Partnership scheme to help small businesses. 'I don't feel
guilty about being rich because I worked very, very hard for it. We need
more entrepreneurs, not fewer, and when people achieve some success we
should praise and cherish them.'

Mair Barnes

Mair Barnes, former CEO, Woolworths

Mair Barnes took the country by surprise as the first woman managing director of Woolworths plc, a nationwide retail chain that was so much a household name it had a nickname – 'Woolies'. The danger of household names, as evident from the recent turmoil of another great one, 'Marks & Sparks', is that they become complacent and need a shaking-up. Mair Barnes knew exactly what had to be done to steer the company away from its loss-making course towards one of sustained profitability – and she did it.

Mair Barnes came to Woolworths when she was 40 years old in 1985. She was 'quick and commonsensical', and experienced in retail marketing. She joined the board of F.W. Woolworth as managing director of its super-store division. She described the chain as it was at that time with wry insight. 'It was the shop of last resort, wasn't it? It was where you went if you couldn't get things anywhere else. It was where the pensioner got a quarter-pound of butter or two rashers of bacon, where tramps could keep out of the rain. It hadn't moved with the times; it hadn't looked beyond its own doors; it was bleeding to death.' The company was so weak she had to help fight off a hostile takeover bid by Dixons in 1986.

Within two years of her arrival at Woolworths plc, where she was merchandise director, she was given the top job in 1987. Being outspoken had never been a problem for the articulate Londoner with Welsh roots. She told the then group chairman Sir Geoff Mulcahy that she was unhappy with the company's direction and where she felt it had come off the rails. He agreed with her analysis and decided to make her managing director. She reported directly to him.

A year before she took the top job, personal tragedy struck. Her husband was in a car accident in October 1986 and suffered permanent brain damage. They had been a dual career couple. Her stepchildren lived mostly with their mother. But now she had an invalid husband to care for. 'Geoff Mulcahy could not have been better about it. He was extremely generous. If the best brain surgeon in the world was in New York, then he would fly him to New York', she recalled. At a time when making phone calls from hospitals was difficult, he gave her his own personal credit card number so she could stay in touch with all aspects of her hectic life from a phone box. 'I was in a fairly stressed state. I did not want to be stuck in a hospital in Shrewsbury any longer than the month or so I was there. I wanted to get on with the real world. So it was in everybody's interest to get me back to London and back to work. I had the good fortune of having a driver to take me twice a day to the London clinic, where they had transferred my husband for continual medical care. Her injured husband was not able to work again, but after extensive medical treatment for a year he was able to look after himself at home.

'One minute I had an intellectual partner, and then not. You go through all those traumas about what is the best thing. It is very sad but you find a way to make it work.

'His three children were all living with their mother – one of them had started university. They were all teenagers. Did it influence my life? It probably changed my perspective on certain things – about what is important. It has also made me much more aware of other people's difficulties. For example, when I see someone misbehaving or doing something odd on the London tube, I now give them the benefit of the doubt, and think perhaps they have been brain damaged. I am now more thoughtful as to why people do certain things. From time to time it has added to the pressure as to the things I have had to consider, the decisions I've had to make. Obviously the decisions were down to me. I make all our travel plans for holidays and travelling is more complicated.'

She carried on with her work life and accepted the promotion to the top job the next year. Her leadership of Woolworths could hardly have been more visible or more effective. She transformed the company from a £5 million loss-maker to a £45 million profit-earner. She became Veuve Clicquot Business Woman of the Year for 1988. The award was presented in April 1989 by Sir John Hoskyns, the Director-General of the Institute of Directors at their headquarters in Pall Mall.

The press wanted to probe her personal life as the first woman to have the top job. She responded by saying that she had a husband and three grown-up stepchildren. Any more information was as irrelevant to her abilities as a businesswoman as it would be to ask Sir John how he managed his domestic life. She maintained at the time that she was not in favour of positive discrimination, despite the fact that there were no other women on the board. 'I'm more interested in ability than in whether people wear skirts or trousers. We had a very capable buyer who had managed to fit her two babies in outside the buying season, and we allowed her to work temporarily from home. That's just common sense.' She does, however, admit that winning the award was 'a catalyst for making me more aware of women in management issues'. The honour from outside was widely welcomed in Woolworths and the company made much of it as it celebrated the success of its turnaround.

Her strategy was to streamline the company, ruthlessly discarding many of the retail lines that were unprofitable and out of date, while concentrating on what Woolworths were famous for. Her gift was knowing where to cut deep into product lines. She dropped food and adult clothing, for example. She also knew how to market retail products. She built on the company's strengths in selling children's clothes by bringing in the 'Ladybird' brand, sweets, toys, home entertainment (videos and CDs), stationery and kitchenware. She reorganized the company to meet its streamlined product range and got a third of its 800 stores looking bright and successful again by refurbishing them. Woolworths' 30,000 employees at the time felt the impact of her charismatic yet practical leadership. She developed a company creed to focus their commitment. She redesigned their training programmes to bring them in line with the company's new requirements and vision. She personally hired Dianne Thompson as a marketing manager and helped to develop her talents and skills. She had noticed Dianne Thompson's ability early and was not too surprised to see her later win the Veuve Clicquot Business Woman of the Year Award in her own right as CEO of Camelot.

She launched an in-company magazine called *Good Idea!* in conjunction with Redwood Publishing, an arm of BBC Enterprises. The relentlessly cheerful magazine, with its features on stars, fashion, beauty and health, cookery and competitions, was printed in over a million copies and sold for 25 pence or given free to customers when they spent more than £5. Mair Barnes said at the time that *Good Idea!* was 'an opportunity to give our readers and customers a more detailed look at Woolworths, our stores, our products and our people'. In fact, it gave the giant retailer a chance to promote its products whilst making their customers warm and happy about spending their money at 'Woolies'.

She was well rewarded for her efforts. A survey published in 1993 identified her as one of Britain's fifty best-paid women. Her high profile in the business world and her handsome reward package put paid to the old warning that if a girl didn't study hard at school she'd end up working at 'Woolies'. It did irritate her to receive letters addressed to her as 'Mr Mair Barnes' from people who could not imagine a woman at the head of the famous company.

Seven years into her role as managing director she was still showing improved profitability. Her last full year in the position showed a record £77.8 million profit on sales of £1.2 billion. Suddenly she resigned her positions as managing director and executive board member for 'personal reasons'. Having been once tipped to eventually succeed Sir Geoff Mulcahy as Group chairman, it seemed an unlikely reason for going. The press speculated that she had been the victim of a boardroom coup orchestrated by Alan Smith, a former Marks & Spencer store director who had become Group chief executive the previous year. He had been paying particular attention to the Woolworths chain in his management reorganizations.

'In terms of my personal relationship, he was fun to be with, but in terms of my respect for him (as a senior manager) and therefore presumably his respect for me, we were not ideally suited. I thought he started to undermine me. The Woolworths bit of the Kingfisher organization was the only bit he knew as it related to his past experience, working as he did in Marks & Spencer in its heyday. He couldn't look outside that box or adjust to a very different business. That was perhaps one of the reasons that he did not survive longer than another ten months after I went.'

She did not look back. She went on to collect an impressive portfolio of boardroom positions. She took up a non-executive directorship at the menswear retailer, Fosters. She became executive chairman of Vantios, the pan-European optical group and the parent company of Dollond & Aitchison. She joined the board of the Spanish optics company General Optica International. She was appointed a non-executive director of George Wimpey plc. Her boardroom appointments included the board of Scottish Power, a leading UK multi-utility company. In June 2001 she retired as a non-executive director of Abbey National plc after nine years on the board. Abbey National was her first appointment as a plc non-executive director, begun while she was still managing director at Woolworths.

Family background and education

Mair Barnes has deep Welsh roots, despite being born in North London. Her family of five attended the local Presbyterian chapel and spoke Welsh at home. She was a middle child. She was competitive with her siblings, but always won. She inherited her grandfather's eloquence. He was the Revd D.S. Owen, the famous Welsh preacher and folk hero to the big Welsh community in London. 'He was a larger than life character. I may have inherited something of his way with words.' The Welsh community in London had strong links to the dairy industry and ran many dairy stores.

She went to Hornsey High Girls School in North London, where she became head girl. She was comfortable with the academic world and did well in all subjects. She had a quirky sense of humour that helped make her popular with her classmates.

She went on to Bangor University in North Wales to read for a degree in biblical studies. She might have gone on to teach religious education. Instead, when the milkround arrived at Bangor University during the spring of her final year there, she accepted a traineeship offer from the House of Fraser.

Early career in retail

She was sent to Harrods at Knightsbridge. Her first job was selling Fieldcrest co-ordinated bed and bath linen for those who could afford en suite bathrooms. Next she ran the training for the Way In boutique. She moved on to the Robert Carrier cookshop, which featured the brown earthernware pots that her own mother had thrown out, preferring the new Pyrex line.

She went to the Kendal Milne store in Manchester. There she introduced the store to the cookshop idea. Kendal Milne was called the Harrods of the North.

She went next to Howells in Cardiff, as the store's first woman manager, with the instruction to liven up the place. There she decided to have a new grand opening and invited celebrities to mix with customers over a glass of wine while they watched demonstrations of new products. She remembered how people flocked to the store, causing traffic jams. 'Bringing people into a store is like inviting them into your home: you make it welcoming and entertaining. My role was just to create an environment where ideas like that flourished among the staff', she recalled.

Her last senior post with the House of Fraser Group was as managing director of its Dingles department store group, a post she left in April 1985 to join the board at Woolworths as managing director of the company's superstore division. She had been with Fraser since they had recruited her from university. Fraser's loss was Woolworths' highly visible gain. In two short years she was running Woolworths. Within three years she was the Business Woman of the Year.

She never lost her common touch, no matter how high her office. When people came up to her and confided that they worked in Woolworths on Saturdays, she 'always asked them, "And did you pinch the Pic'n' Mix?", and they always blushed.'

Gender and the Business Woman of the Year Award

Mair Barnes was 44 when she won the Veuve Clicquot Institute of Directors Business Woman of the Year Award for 1988, which was presented on 16 March 1989 at the Institute of Directors headquarters on Pall Mall in Central London. It was a big occasion for her. She was one of the few corporate managers to win the award, which had become associated with successful entrepreneurs, for several years. The selection panel cited her many achievements in her three-year tenure at Woolworths. As managing director she had turned a loss of £5 million into a profit of £45 million for the year in question – 1988. She had the number of suppliers reduced from 8,000 to 1,000.

She had reformed the training programmes for many of the 30,000 staff in the company that produced a turnover of £1.1 billion. And she had overseen the refurbishment of 200 of the company's 800 stores and had scheduled the refurbishment of 70 more stores in 1989. Woolworths contributed 33 per cent of the retail profits of Woolworth Holdings, which was soon to change its name to the Kingfisher Group.

She continued the strategy developed in late 1985 of specializing in five leading markets. Under her leadership Woolworths became number one in the toy market with a 12 per cent market share. She wanted to improve the company's offering in toys, especially in the under £10 category. To demonstrate the company's serious intent she acquired the Chad Valley brand with the plan to create its own original line of benign toys.

Woolworths had captured 6 per cent of the confectionery market and had made a move to increase its share of the entertainment markets for pre-recorded videos and chart music.

On the gender issue, Mair Barnes said, 'There is still a failure to recognize women's ability. However, I cannot say I spend much time thinking about whether attitudes are changing. I am not particularly aware of it and it would be difficult for me to detect a trend. I have been a "woman in a man's world" for so long that it does not become a talking point in my daily life.'

Her chairman Sir Geoff Mulcahy was very pleased with her winning the award. She shared a large bottle of champagne with the people she worked with. But she was a busy woman, in the middle of a huge change programme, and enjoyed the award more in hindsight. It gave her more to do as she became involved in many after-dinner speeches and similar engagements. The following year she was invited to speak at the dinner in honour of the South African Business Woman of the Year, the first woman to do so and the first person from outside Africa.

She herself never had a mentor. It was not fashionable at the time. Today Mair values mentoring, and as non-executive director she has gone behind the scenes in some of the companies and done a bit of mentoring for others. She does not believe that women needed to be fast-tracked or given preferential treatment. However, she would encourage them to show courage, and to look for opportunities to turn things round. 'You have a right to be here' was her advice. She believed in using networks. She made it her personal mission to help men feel more comfortable in the presence of senior women managers. She was intolerant of playing organizational politics, and intolerant of those who did.

Management style and leadership

The key management principles Mair Barnes lives by are reflected in her own development as a senior manager. She enables people to run projects aimed at increasing profitability while achieving career success. She believes in helping staff stay goal-oriented and focused on important matters. She believes in employee participation at all levels in the company and tries to foster it.

'I liked to surround myself with people who were good at those things I was not good at. I enjoyed building a diverse team that was dynamic and full of brain power. I did not have a big ego. I was impressed by the McKinsey guys with their strategic insights into the business. I liked a tough approach to targets. I was good at retailing – that's where my contribution came from – retailing.'

Leaning into the future

Mair Barnes left Woolworths in 1994 to begin a more contemplative period in her career. 'I realized after a lot of thought that I did not want another chief executive job where one works full-time, flat out eighteen hours a day. I also did not want to get typecast as a shopkeeper. There is nothing wrong with being a shopkeeper. I was trying to diversify out of the retail business. Later someone offered me the opportunity to become chairman of a pan-European optical group called Vantios that operated in Switzerland, Italy, Portugal and Spain, all over Europe. The company had 600 outlets and was the market leader in Spain and Italy. In the UK it was Dollond & Aitchison. Their headquarters was in Birmingham.

'It was great working with people across all those different cultures and also with the venture capitalists in the City who backed the company. In its day, it was one of the biggest venture capital deals in Britain as CVC, a management buy-out from Citicorp, bought the business from Gallahers. Being chairman gave me an opportunity to take some traditional brands and bring them up to date, and to help shape the future of the business and lead it to a flotation. It really was much more of a leadership role and it was part-time. I was the chairman, not the managing director. I had MDs in all the countries and I could not have my hands on the business as I did when I was chief executive at Woolworths. I sold off part of the business at the end of 1998 and another part a year later in 1999 and the final bit of it in early 2000. I then had the great fun of making myself redundant.'

She is now 57 and has over a decade of boardroom experience to call on. 'I like this business of dabbling in very different companies in different sectors of business and commerce. I would like to continue doing it. I've enjoyed my work in retailing enormously. I felt I wanted to give something back to retailing because I took so much from it in my career. But I also want to learn something new. I think that it is important to keep a global perspective and not limit oneself to the UK. I have travelled much to many different places. I am just finishing a report on Australia for a South African company, which kept me in Australia for three weeks last month. I find that sort of thing very interesting. What do I see going forward? I suppose never having had major career plans, I don't mind keeping my options open to suggestions. I suspect it will be a variation on the current theme.'

She works with the Department of Trade and Industry (DTI) on a number of issues including directors' remuneration. She has also worked with the Non-Executive Directors Forum based in Milton Keynes, which started about five years ago. 'I've taught on some of their programmes and, of course, think that they are important. It's about sharing experiences along the themes we have been discussing in this interview. It's about people learning from each other and then sharing that information across their own boards. There is never one perfect way. If you can actually share your experiences with people, it is very helpful. In terms of boardroom experiences, I've been there. Certain things I would do differently now.'

She does not feel that the government should legislate for more women on boards. That would only increase the zone of discomfort men have about females being on boards. 'I think it just has to come naturally. I would like to encourage men to open their minds a bit more. It is not that frightening and we are not that difficult.

'Yasmin Jetha, the first Asian woman on the board of a major British company, had just come onto Abbey National's board as I was leaving it. I had been there nine years and I am sure that Yasmin is perfectly capable of fighting her cause there, as I had done.'

Sophie Mirman OBE

Sophie Mirman OBE, founder, Sock Shop and CEO, Trotters

Sophie Mirman went from being a trainee manager at Marks & Spencer to stunning success in the retail fashion business with Tie Rack and Sock Shop to the ownership of just two children's wear shops in ten years. It was a roller-coaster ride that left her in turn breathless and bruised.

She learned about the retail trade from the ground up – first as a 10-year-old, delivering millinery creations made by her famous mother in beautiful black boxes with white trim around them at two shillings and sixpence a box in central London; then in the Marks & Spencer typing pool as a 17-year-old; and then, only 19, she became Lord Sieff's secretary. When she told him she wanted to be the first woman on the M&S board, he took her ambition seriously and mentored her away to learn the business, starting as a sales assistant and later as a management trainee for Marks & Spencer in the UK and in France.

She made use of the M&S experience – and took it much further – in her first entrepreneurial effort as the founding general manager of Tie Rack, launching the company's original three shops in London for South African businessman Roy Bishko (whose idea it was) over a three-month period in the run-up to Christmas 1980. Out of necessity, she accelerated her learning about the retail trade to include purchasing as well as marketing, making trips to Italy to buy the silk ties and other items for the three shops. The three shops – on Bond Street, Oxford Street and in Knightsbridge – were very successful and she was immediately promoted to the job of managing director of the expanding chain of Tie Rack shops. With her share of the turnover she was earning over £60,000, but her use of a bicycle was an embarrassment to the founders. They asked her to select a company car of her own choosing and were astonished when she ignored their urgings to choose a BMW or Mercedes and decided on a Citroen 2CV.

Eighteen months later she had an original idea of her own – the Sock Shop chain. Her idea for the shops arose out of her own frustration. 'I had a particular dress on and I wanted a pair of cream woolly tights to go with it so I went to practically every store in London and could not find the tights I wanted. The hosiery departments in the stores were always at the back of the stores and inconvenient to get to for something as necessary as socks and tights, which should be as easy to buy as newspapers. My experience was not unique but, I believed, something I shared with thousands of other frustrated customers. So I went to Roy Bishko and his South African financial backers and told them of my idea of setting up a chain of shops alongside Tie Rack to sell just hosiery. They thought it was the most ridiculous idea they had ever heard of and that it would not work. They dismissed the idea without even considering it.'

She had already had arguments with the owners about the way they treated people who worked in the shops. If they felt a person's face didn't fit they asked her to sack the shop assistant. She didn't agree with the approach. It collided with the values she had learned at M&S. 'I had been taught that good human relations and respect for people were the only way to do business, and that was the way I operated.' The way they treated her own original idea combined with her grievances over how to deal with people to help her make the break. It was a wrench for everyone as the Tie Rack business had been built around her. She was the figurehead. She handled the press and had excellent relations with the media. Under her leadership the company had expanded to fifteen shops. She left Tie Rack, taking the company's financial director Richard Ross with her.

Together they started Sock Shop with just one shop in the Knightsbridge Underground station on 16 April 1983. Like Tie Rack it was an instant success. Both businesses captured the London commuters' imaginations and served their needs for a new tie, a pair of socks or a replacement pair of tights, or a small present for oneself or for someone at the office. As she had done in her early days at Tie Rack, she was back riding a bicycle to work with a big basket for carrying stock, but soon she bought a red van with 'Sock Shop' painted on it.

Sock Shops sprang up across London – usually in underground or railway stations. Sophie Mirman and Richard Ross, the founders, enjoyed phenomenal success with over a hundred shops, becoming one of the wealthiest couples in the UK. She became Veuve Clicquot's Business Woman of the Year for 1987. Richard Ross, by now her husband, quipped at the award ceremony: 'Behind every successful businesswoman there's a man without a chip on his shoulder!'

But – as with the dot com phenomenon – the demise of the Sock Shop business was as sudden as its initial success. According to Sophie Mirman, four separate events converged to bring the Sock Shop into administration. The first was the doubling of interest rates, which for a company as highly geared as Sock Shop spelt instant danger. The second was the weather: two hot summers in a row left the business vulnerable as women bared their legs to the sun and purchased fewer of Sock Shop's products. At the same time the dozen shops opened in Manhattan failed. The UK business was further crippled by a series of wildcat strikes in 1988 by the rail workers' union which closed down the rail and tube stations in London, where one-third of the Sock Shop stores were located, for one day each week.

Fortunately for them, Sophie and Richard (who had married during their decade of success) had taken some of the money out of Sock Shop. When the business collapsed, they put on brave faces and immediately tested a new idea Sophie had of creating a shop for children, where the parents could do one-stop shopping for them. They called the shop Trotters, and located it on the King's Road just behind Peter Jones, a John Lewis department store. Trotters had a children's hairdresser on site to cut their hair while they sat in a space ship. There was a shoe department well stocked with Start-rite shoes. A book nook, a juice bar, a selection of educational toys and a large clothing department completed the child-focused shop. The concept was successful enough to warrant another shop in Kensington High Street set up and run by Sophie and Richard. Their success also prompted Tim Waterstone of the book store chain to set up a similar children's shop of his own called Daisy and Tom, located cheekily on the King's Road a few minutes away from Trotters. Can the British public look forward to a chain of Trotters stretching across London and beyond? Sophie Mirman says no. She had already 'done it once' and it understandably left her 'bruised'.

Family background and education

Both of Sophie Mirman's parents were French. They chose to come to live and work in London just before the Second World War to pursue careers in the fashion business. Her mother was a famous milliner. Through her connection in the fashion world – she made hats for all the Dior shows – her father came to work for Christian Dior's UK company and became a vice-president with the French firm. Her mother was a royal milliner with her business located in the family home, 'a big house in Chesham Place, just off Belgrave Square', as Sophie remembers. 'I was brought up in an environment where I always saw both my parents work', she said. 'Half of the house was for their business use and the rest was where we lived.' Her mother's hats were famous and in demand and often graced the covers of *Vogue* magazine.

Did she inherit her parents' artistic genes? 'My mother could fiddle with a hat and make it into an extraordinary creation', she recalled. 'But if I touched it, it would turn into a complete disaster.'

Her parents did not seem to mind her lack of artistic talent. She was an only child, born late to a mother in her mid-forties who had almost given up the idea of children of her own. It meant that she was treated like a small adult from an early age. There were no children to play with in her own family. 'Although I had lots of friends, if my parents went out to supper, I would go with them.'

From the ages of 5 to 17 she attended the French school in West London – the Lycée Charles de Gaulle. She left with her baccalaureate to attend a bilingual secretarial college.

When she was only 13 years old, Sophie experienced a trauma that scarred her young life.

'Three of us were in the car – my father and mother and I and my dog. We were driving along a country road on a Sunday afternoon and my father lost control of the car and it crashed into a field in the middle of nowhere in the countryside. In those days people did not wear seat belts. Both my parents were thrown through the windscreen and badly injured. I saw my parents in this terrible state, unconscious and lying in a field. I was sitting in the back of the car and was not injured. So I climbed out of the car window with the dog and ran about a mile up the road to the nearest house for help. I told them my parents had had a very bad car crash and asked them to call an ambulance, which they did. They drove me back to the scene of the accident. My father had put out his arm to hold my mother back, but he went through the windscreen and was bleeding badly from the cuts and was only semi-conscious.

'Because my parents are French we had no family in England. I was sent to stay for three weeks with friends who kindly looked after me while they convalesced. It was ghastly seeing my parents so badly injured and having to take responsibility for their rescue and then being on my own for three weeks while they recuperated. I think that made me instantly grow up. I had to deal with it. I had to cope on my own. There was no one else there. I had to do it on my own. I'm sure that was the turning point in my life. All of a sudden I became an adult. The traumatic experience stopped me from going through any turmoil in my teenage years.'

Both parents recovered and went back to work. Her father had facial scars from the accident and suffered from it as it combined with a general weakness he carried with him all his life due to having TB as a child. 'He died when he was 74, which is extraordinary considering his life-long illness', she said.

She finished her secondary schooling at the French Lycée and won a place at the London School of Economics to study Russian and Economics. Why Russian?

'I guess it was stubbornness. At the Lycée we had the option of Spanish, Italian, German or Russian. Everyone else was doing Spanish, Italian, or German, and three of us thought "What the hell, we'll do Russian." '

It was in retrospect a foolish decision as she never used the language and, of course, found it immensely difficult as it had its own alphabet and nightmare grammar. In the end she did not go to LSE or any other university. Instead she went to work. She felt that since her father was ill by then and finances were tight in the family, she should start a career instead of spending four years at university. In that time she felt she 'could climb up a career ladder and earn a decent living'.

Up until then her work experience had consisted of delivering hats for her mother, being in a typing pool in summer jobs, translating letters from English to French and teaching French to the children of the rich. 'When I was about 15, I decided that I needed to earn pocket money. My parents had a flat in Brighton and we went there at weekends. So I put an advert in the *Brighton Evening Argus* saying "French student wishes to give French lessons", without any idea as to the connotation of "French lessons".' Only one of the fifty phone calls she received was about learning a language. It came from three old ladies who paid her 50 pence for an hour of French tuition at their home. It was hardly worth it. But it led on to tuition at a £1 an hour. When it came to an interview with a Greek shipping magnate she thought she'd charge him £1.50 per hour to tutor his 10-year-old son. But a friend of her father told her to charge £5 per hour. She thought it was an outrageously high rate for a 15-year-old to charge, and went to the interview hesitant about her rate. But during the interview in a Hyde Park flat, the boy came in and asked his father for pocket money. She watched him produce a wad of notes and peel off a few for his boy. That emboldened her, and when he asked her rate she said £5 per hour. He agreed without hesitation to her teaching his boy five days a week. It was her first experience of earning real money and she liked it.

Her maturity and appetite for early responsibility showed through later when at 17 she attended a bilingual secretarial course at a secretarial agency. The woman in charge of the office let her take over the business when she went on holiday. It was a 'wonderful experience' for her 'actually being responsible for the business and having to be there on time and banking receipts at the end of the day'.

Training and mentoring at M&S

Her first real job was at Marks & Spencer on Baker Street. 'I spent two weeks in the typing pool, which I absolutely hated. Then I worked in various departments, including the economic information unit. I provided information to the board on what was happening in the outside world. I had contact at that stage with Lord Sieff and used to take mail into his office. One day a job vacancy came up in his office and I applied and got the job as his secretary. That started me off on my career path. He was a wonderful man and we got on very well. He was a great inspiration and a mentor for me.

'One day he said to me, "What is your ambition, what do you really want to do?" And I said that I wanted to be the first woman on the Marks & Spencer Board. He took me very seriously and did not laugh at me and said that if that was my ambition I couldn't stay working for him any longer. I would have to go out and learn the business. He arranged for me to go out and look at all aspects of the retail trade – the buying side, store management, staff management, merchandising. He thought I'd make a good buyer – that my skills would lie there. But I didn't fancy the buying side of the business and decided to go into store management. People usually go from store management to head office. I was going counterclockwise from head office into the stores. I went off and did a store management course. It was first-rate training, very exciting and the best around then. There was a very structured career ladder and I started off sweeping the floors at 7.30 in the morning, then moved on as a sales assistant working in the warehouse, and so on until I learned every aspect of the business from the ground up. I spent four years in store management, very slowly climbing up this steep career ladder. It was frustrating because I wanted to move up faster than I was allowed to. I was sent to various stores in the UK and then to Paris where M&S had just opened up business. That was wonderful. It gave me total independence from my family. I was on my own in Paris for about a year.

'The work ethic and the style of management are different there. You spend the first half-hour shaking everyone's hand in the morning and it's very formal, you're not on first name terms.' She was in charge of a department and wasn't comfortable with older people calling her Miss Mirman. It took a while for her to make interpersonal relationships even slightly less formal. Just as she was settling in to her new-found independence, her father fell very ill and she had to go home to London to help her mother look after him. He went into hospital to die there six months later.

She wanted to work for M&S in London. When the personnel manager tried to send her to Glasgow, she had a word with Lord Sieff and a place was found for her in Croydon. Grateful for the excellent training in the retail trade, but not happy with the speed of her progress in M&S, Sophie Mirman began to read the wanted ads. She found an ad in the *Camden Times* for a retailer to start up a new business.

Entering the entrepreneurial experience

She went for two interviews at the time. One was to become a buyer of all French foods for Europa Foods' forty stores in London. The other was to set up three shops selling ties. She was offered the Tie Rack job the day after her interview. The chairman of Tie Rack was impatient when she said she wanted to think about it. He phoned her five times over the weekend to see when she could start, and seemed desperate.

Having just lost her father, Sophie was not in her most confident mood. 'They were looking for someone to set up the whole retail operation and I felt I didn't have the relevant experience – not for the whole thing. They wanted someone to do the buying and the merchandising, recruiting staff, dealing with shopfitters, etc. My experiences in the retail trade were all at Marks & Spencer, which is a fairly cocooned environment, looking at very specific areas of the business. So I decided to go along and to ask for a salary that they would not agree to and if they said yes I would give it a go.

'When I think about it – that was 1980 – it was a most extraordinary way of starting a business. I didn't have all the attributes. Nor did these two South African financial backers. It was Roy Bishko's. They had a chain of shoe repair shops in Oxford Street and they had arranged a little corner of one of the shops for selling ties. The ties sold so well that Roy had the idea of setting up the tie shops and developing a chain of shops. The target was to have three shops opened before Christmas and it was already October and we had to get the shops ready and buy for them.'

Sock Shop, Trotters and after

To raise money for Sock Shops' first store Sophie Mirman and Richard Ross had put an ad in the *Herald Tribune* asking for venture capital, but nothing came of it. In the end they borrowed £45,000 from their own bank manager through a government business development scheme. In 1987, when Sock Shop went public, they had fifty stores and the offer was over-subscribed fifty-two times. Peter was appointed corporate development director and, in a neat twist, her mentor, Lord Sieff from M&S, accepted a position as a non-executive director. Share prices doubled on the first day of trading. The number of stores passed the one hundred mark. Lord Sieff liked going around to visit the shops with Sophie, talking with the staff over tea or coffee and enjoying the small scale of the operation in contrast with his own sprawling stores.

Apart from purchasing their London home, the couple lived moderately without lavish displays of wealth. They found the experience of being listed among the wealthiest Britons very embarrassing. By the end of 1989, with the company in administration, Sophie Mirman and Richard Ross had lost £70 million. They left the company the following year.

Her new retail idea came shortly after when she was taking her own children shopping. Little William went into a screaming rage when a hairdresser tried to cut his hair. He was frightened and wouldn't settle down. Her daughter, Natasha (eighteen months older than William) could not find the pair of shoes she wanted in the right size. 'Why not create a child-centred environment to meet all their needs in one place?' she thought. In October 1990 they opened Trotters on the King's Road in Chelsea.

In October 2001 Trotters is still thriving. There are six or seven shop assistants in each shop and three hairdressers. One of them is busily cutting a boy's hair as he sits quietly in a starship rocket. At the rear of the shop other children are being fitted with their choice of Start-rite shoes from a wide selection. Stock levels are kept high in all sizes. There is a huge toy car to play in. Galt educational toys and puzzles line one wall of the shop. The opposite wall contains children's books for sale and a juice bar for refreshment. In between are a half-dozen clothing racks carrying shirts and trousers and jumpers and jackets up to size ages 10–11. One entire display is of orange and black wizard capes for Halloween and orange capes that can turn a child of any size into a walking pumpkin, with even a flap for a lid for his or her head. The shop windows opening onto King's Road are brightly decorated for Halloween. A point-of-sale terminal at the front of the shop is busy as mothers and nannies with their children enter into the spirit of the place and make their purchases.

Sophie Mirman is not in the shop today. She is meeting a buyer in the company's offices in a new, shared building further along Kings Road. She is studying the quality of the garments the salesperson is showing her. Nearly thirty years of retail experience are at work here as she looks through the garments. She shows the salesperson the same charm and care she has always focused on the customer. It's a pleasant encounter for both. Richard Ross is there too, in a separate office, still doing the accounts, still managing the finances for her.

Anita Roddick OBE

Anita Roddick OBE, founder,
The Body Shop

' I'm probably one of the few international retailers to be baton-charged and tear-gassed by American policemen during the World Trade Organization meeting in Seattle in November 1999', she said, waiting for the understatement to take its effect with the timing of a skilful campaigner making her point from her international headquarters in Littlehampton, West Sussex.

Anita Roddick is the most successful, outspoken and controversial of all the Veuve Clicquot Business Woman of the Year Award winners. With nearly 2,000 outlets in forty-nine countries her company, The Body Shop, now in its 27th year, is the most consistently profitable retail enterprise to date created by a British woman. A business begun out of necessity in Brighton, so that she could support herself and her two little girls whilst her husband was on a year-long adventure, has grown into an internationally recognized example of how business success can be combined with ethical behaviour. Her leadership of a company that incorporates community services, ecological concerns and social justice issues has attracted worldwide attention for nearly three decades.

Anita Roddick is an articulate proponent of the causes she believes in. She considered her latest of three books – *Take It Personally: How Globalization Affects You and Powerful Ways to Challenge It* – to be the most important statement of her views to date. The other two, *Body and Soul* and *Business as Unusual*, chart her success with The Body Shop over the first twenty-five years. All three books make the case for business ethics. *Business as Unusual* is dedicated to her three grandchildren, Maiya, Atticus and O'sha, 'in the knowledge that they'll end up like their parents and grandparents (and of course Mother Jones) – ballsy, truth-telling, free-thinking, heart-bleeding, myth-debunking, non-conforming and hell-raising activists'. She sees herself as a campaigner as much as a businesswoman.

During autumn 2001, she launched her 'business journal' *New Academy Review*, in collaboration with KPMG and the University of Cambridge Programme for Industry. It is the only international journal for corporate social and environmental responsibility. She sees the journal as being 'in direct conflict with *The Harvard Business Review*'.

A year earlier her speech, 'Beautiful Business', calling for corporate leadership founded on social and political action, delivered to the RSA on 29 March 2000, was published in the *RSA Journal* on 4 April. In her speech she said: 'Leaders in world business are the first true global citizens. We have world-wide capability and responsibility. Our domains transcend national boundaries. Our decisions affect not just economies but societies; not just the direct concerns of business but world problems of poverty, environment and security.

'Open up a typical management book and you will find it hard to avoid words like leadership, team-building, company culture or customer service', she said. 'However, you will be lucky to find words like community, social justice, human rights, dignity, love or spirituality – the emerging language of business.'

In the speech she sums up her experience of business as a vehicle for social change. 'Many of us in this movement [for social responsibility] would rather have slit our wrists in the sixties than ever be seen as corporate leaders. Most of us were entrepreneurs who, with the zeal of the convert, say that business wasn't just financial science, where profit was the sole arbitrator, it was more about participating in political social activism; using products as emissaries for social change or stores for leveraging our customers on social action. In short it is about bringing your activism to work.

'When I look at my business, I see there are no rules to rely on and no signposts to the future. No one has been there before. That gives us enormous freedom to experiment towards what we want. It is a tense exercise trying to run a business with a difference, incorporating social and environmental change in everything we do, all over the world, every day we are open for business.' Her vision of the role of a modern business has won her global support, admiration, awards and recognition as well as criticism, rejection and ridicule. It goes with the territory – the moral high ground she has claimed for herself over the years.

The Veuve Clicquot Business Woman of the Year Award

The Veuve Clicquot Business Woman of the Year Award for 1984 was the first public recognition Anita Roddick received from her peers. 'It was my most important award because it was the first and it was fabulous. It was a whole different level of people that gave me the honour – people whose company I hadn't shared before. It was publicly so well done. I actually enjoyed it more that I did receiving the OBE', she recalled.

Dozens of awards and honorary doctorates have followed. The Body Shop received the Business Enterprise Award in 1987 from the Confederation of British Industry, and collecting the award gave Anita Roddick another chance to challenge business leaders to 'push the limits of business, to change its language, to make it a force for positive change'.

The businesswoman and campaigner, of course, are the same person in Anita Roddick's mind. Business agendas should be fused with social need and boundaries between company objectives and personal values blurred. As she put it: 'In terms of power and influence, you can forget the church, forget politics. There is not a more powerful institution in society than business – I believe it is now more important than ever before for business to assume a moral leadership. The business of business should not be about money, it should be about public good, not private greed.'

Involving the customer

The commitment to The Body Shop customer goes beyond good value for money and friendly, efficient service to include an open invitation to join community projects and social causes. The shops have posters, leaflets, poster boards and suggestion boxes to involve their customers in a range of issues and good causes. One cannot obtain a franchise from The Body Shop to run a retail outlet unless the applicant can demonstrate current involvement in local community issues, a plan for further community service and a commitment to the company's core values. These are clearly spelled out:

- Against animal testing
- Support community trade
- Defend human rights
- Activate self-esteem
- Protect our planet

Not surprisingly The Body Shop customers are encouraged to follow a classic model for social action in which they see, judge and act. She follows the model herself and has led the way with projects to create employment in a poor area of Scotland, where she built a soap factory, and in London, where she helped launch the magazine *The Big Issue* which is sold in the streets by homeless or troubled people or simply the unemployed.

'We used to buy millions of bars of soap from a European supplier. The quality was good and they were cheap, but we learned that they were cheap because our supplier was using cheap immigrant labour. This directly contradicted so much of what we stood for and offended so many of our principles that we decided to make a change. It also presented us with an opportunity to help a community in distress. We built a soap factory called Soapworks.

'We could have set it up in a safe suburban industrial park, but I would rather employ the unemployable than the already employed, so we located it in Glasgow, in Easterhouse, an area of extreme deprivation, and what is more in our own backyard. It was a moral business decision that worked.'

She is careful when sourcing the raw materials for her products to respect the ecology of the countries involved and to give the providers of raw materials a fair price, and whenever possible, an opportunity for development.

One of the most spectacular campaigns of The Body Shop, directed by Anita Roddick, was aimed at stopping the burning of rain forests. As a prelude to its four-year campaign, The Body Shop displayed rain-forest posters, published by Friends of the Earth, in all its shops. This was followed by a year of intensive education on rain-forest issues. In years two and three Anita Roddick launched a sustained campaign for the rights of indigenous tribes. Then in year four she promoted solutions to the problems The Body Shop had been studying, namely reforestation and the management of sustainable resources. An immediate action of the campaign was to stop the annual burning of the rain forests that took place during the dry season between July and September.

The Body Shop protested the fact that an area of rain forest larger than Great Britain had been set ablaze to clear land primarily for cattle ranching in 1988. The burning had wreaked havoc on the Indian population, destroyed wildlife and plants, and contributed to the greenhouse effect by releasing tons of carbon dioxide into the atmosphere. Within weeks, at the climax of the campaign, The Body Shop had collected more than a million letters to the president of Brazil demanding that his country stop the burning of the rain forests. These letters were hand-delivered *en masse* by Anita Roddick and 250 members of The Body Shop to the Brazilian Embassy in London amid massive media coverage. Eventually Brazil responded with dramatic new measures to limit the destruction of the Amazonian rain forests, including a two-year moratorium on the felling of mahogany and virola, two of Brazil's most important tropical hardwood trees.

In 1990 The Body Shop launched its Romanian Relief Drive to work alongside Romanians in aiding the derelict institutions of the Ceauşescu regime. This has since become Children On The Edge, and every year members of staff participate in a summer playscheme in Romania. Two years later the successful scheme expanded into Albania, Bosnia and Kosovo.

The Body Shop management turns its shops into action stations for human rights and for encouraging customers to speak out on issues which affect them. 'We are a campaigning company – it is in our DNA', was how Anita Roddick put it.

To mark the 5th anniversary year of the Universal Declaration of Human Rights, The Body Shop joined with Amnesty International to run the world's largest citizens' movement for human rights. Over 12 million people made their thumbprint marks on human rights pledges – 3 million of the pledges were made by The Body Shop customers in thirty-four countries. The Body Shop collected 9 million Amnesty signatures. Eight of the twelve Amnesty defendants claimed that the campaign helped them directly. Two defendants were released from prison and three others were able to attend the anniversary events in Paris. It was the third campaign The Body Shop undertook with Amnesty International under Anita Roddick's leadership.

Family background

Anita Roddick's roots are in a small seaside town called Littlehampton, in West Sussex, where she based the international headquarters of The Body Shop. Her Italian parents immigrated and settled in that seaside town and Anita was born there in 1942. Her mother and father owned a café in the town centre called the Clifton Café.

'My mother was the cook and my grandmother peeled potatoes in the garden at the back. As soon as we were old enough, all of us children were expected to help in the café after school and at weekends taking orders, clearing tables, washing up, buttering endless slices of bread, operating the till.' The café served basic food from early morning to late at night and did a brisk business at weekends from the day-trippers coming to enjoy the seaside town.

'As a child I was seen to be an outsider. Many Italian males were interned as the enemy in camps throughout the country. My mother and her family came here and were among the first Italians in this blue-collar area. Even when I was small I realized we were different from English families. We were noisy, always screaming and shouting. We played music loudly, ate pasta and smelled of garlic. My grandmother would sit outside on the front doorstep doing crochet; my grandfather made ice cream in a garage at the back of his house. I never thought we were poor, but I never thought we were rich.

'At home we all slept in one room and rented off the other bedrooms to make money. Lidia and Velia [her sisters] shared one bed, my mother and I shared another, and my father slept in a third bed behind a curtained partition.' They were too poor to go on family holidays, as their English neighbours did.

Her Uncle Henry was off working in America when she was small. She met him again when she was 5 years old and her mother, a strikingly beautiful woman, had taken her and the other children on a trip by train to her village in Italy. To the children's surprise Uncle Henry turned up in the same village. He was a romantic figure and played the mandolin for them.

Later, back in Littlehampton, Anita, who was 8, and the other children had another surprise when their mother divorced her husband, Donny Perella. Uncle Henry, his first cousin, bought the Clifton Café from him.

He transformed it into an American-style diner with a long, aluminium bar and high stools. The diner had pinball machines and a jukebox. It served ice cream sundaes with knickerbocker glories and Coca-Cola. Drawn by the novelty of the place, people of all ages, but particularly the young, made the diner a success. Unfortunately, Donny Perella died a year after the divorce.

Her mother quietly married Henry in a civil ceremony and only informed the children afterwards. He was an inspiration to young Anita with his love of the arts and theatre. He encouraged her to read widely, including Eugene O'Neill and John Steinbeck, but would not let her read his copy of Henry Miller's *Tropic of Capricorn*. Eighteen months later Henry died of natural causes. Devastated by his death her mother continued to run the diner with the help of her children.

'My mother is a pre-eminent storyteller. I think that stories from your family, about your family are more magnificent than anything that you can read in the Bible', Anita Roddick said. 'My own life as a child was dominated by storytelling. There were no children's rhymes or riddles for us. Instead, my mother told us stories of romantic love and deep feeling, stories of life on the farm in southern Italy.' Anita continues the family tradition. At her California home she has a step designated as 'the storytelling step' and from it tells her own grandchildren wonderful stories.

School days

There is a British TV commercial that features a number of celebrities in turn shouting out the name of a person unknown to the viewing audience. At the end, a 'voice over' reveals that all the unknown people are teachers who had greatly influenced the famous people. Anita Roddick remembers the names of the teachers, otherwise uncelebrated, who influenced her most.

She went to the local Catholic school, St Catherine's Convent. She was inspired by one nun there in particular, Sister Immaculate Conception, who taught her a sense of social justice by serving food to local tramps. And later at another school a lay teacher named Miss Springham. 'What they gave me was an education and – these are not the words that I would have used then – social justice. They allowed me to read everything from the writers of the 1930s – especially Steinbeck, who was not part of the curriculum. The sister, who is still alive today, made us look after the tramps with respect, calling them "Knights of the Road". She changed our thinking by language, and she – more than anyone else – taught me about the power of words. Wittgenstein said: "words create the worlds". It's the same in business. Change the language of business and then you can change behaviour. Using powerful words like "love" and "care" in a business environment or organizational context is very interesting.'

Anita failed her eleven-plus exam, 'but there was no great drama about it because I honestly don't think my mother understood the difference between a grammar school and a secondary modern'. She attended Maude Allen Secondary Modern School for Girls. In her second year there she was finally fired with a desire to learn and began to exploit her potential.

'My teachers were exceptional', she wrote. 'They encouraged me, indulged me, let me get away with murder and didn't try to stamp on my personality. They recognized that I was different and let me be so. It was like *The Prime of Miss Jean Brodie* – they made me feel special, creative, original, inspired me to write, inspired me to act, supported me in everything I wanted to do and treated me like a young adult. Those teachers are indelibly printed on my memory – I can clearly remember Mr Kirk, who introduced me to the '1812' Overture, and Miss Springham, who advised me to read Dylan Thomas and John Steinbeck.'

At this time the shocking truth about Uncle Henry being her (and Bruno's) true father was only hinted at. 'I knew, of course, that my mother loved all her children, but I sensed that Bruno and I were somehow special. In those days I never guessed the truth about my Uncle Henry, although with hindsight I can see she gave me plenty of clues. She would often say I was like Henry in one way or another – just little things like the way I ate an apple or sat in a chair. She told me that Uncle Henry always reassured her about me, telling her that there was "something crazy" in me but that I would do great things . . . "Be special," she would say, "be anything but mediocre." I think she must have been echoing Henry's words, for her English was far from perfect.' Her mother didn't tell her the truth until she was 20, but it didn't harm their relationship. Anita is 59, and her mother, who is 87, still lives in the same house she shared with two husbands and her children.

Anita Roddick got good GCEs and won a place at Newton Park College of Education at Bath. She went off on the train to Bath to study to be a schoolteacher, looking like 'a middle-aged matron'. (She had also been offered a place at the Guildhall School of Music and Drama, but her mother wanted her to be a teacher not an actress.) Anita Roddick decided to combine the two and become a dramatic, dynamic teacher of English and history.

Newton Park College is a large Georgian mansion. She studied history and education formally, but her three years at the college were also an awakening to aesthetics. Through another teacher, Elizabeth Newman, Anita the student discovered 'how to understand and appreciate art and design. It was through her that I developed an "eye", an instinctive appreciation of aesthetics.'

During her final year at the college, her mother sold the Clifton Café to one of her uncles. She bought a nightclub located above a dry cleaners and butcher shop in the centre of Littlehampton, and named it El Cubana. It was a place where she could create a *faux* Spanish atmosphere celebrating life and hold court. From the shabby nightclub, Anita Roddick learned the importance of creating a style and the power of music.

She sailed through her student teaching days enjoying her ability to create imaginative and effective learning experiences for her students. She won a scholarship to study in Israel for three months to complete her thesis, an educational one on 'the Children of the Kibbutz' and a historical one, 'the British Mandate in Palestine'. She actually worked on a kibbutz on the shores of Lake Tiberias. She describes the trip to Israel in 1962 as 'a seminal experience, one of the best things that ever happened to me'.

After graduating from college, she got her first full-time teaching job in a junior school, but before she could take up the post she agreed to meet one of her friends from Israel in Paris for the summer holiday. Once in Paris she took a job working in the library of the *International Herald Tribune* and stayed for nearly a year, cancelling the teaching job. Back in England she taught near her home for two terms and then took a job teaching English and history in a comprehensive school near Southampton.

Backpacker

Although Anita Roddick enjoyed teaching and was very good at it, she resigned her post to travel. She went to Greece for a summer holiday and returned by way of Geneva. There she found work as a researcher in the Women's Rights Department of the International Labour Organization based in the UN. After one year she was ready to spend her savings on an adventurous trip. She took a train to Southampton and a boat to Tahiti, the New Hebrides, New Caledonia and Australia. She worked for a while in Sydney to earn enough to continue her travels to Réunion, Madagascar and Mauritius en route to South Africa. Wherever she travelled, she collected the beauty secrets of the native population. She was impressed by the way they used natural substances for skin and hair care.

When she arrived back at Littlehampton after her worldwide travels, her mother had already found a husband for her – 26-year-old Gordon Roddick, like her an adventurous spirit who had already tin-mined in Africa, sailed down the Amazon in a canoe and farmed in Australia. A middle-class Englishman, this tall thin man had trained as a farmer and was doing some farming in the area. He preferred the El Cubana to the local pubs. Anita Roddick's mother, Gilda, mothered the young man and shared her daughter's letters with him for about six months. By the time Anita came back home he was already half in love with her.

Four autumn days spent talking with each other whilst walking around Littlehampton led to Anita's decision to move in with him. She also wanted a child and took a job teaching just before and during her early pregnancy. In August 1969 she gave birth to her first child, Justine. Fifteen months later she was pregnant with her second, Samantha.

Life-time partnership and the first 'The Body Shop'

The Roddicks made a short trip to San Francisco to see friends and to show them their first child. They then drove to Lake Tahoe in Nevada and from there on a whim decided to go to Reno. Seeing marriage parlours lining both sides of the street in Reno, they decided on the spur of the moment to get married. It cost $25 at the Town Hall. In Reno divorces are granted almost as quickly as marriage licences, but the Roddicks' marriage has endured the double test of living together as a couple and working together as business partners for approaching four decades.

The Roddicks' first business together was a bed and breakfast place in Brighton – a Victorian house they had completely renovated. But the hotel business was hard going with the two of them working at it, impossible for one to do alone, even with Anita's deeply ingrained work ethic. When Gordon announced that he wanted to hit the road again alone and ride horseback from Buenos Aires to New York City, Anita declared that she would only agree to it if she had a way of supporting herself and her two young girls.

Setting up the first 'The Body Shop' outlet in Brighton in March 1976 was the answer to this family financial need. It was an immediate success. No one could have imagined that such a small, homespun operation would grow into a global enterprise that would transform the health and beauty market. Later, under her leadership, The Body Shop would challenge corporations everywhere to develop more moral and ethical dimensions to their strategies. It did not start with any grand design. Together Gordon and Anita Roddick were able to borrow £4,000 from the bank, using their home for collateral.

'Everything was determined by money, or rather a lack of it. A local student designed the logo for £25 and I got friends to help with filling the bottles and handwriting the labels. I painted the whole place dark green, not because I wanted to make an environmental statement – the word "green" was not a metaphor for the movement then – but because it was the only colour that would cover up all the damp patches on the walls. The cheapest containers I could find were plastic bottles used by hospitals to collect urine samples, but I couldn't afford to buy enough so I thought I would get around the problem by offering to refill empty containers or fill customers' own bottles. In this way we started recycling, reusing materials long before it became ecologically fashionable. Every element of our success was really due to the fact that I had no money. I ran my shop just the way my mother ran her house in the Second World War – refilling, reusing, and recycling everything – and what we did in that first year was a thumbprint for the differences that would set my company apart.'

The first employees of The Body Shop were friends of Anita Roddick, who shared her values about natural products and her anger about women being exploited by the big cosmetic companies. They were tired of paying more for elaborate packaging than for the products inside. As the shop's reputation grew, several of these friends wanted to open their own shops in other towns. So the second shop was opened in nearby Chichester and the third one in Bognor Regis. One of her friends had a boyfriend who was a mechanic and owned a garage in the area. He had £4,000 to invest in opening the third store, but wanted a share in the company. Anita wrote to Gordon about it and when the letter eventually caught up with him on his travels he wrote back to say, "don't do it", but it was too late; she had already agreed to give him a share in the company's equity. Today Ian McGlinn still owns his share in The Body Shop. Anita Roddick does not resent what must have been one of the best investments made in the last century.

'I have just been talking with some young entrepreneurs in England and I assured them that you can make the money and invest it and have it work for you – it's a way of owning without control. I think the notion of control is a very masculine thing. I'm not positive, but I think it is gender-specific.'

The number of stores as recorded in The Body Shop International plc 2001 Interim Report totalled 1,917, of which 507 were company-owned and the remainder franchised. The idea of franchising the shops came about spontaneously shortly after the launch of the first store in Brighton. 'When Gordon came back he said, "this is a good idea", and we did not even call it franchising. It was the early eighties and we still called it self-funding. A person would come to us and pay some money and they would have to find their own shop and their own decorations and then buy all the stock from us, and we made our money by wholesaling the stock.'

There is a replica of the first 'The Body Shop' in Brighton in the company's headquarters. It is a focal point for the daily bus tours of the international headquarters, which are a popular, year-round tourist attraction. Within the huge pagoda-like structure that houses the central administration building there is another replica building – that of Uncle Henry's American diner, where employees can get breakfast of toasted bagels and cappuccino before starting work or a quick subsidized lunch. Since January 1990 there have been purpose-built crèche facilities available on site that cost the company nearly £1 million to build.

Going public

Going public with The Body Shop was a way of securing better High Street shop locations by raising the company's profile, and also a strategy for the Roddicks to gain independence from their partner Ian McGlinn. 'We had begun in the mid-seventies and now in the eighties we could not get High Street positions because we were not taken seriously enough. We also needed the money to build up the manufacturing side of the business. We wanted to control the entire life cycle of our business and to have a total vertical integration. We wanted to make sure that the ingredients were not tested on animals and that The Body Shop made a lighter footprint on the environment.

'Gordon was very opposed to going public. He said he would need at least two years to prepare the company for flotation, to put our house in order and to install a new accounting system. At that time our infrastructure was virtually non-existent, I handled all the product development, design and public relations; Gordon dealt with all the legal and financial matters – things like leases and franchise problems – with the help of a local solicitor and firm of accountants. He wanted to make sure that he understood the nuances of going public and that there were no risks to our retaining control. He refused to be rushed. Only when he was sure he knew as much about the flotation as anyone else in the great financial world did he give it the green light.

'There were hundreds of meetings with guys in city suits using jargon I couldn't understand. The meeting I remember best is the one when someone from our stockbrokers, Capel Cure Myers, came down to Littlehampton to explain to the staff what going public would mean. It was a wonderful scene. All the staff, about forty of them, were sitting on chairs in the warehouse listening to a man in a pinstriped suit talking about the Unlisted Securities Market – I don't think a single person in the audience understood a word of what he was saying. Certainly my mum, who was sitting in the front row, had no idea what was going on . . . To this day we still haven't mastered the art of explaining the intricacies of shareowning, even though everyone who's been with us for a year can become a shareholder.'

In April 1984 the flotation of The Body Shop took place. The price was set at 95p for a 5p ordinary share. BBC TV filmed the trading at the Stock Exchange – the first time TV cameras were allowed to film there. The price climbed throughout the day, stopping at £1.65. 'Someone turned to me and said, "The Body Shop is now worth £8 million and you are worth £1.5 million." I couldn't take it in.'

After a celebration that night at the Hippodrome in London's West End with the City people who put together the deal, the couple drove southwest to Littlehampton. 'Driving home late that night, Gordon and I talked over the day's events. What had happened was a benchmark, we both recognized that. We were now major shareholders in a public company which looked as if it was going to grow and grow. We were millionaires, but neither of us could really grasp that notion as being a measure of success.

'Before the flotation, Gordon and I had been so busy just running the business, helping to open shops, keeping them supplied and keeping pace with expansion, that we had never really stopped to consider the wider implications of what we were doing . . . The beginnings of The Body Shop had been a balancing act – balancing time with the kids against time with the business, balancing taking risks against caution. I looked on the business as a kind of personal playground, as well as something that provided self-esteem and money for our survival.

'To me the desire to create and to have control over our own life, irrespective of the politics of the time [she was toasted as one of "Thatcher's children" to her great irritation] or the social structures [the flotation took place in the middle of the miners' strike], was very much part of the human spirit. What I did not fully realize was that work could open the doors to my heart.

'Today I am convinced that the enemy of our relationship with the City is not the City itself, with its constraints and templating and financial demands, it is ourselves. Being a very strong ethical company and a campaigning company has never deterred this business. The biggest obstacle to our success has been our own bad decisions. There is no doubt about it. Whereas most global companies our size would spend £10 million on advertising, The Body Shop has never spent a penny on it. Every blank space is an opportunity to tell a message. That's why my trucks are moving billboards. Cheap ones too! We have our own human rights department and our own social audience, so none of that is a problem. When we have a problem it's because we have lessened the role of communications and have accordingly made stupid decisions on product development. The customers do not like daft products and daft decisions; they do not object to our ethical stands.'

The community dimension

After the flotation Anita and Gordon Roddick were concerned that 'they would now be measured by their personal wealth and the wealth of the company, not by how many people we were employing. We were both in our forties and not easily impressed by the celebrations in the City; we asked ourselves: "How do we keep human?" We decided to set up a volunteer department with our employees. Most of our people were in their mid-twenties, with the strength and health of young adults. Community volunteering was the answer. We said that every shop had to do community volunteering, which we would pay them to do. We found this amazing teacher at one of my kids' schools and the teacher agreed to audit the shops to make sure they didn't go cleaning golf links, but found better community projects. It was phenomenal. There was this energy and enthusiasm which when it comes from the heart is unstoppable.'

Imitation: the highest form of flattery

Anita Roddick's success with The Body Shop set off a wave of 'me too' natural products. Mainstream competitors like Boots, Woolworths and

Superdrug, launched their own lines of natural products to blunt and erode the competitive edge of The Body Shop. Specialist shops in flagrant imitation of her chain sprung up everywhere. Lush is the latest in a long line of copycat shops. Sales people in Lush shops will slice soap for their customers like cheese at a deli counter in a supermarket. Everyone seemed to be looking for a slice of The Body Shop market. Anita Roddick admires some of Lush's ideas, but said that she could not stand going into their shops because of the smells. 'It hits my respiratory system; I gag', she said.

Imitating The Body Shop was particularly blatant in America, it contributed to a loss-making situation there for many years. 'The story of our start-up there would make a good chapter. "Taking a Bath in America" it's called', Anita Roddick said relishing her pun. 'We opened up with the infrastructure in America for almost a hundred shops. The competition was as instant as it was enormous. We thought when we entered America that we were sacrosanct, untouchable and that we would be able to open an entirely new market with barely a second thought. What we didn't antici-pate was how fast the competition would come in.'

At first she entered the New York area with company-owned shops only and everything seemed fine. 'When we entered the US market in 1988 we opted to open our own stores rather than immediately to get into fran-chising, to give ourselves time to adjust to the new market.' The sampling won great press for The Body Shop, which also initially made money. But the company was soon sucked into the shopping mall way of doing busi-ness and that was an entirely new experience for the British shop-openers whose *naïveté* was soon exposed.

'Towards the end of the same year The Body Shop began franchising there – 1990 – Leslie Wexner, a retail mogul who just takes an idea and copies it, opened his first Bath & Body Works shop. Within 18 months he had 100 stores grossing $45 million a year. He became our number one competitor. We managed to stop him copying the look of our shops, but within another 18 months there were about another 30 different look-alikes of The Body Shop that developed their own lines of fruity potions and sold them for less than we could. We were struggling. Wexner was the worst threat, as he must own a third of every mall in the country. We were a shop-opening company. We had no strategy to cope with a copycat competition that was so fast and furious. We had not thought what would happen if Wexner decided to turn one unit in each mall into a copycat of The Body Shop. Immediately we had 500 shops competing with us. We thought that people could separate the real thing from the imitations, but in America that kind of discernment was absolutely irrelevant.

'To make matters worse we had located in the malls instead of in urban streets, only to find that the mall owners did not allow us to do a lot of our campaigns. They did not want us to put up many of our posters.' Mixing politics with shopping simply did not go down well in the malls.

Anita Roddick's unshakeable commitment to not testing on animals also created difficulties for the struggling company in America since about half the ingredients available for their products there had in fact been tested on animals and therefore could not be used. Sourcing the raw materials from developing countries was a difficulty for The Body Shop. Finding new products to meet the consumers' insatiable appetite for novelty was also difficult. There were problems with how The Body Shop structured their franchising that cut into their margins. They had to learn to live with the American concept of never-ending sales, when in the UK they didn't have sales. In the end, after over a decade of struggling in the American market, after a serious re-engineering exercise, The Body Shop has prevailed with about 400 shops across America.

Anita Roddick summed up her American experience in these words: 'I am always entranced, seduced, mystified, infuriated, and challenged by America. I love the enthusiasm there, the willingness to take risks, to experiment, and some of our most enterprising and amazing franchisees are American. I love the politics of dissent in America, its labour movement history and its community movement. I have also met more heroes in the United States than in any other place in the world.'

Gender-based barriers to success

Anita Roddick encountered some barriers to her success in business earlier on because she is a woman. Her start-up money for the first shop didn't come until she approached the bank with her husband and used the collateral of their property to underpin the bank loan. 'There are certain self-imposed barriers – one of which has to do with women and money. Analysing money and being careful about it and understanding how money works and all the systems connected with it is not something that comes naturally to many women entrepreneurs. Most are interested in marketing or sales.'

She now has plans to produce a series of tapes and booklets to help women entrepreneurs get started. 'Not as nutty as Tom Peters' stuff, just the fifty things you need to know to actualize a good business idea', she explained. It will include creative ways of raising money and imaginative ways of marketing.

Other barriers included giving away power too easily and not liking to argue or confront. 'Women also aren't as unimaginatively loyal as men are. Men have this loyalty to their peers and to their group. You can say to someone, this has happened here or he's not the right person for the job, or it's killing him, and if that someone is a man or a group of men, they say "No, no, we have to support him, see him through this spot of bother." I don't think women are like that.'

She has her own view about the paucity of women on the board. 'I have another point of view. I think that women do not want to be on the boards of companies. They have seen the organizations and they have seen their values and they say it is not my style – nothing I want to be part of. Anyone who – like me – goes to board meetings knows that it is frigging dull. The board meeting is not the narrative of the business; it is simply financial science. Until they move that financial science away and talk about what the role of business is and bring out personal testimony – who would want to spend time at their meeting?

'The history of the past few centuries has done little to repair the self-esteem of women, and in our own generation there are so many pressures to undermine it – a beauty industry making women dissatisfied with their bodies, an economic system that is often stacked against them, a set of hierarchical traditions designed to exclude them. But paradoxically, it looks as though the next few generations will need women – and so-called 'feminine' strengths – more than ever before.

'In spite of their best efforts, I don't believe that there is much chance that the proverbial "glass ceiling" is going to be shattered in my lifetime. Some reports indicate that if women continue to progress in business at the current rate, it will be 500 years before they have equal managerial status in the world, then another 475 years before they hold equal political and economic status to men. Nearly 1,000 years to go isn't progress. But I also believe that there are ways to work around the problem and my own career shows that it's possible – though even the traditional male structure is still in place waiting to reimpose the status quo.

'My daughter Sam, who is 29, with no business training and dyslexic, a school leaver at 17, has just opened her own shop in Covent Garden with two other girls from school. It's one of the most exciting concepts of a shop I've seen – women and sexuality. So it is not your Ann Summers type shop. It is brilliant and witty and smart and irreverent, and dazzling and different. If she can get the pricing right, she will use this as a base for campaigns and she will turn that horribly, tacky industry into something joyful, just as I turned the beauty business into something more relevant than just sloshing something onto your skin to make you look young.'

Personal meaning of success

Anita Roddick has written an entire article on her personal meaning of success. She sees it as 'a movable feast'. 'In the early days it was survival and earning the income to oil the wheels. Then it becomes a relationship between wealth and status. Now for me, it is about how to keep this company alive and brilliant when I have gone. I've had the platform of The Body Shop for over twenty-five years and if I move into another arena, how do I make that a success? Number one, I do not want to start up another business. I want to make it an enterprise or a co-operative. So my personal definition of success does move.'

She has already started The New Academy of Business based at Bath University, where she lectures to management students from around the world who want to learn about creating socially responsible and ethical companies. From small beginnings there is already a global network of like-minded business people doing research projects and sharing ideas and data. 'We have set up Respect Europe, which is a management consultancy firm for socially responsible businesses.' Her website – AnitaRoddick.com – helps communicate the messages from the management network.

She drives her Volkswagen to work. 'My car is ten or fifteen years old and it has anti-globalization stickers on it.'

She has a fine house in West Sussex which she readily shares with other campaigners from Greenpeace and G8. 'I have a wonderful house and great status and I live a fairly hedonistic lifestyle, but it is all about community. We have a house in Santa Barbara in the so-called gated community – the gates are there to keep out the poor. Until you change the financial institutions and until you move from the suicide economy, which is about extracting all the resources and making money for a few people and not genuinely thinking of creative ways of transforming society and business, the gap between the rich and the poor will continue to widen.

'I have never argued with the City in my life. I have shocked them. There is no culture for reflection in business, none! You are measured by this very unimaginative band called profit and loss, or the financial bottom line. I demand that the financial bottom line include human rights and social justice and community development. I demand it in this company and if they do not like it they can buy shares in L'Oreal.'

Debbie Moore

Debbie Moore, CEO, Pineapple

Debbie Moore, founder of the Pineapple brand fashion wear and the Pineapple Dance Studio in London's Covent Garden, has been in business for twenty-two years and is still going strong. On 5 November 1982 she became the first woman company chairperson to walk out onto the old Stock Exchange trading floor to celebrate her company's flotation. For this historic event the former model was wearing her own creations – a batwing-sleeved sweatshirt, a ra-ra skirt and black leggings. Forty per cent of the company's one million shares were offered. At the end of the first day of trading, the share price was £1.00, almost double the issue price of 52p. The issue was over-subscribed several times. The following year, 1983, she opened the Pineapple Dance Studio in SoHo in New York City, financing it with a rights issue.

As Pineapple grew, Debbie Moore became a role model for women entrepreneurs. She was Veuve Clicquot's Business Woman of the Year for 1983. The accolade was important for her personally and put her in the same league with the two other women entrepreneurs she respected most, Anita Roddick, founder of The Body Shop, and Sophie Mirman, who started Sock Shop. 'My daughter, Lara, was pleased to see reports of the Veuve Clicquot award in all the papers, and she enjoyed the giant pineapple-shaped cake the chef at the Institute of Directors had made specially for the occasion', Debbie Moore said. 'It is such a prestigious award and led to other marvellous things happening. I was invited to Number 10 by Margaret Thatcher. I was also invited to Buckingham Palace that year for a reception for achievers with the Queen and Prince Philip.'

Pineapple back from the brink

Unhappy with the City's narrow focus on increasing profitability, on 21 January 1988 Debbie Moore bought back Pineapple dance and fashion in a management buy-out. By then the dance and fashion part of Pineapple had been relegated to being just one of the seven subsidiaries of the Pineapple Group, an Anglo-American marketing services company. It was the only company in the group not making a profit.

A grim sequence of events had been unfolding. First the market had lost confidence in Pineapple and its share price spiralled downward throughout 1985. Then Debbie Moore herself lost confidence in her own abilities. She had been away from the business, giving top priority to her daughter's recovery from a serious illness. In her absence others had taken charge and they were not keen to refer decisions to her again when she returned. To add to the difficulties, against her instincts, she used a specialist retail recruitment agency to assemble a new management team. It did not work; old problems were not solved and the ill-chosen team members created new ones.

Her accountant husband, Norris Masters, made matters worse by coming into the business full-time at the beginning of 1985. He held 300,000 shares in Pineapple (his half of the 600,000 allocated to the married couple when the business went public) and wanted to look after his interest. But their marriage was breaking up and they separated at about the same time he came to Pineapple, making things awkward. To buy a dance shoe manufacturing company, Norris Masters sold some of his Pineapple shares. This action, combined with a decline in profit the previous year, helped to undermine confidence in the company. Pineapple developed cash flow problems. A supplier had a 'winding up order' issued against the company. When the time limit for payment expired, the Order was printed in the *London Gazette* and circulated to the banks and financial institutions. Pineapple's bank withdrew the company's working facility.

In keeping with the axiom that the best defence is a good offence, Pineapple went on the offensive through a new rights issue and an aggressive acquisition strategy. Non-executive director Peter Bain had been on the board of Pineapple plc since early 1984, as a result of Michael Ashcroft, Chairman of ADT, underwriting the company's first rights issue to buy Broadway Pineapple. He was a specialist on acquisitions with a proven track record. Within eighteen months he began buying, on behalf of Pineapple plc, six British and USA companies that provided the whole range of marketing services. He was able to convince Pineapple shareholders that this was the way forward, and raised the money for the purchases through a new rights issue. Soon the Pineapple Group was showing profits again, apart from the dance studio and fashion part of the business.

At this point Debbie Moore made her offer to buy back the dance and clothing part of the company for just £1. Of course, there were costs. She had to sever all her financial interests in the group. The Broadway dance studio property had to be sold for £3.5 million, nearly triple its cost three years earlier. Debbie Moore also had to deal with the dance and clothing part of Pineapple's half-million pounds in earlier losses subsidized by the Pineapple Group. The only challenge to her bid at the Extraordinary General Meeting was her ex-husband Norris Masters, whose offer to buy the company at its market value was rejected.

There followed a period of serious examination of the business she bought back. She decided to drop Pineapple's wholesale business and to concentrate on retail and mail order trade. She opened up new markets in Japan. 'By the autumn of 1988, I had given each of the centres a facelift, built a new management team – a mixture of old and new faces – and there was a great feeling of renewed energy', she recalled. Perhaps the most valuable lesson she learned was that reassessment in a small business is a continuous process.

In the mid-1990s she restructured the business again to concentrate on her strengths as a fashion designer and manufacturer of affordable casual wear. By autumn 2001, most of her manufacturing was done abroad in Bangkok or the Czech Republic. Her famous fashions of the 1980s were enjoying a comeback. Besides producing the Pineapple basics, Debbie Moore was reintroducing the ra-ra skirt in a lightweight fabric instead of the original fleece, footless tights that are longer and looser, and a smaller version of the batwing sleeve. 'We've also fitted garments more closely to the torso', was how Moore put it. 'They are more Prada-esque for 2001.'

The Covent Garden dance studio was thriving, fully booked in October/ November 2001. Cliff Richard was getting ready for a tour and used the studios for his rehearsals. Cher had dropped in to workout the same week. The studios were bustling with dancers and performing artists from around the world. One teacher was training Japanese students in ballet. Try-outs for a new musical were underway in another studio. She had fifty Pineapple concessions in Miss Selfridge stores nationwide, six Twist outlets stocking more formal jersey women's wear and a new label at Debenhams, 'Pineapple by Debbie Moore'. There was the launch of a new range of fashion aimed at the youth market and labelled 'Mai Mee'. Taken together all these developments indicated that, in the high-risk fashion business, she has not only survived but prevailed.

Family background and early career

Debbie Moore came from a working-class family where her father was a plumbing contractor and her mother a clerk in a mail order company and later in a tax office. She had a bright older brother, 'a whiz with computers', who went on to get a Ph.D. The family of four lived modestly in a suburb of Manchester. Her mother is 80 now and she and her husband still live in the same house they moved into when they married.

Debbie passed her eleven-plus and went to grammar school. There she had to struggle to resume her studies after a severe bout of whooping cough when she was 14. The illness caused her to miss three months' schooling and set her far behind her classmates. So she transferred to a commercial college. Her luck improved at age 15, when a classmate put her name forward for a modelling competition for *Honey* magazine. She won it. As part of her prize she was enrolled in a fine modelling school in Manchester and trained in the art of modelling by Sheelah Wilson. 'You learn to walk in six-inch heels on polished floors and to go up stairs and turn – that sort of thing', she explained. 'Twenty-five pounds worth of clothes from Courtaulds was also part of the prize', she said. Her first modelling assignment was for UK *Vogue* magazine. She undertook regular work with the clothing company Courtaulds and was paid £5,000 a year. Then came jet-set assignments – the first, in New York City, was sponsored by *Honey* magazine.

Later came more work in New York, Washington, DC, and Philadelphia. The more routine modelling was in Liverpool, Bradford, Leeds and Manchester. But there were exotic locations, especially for the travel companies, like Ibiza, Majorca, Torremolinos. She was doing something she liked – travelling – and meeting exciting people from the fashion and entertainment worlds. At home in Manchester she mixed with a trendy group of friends that included David Bailey, the photographer, and George Best, the football celebrity. She went to the Cavern in Liverpool. It was heady stuff for a teenage model.

An early marriage to photographer David Grant followed in 1965 when she was 19. By then she had become the 'face of Revlon' and was earning £10,000 per annum. The couple first rented a flat in Altrincham and then bought a large stone house on the moors. It was 'like something out of *Wuthering Heights* and he was my Heathcliff. I kind of imagined this is where I would live and have children. And then one morning my husband decided to go to work and not come back.' It was a brutal and unexpected end to a marriage that once promised so much. She and David Grant were filmed for a Granada TV series *This England* in a programme called *Model Couple.* The marriage had lasted only two years. She was shattered by his desertion. 'It prompted me to throw myself into my work to get over it.'

She knew that the best jobs – those that involved travel abroad – were in London. She had friends there who kept inviting her to stay with them until she found her own flat. She didn't quite know how to tell her parents she was going, but when she finally did, 'they said "it's about time; you're not going to get any further here, good for you; get on with it"'. She moved to London where she met with more career success.

'I travelled the world and met all kinds of interesting people. It was a demanding lifestyle, but I enjoyed it. I'd get back home late from a shoot to find a message from my agent that I was on the 7 a.m. flight to Milan in the morning with two evening dresses.'

But like all models, Debbie Moore wondered what she'd do when she was over thirty and the modelling slowed down or the assignments stopped. In the many hours waiting on sets for photo shoots, she talked with other older models about the future. She remarried, and had her daughter, Lara, in 1974.

'People I worked for often complained that the younger models were appallingly unprofessional, turning up to photographic sessions with unwashed hair, no accessories, etc., so together with Eve Pollard (then a fashion journalist and later a famous editor) I was seriously thinking of opening a modelling agency and training girls in the same way I had been trained by Sheelah Wilson', she explained. 'My modelling career was going well, but I knew it wouldn't last and I decided I wanted to run my own business. I had been modelling for about seventeen years by this time.' But before she could act on the modelling agency idea, she saw another opportunity and pounced on it.

First business

Towards the end of 1978 the dance studio she attended in Covent Garden 'to keep slim and sane' suddenly closed down with only a five-day notice, leaving hundreds of members like herself, teachers and dancers and other professionals without a studio. She helped some young dancers collect over two thousand signatures on a petition to try to keep the Dance Centre open but failed to do so. At the same time she took the names and addresses of dance teachers who were potential clients for a new club. 'I had started thinking about setting up something similar – obviously there was a huge demand and in many ways it seemed a very easy business. It is basically a space-letting operation – all the teachers are self-employed and simply rent studio space from you.' She began looking in earnest for a new place in the same area close to theatres and the Opera House.

The Covent Garden fruit and vegetable market had completely relocated to its present-day modern warehousing on the other side of the Thames, leaving many large buildings vacant. Through a photographer friend, who was looking for rented space, she found the abandoned pineapple warehouse that became her first business premises and today still houses her famous Pineapple Dance Studio. 'I went and looked at this derelict pineapple warehouse that was full of dead pigeons and felt instinctively that, despite its appalling state, its potential was enormous', she said. The photographer wanted the first floor, leaving the basement and ground floor for her. 'It was about 7,000 square feet – the minimum I needed; 10,000 would have been better, but I went ahead anyway.'

Having the names and phone numbers of teachers and dancing instructors from the previous dance studio was a great advantage, as was having the names and addresses of former dance studio members from the petition they signed. 'I had lots of journalist contacts from my modelling days. So I could phone people and tell them what we were doing . . . At a party, I overheard journalist Celia Brayfield discussing the fate of the Dance Centre, so I introduced myself, and told her that we had just started the building work at Pineapple. A few days later, a story about us appeared in the "Londoner's Diary" in the *Evening Standard,* and their switchboard was blocked with calls from people wanting to know when we were opening. Suddenly we were on the map!' she said. The business was an instant success in its first year – 1979 – and Debbie Moore drew a salary of £35,000.

Soon their success meant that they needed more room. She paid the photographer £30,000 to move from the first floor he occupied to the second floor, giving Pineapple the space she needed for professional classes. With the extra room she was able to move the café and double the size of the clothing shop, 'doubling its take'. Later, when the banana warehouse next door was vacated by Kobi Jeans, she seized it in a matter of hours, bypassing her own accountants, to keep it from becoming a wine bar. She expanded her clothing shop into the former banana store, again 'doubling the take' and giving her room to do the wholesale operation properly.

'Although I didn't know it at the time I opened Pineapple Covent Garden, design and image would become one of our strengths as the company grew and developed. I knew nothing about graphics, but just knew that I wanted the name written like the Ritz Hotel – early 1940s style. Women are more instinctive than men, and you must just open up your mind and be prepared to back your instincts', Debbie Moore later recalled in a book she wrote in 1989 to help other women make a start in business. The book, filled with chatty advice from her own experience (and the experiences of others like Anita Roddick and Sophie Mirman), was called *When a Woman Means Business*.

At the start of the fitness boom late in 1981, Debbie Moore decided to open a second London Pineapple Dance Studio in Paddington Street, just off Baker Street. She needed it to give her teachers the teaching hours they said they required as she had run out of space in the Covent Garden studio. She opened Pineapple West, just as other people, in imitation of Pineapple, were opening up studios and trying to lure her customers away. It was a case of grow bigger or lose it all to the larger rival studios springing up.

Making it big in New York City

The New York City–Broadway Pineapple Dance Studio followed. At first it must have seemed impertinent for Debbie Moore to open a dance studio there in what was the acknowledged dance capital of the world. One London journalist accused her of 'hauling coals to Newcastle'. But dancers in New York told her that there was a need to pull all their disparate activities together in one dance studio, instead of criss-crossing the city for rehearsal space, fitness centres, danceware, lessons, etc. She discovered it was true and found an amazing building to buy in SoHo before it was gentrified. 'It was 200 feet long and 40 feet wide, with no pillars to break up the floor space, and windows on three sides so the natural daylight was superb', she remembered. She bought the building on Broadway for the dance studio from a Russian immigrant who dealt in Russian art.

She rented an apartment for her manager to live in and, most importantly, employed the man to run the studio – Steven Giles, a dancer, who had worked for two years at Pineapple Covent Garden and wanted to live in New York. It was a key appointment because Steven Giles ended up putting the New York studio together when Debbie Moore had to attend to her sick daughter. 'While the New York studio was being built Lara was ill and I couldn't go there to manage it.' She raised the money with a rights issue and a year later opened the studio. Media coverage included Debbie Moore appearing on breakfast TV *Good Morning, America* and on *Lifestyles of the Rich and Famous*.

Hardly had she come back from buying the New York building when Debbie Moore noticed a building for sale in South Kensington. Buying and saving the building, which had last been a church, proved irresistible to her. The business reason for the purchase was to give Pineapple – with three dance studios – more space and competitive advantage by completing its coverage of central London. The building for her South Kensington Pineapple Dance Studio was bought through the Business Expansion Scheme, which allowed investors the chance to offset their investments against tax.

Creating the Pineapple global brand for clothing

Debbie Moore was quick to notice how dancers modified their dancewear to meet their specific needs, with a cut or rip here or there to give them greater freedom of movement. 'We used to customize their dancewear because the legs were cut too low and the necks were too high and they used to cut them and chop them and use safety pins', Debbie Moore explained. She also realized that professionals working in the theatre, and those aspiring to do so, needed clothes to reflect their lifestyle. She first designed a range of functional clothes for them and sold them from a shop within the studio. She also realized that most fabrics were not suited for the wear and tear they gave them. She found the basic 'school colours' of leotards unappetizing. 'When I started out,' she recalled, 'leotards were all shiny and came in colours like brown and maroon. I worked with Dupont, pioneers of Lycra, to establish cotton/Lycra, which had previously been used only for swimwear and underwear, as a fabric for outerwear and streetwear. Working with Dupont, I asked them to work up Lycra into leotards, catsuits and leggings, which I had small contractors doing for me. Then I realized that if you could make leotards out of this wonderful fabric, why not a dress, why not a body and a skirt.

'Then I found this marvellous factory where the pattern cutter had specialized in corsets all her life. So together we worked on blocks, because I didn't go to design school – I had no technical training – but we got this fantastic fit because the fabric was cut right. Later when Lycra became fashionable other fashion houses got the fabric and made a dress out of it and thought that it would go out and in at the right places on its own. But it all has to do with how it's cut and Peggy with her fantastic skills and blocks in those early days.'

Debbie Moore gave dancewear 'street credibility', creating the Pineapple formula – ultimately versatile, easy-stretch separates at low prices. Before then people were used to more tailored clothes. Pineapple created the little black dress that could be scrunched up at the bottom of a handbag and emerge beautifully for a spontaneous evening out. The clothes washed well, did not need ironing and kept their colour and shape.

'Fashion is a notoriously difficult business, so it's best to go into it gradually, as we did. In those early days, we sold a few leotards and leg-warmers which were quite limited then – just white, black, pale pink and pale blue. So we found some outworkers and got them to make leg-warmers specially for us in interesting colours and patterns. We were also making ra-ra skirts, sweaters and ski pants that could be worn in the studio and in the street. Then we started telling the dancewear manufacturers how to make the leotards more exciting and stylish – cutting the legs higher, lowering the necklines and introducing new colours.' When she realized that these companies would sell the greatly improved dancewear not only to Pineapple but to their other customers, she decided to develop her own label, adapting the fashionable dancewear to comfortable streetwear. With no formal training in fashion design and production, she relied on her instincts, networked with friends and contacts to find the quality manufacturers, and made mistakes that took the clothing division of Pineapple to the dangerous edge.

By October 1987 she had opened one of her pilot shops for Pineapple fashions further along the King's Road away from the much more expensive Sloane Square end. The rent was £20,000 per annum with no premium to pay for the rental agreement. When the pilot shops proved successful, she built up a chain of shops. The wholesale and export markets followed and manufacturing expanded. Recognition came with the increasingly successful growth of the business. In the early 1980s, street fashion was greatly influenced by dancewear. Shows like *Chorus Line* and *Cats* and TV programmes like *Fame*, gave dancewear a 'street cred' that boosted Pineapple's products everywhere. Soon she would be selling her products in Japan and Hong Kong, the USA and Canada, and continental Europe

Work/life balance

In the long-running feature in the *Sunday Times* colour magazine called 'Relative Values',[1] well-known mothers and sons or daughters, fathers and daughters or sons, or famous brothers and sisters, talk about each other in a deeply personal way telling the readers how they really related to each other and the continuing impact they have on each other throughout

---

[1] Ann McFerran in 'Relative Values' feature: 'The fashion entrepreneur Debbie Moore and her daughter, Lara Masters, television presenter' (*Sunday Times* magazine, 9 September 2001).

their lives. In September 2001, Debbie Moore and her daughter Lara Masters, a television presenter, told the story of how together they got through Lara's three separate, debilitating attacks of arteriovenous malformation, a rare illness that has left her partially paralysed. Lara, 27, is the first disabled presenter on mainstream British television, appearing on ITV's *That's Esther*. She also writes a column for the disability website www.youreable.com.

In the article the two women – mother and daughter – reveal their devotion to each other. Lara says: 'Mum's had to have a lot of guts to do what she's done, and I've inherited that from her. Both of us have done groundbreaking things, but Mum and I are quite different. She's practical and clear-headed, while I'm more emotional. She enjoys business; I'm more interested in expressing myself creatively.'

When Lara was only 6, she pleaded with her parents to send her to a boarding school as she was an only child. At school she was a very active child, enjoying horse-riding, swimming, acting and dancing. She wanted to be in the performing arts. But in 1980 Lara learned that she had had a spinal haemorrhage and the operation to remove a non-existent tumour from her spine left her paralysed from the waist down. Her mother was told that she would be paralysed for life, but decided not to tell her daughter. Lara got better and in six months returned to school.

Debbie Moore left her business in the hands of others and took time to be with her daughter.

Back at school at age 14, while riding a horse trying for a Duke of Edinburgh award, she suffered another attack. 'I was totally paralysed and in absolute agony. This time the doctors realized what the problem was. They diagnosed AVM', she explained.

This time it was much worse. Her parents spent a fortune on her trying to get the best medical treatment. She had microsurgery to seal the artery in New York City. She recovered enough to return to school. To make matters worse, her father then died of cancer. After four years of stability, her condition began to deteriorate until she had to take to a wheelchair. Her career aspirations to be an actress became channelled into writing, acting and reading scripts for the disabled theatre company Graeae. After an appearance on the morning television programme *This Morning*, she was offered the presenter's job on *That's Esther*.

'Mum and I hang out together on Saturdays, and we go to Thailand together, where Mum does business', she said.

Debbie Moore described her relationship with her daughter through the critical moments of her illness with admirable maternal passion. 'There I was, with a child I loved more than mountains and rivers and seas, paralysed. You feel your child's pain twice as much, and it was as if Lara knew. Once she said to me: "Mummy, it's worse for you than for me" . . . I slept on the settee, and Lara's illness became like a parallel career: I'd find all the best people to talk to, and read every medical journal.

That was my life, and it still is. I had a brilliant assistant at the office. Whoever called me, she'd say I was in a meeting – but in fact I'd be at home with Lara . . . When the time is right, I'm sure she'll walk again.'

Debbie Moore knew that without Pineapple she would not have been able to afford the specialist care her daughter required. As she put it: 'Money can't buy happiness, but if I hadn't had my own business I could never have contemplated taking Lara to New York. There are people who say that the children of mothers with careers are deprived, but in this instance it was only because I worked that I was able to do the best for Lara.'

What was the ultimate affect to Debbie Moore of her interruptions to the business to care for her daughter? 'I think it kept it small. I was at a point where Pineapple clothing would have been some mega-global set-up. For example, when I opened in New York, I had a PR agency there to do the opening. They had just taken on a young woman named Donna Karan, and they brought her down to my shop to show her what I did – leggings that go with the skirt, that go with the body – component-part dressing. *Womenswear Daily* did a big write-up about my revolution in desk-to-dinner dressing with component parts. That's how Donna Karan got her inspiration and of course she's global now with her own roadshow and her own perfume. That's probably where Pineapple would have been by now, if I had been able to devote myself entirely to the business.'

Barriers due to gender

'When I first started and was going to turn this derelict pineapple warehouse into a public building that would probably house about 2,000 people daily, I had to deal with planners and district surveyors and then contractors, engineers and builders. I had to work hard to get beyond the model image to get them to take me seriously.

'Raising money was another area where I was disadvantaged as a woman. I found a bank manager who believed in me and then it was much easier. I do say to women that if you don't get on with your bank manager, go out and get another one. But I realize that it's not the same as it used to be in the old days when you would have lunch with your bank manager.

'If you can't get any bank to loan you the money,' she advises, 'you might be tempted to take on a partner, giving them a share in the business in return for capital. My advice would be to resist the temptation if you possibly can. I don't think it's a good idea to have a partner in the business anyway. It's great to get input from other people, but you want to be the one who makes the decisions. With a partner you have to discuss all the issues and everything takes twice as long. A discussion can soon turn into an argument and partners can soon fall out.'

Leadership style

'I used to have a saying, "Every plan made is an opportunity lost!" Because I felt that if you try to plan your business – indeed, your life – down to the last detail, you are no longer able to seize any opportunity that may arise unexpectedly. Some of my colleagues have always told me how unbusiness-like that was, so I was very pleased to read in his book *The Art of the Deal* that Donald Trump, the New York property-developing multimillionaire, operates in much the same way, if not more so!'

Not surprisingly Debbie Moore, without formal business training, relies on her intuitions. In place of complicated decision-making models, she uses her gut feelings, finely developed over the years. She depends on 'emotional intelligence' which today can be a better predictor of career success than IQ. To watch her interact with her staff at Pineapple fashion offices or at the famous Pineapple Dance Studio is to witness a charismatic leader who draws from others their loyalty, affection and best efforts. She is quick with words of praise, the spontaneous introduction of each member of her staff to a visitor, a warm embrace for an old friend.

Her office is decorated with photos of her achievements, a half dozen awards, including the Veuve Clicquot Business Woman of the Year Award, displayed prominently, pictures of herself and former prime minister John Major, another photo of her with Lady Thatcher, a few photos from her modelling days. She remembered 'winging' a talk one evening to graduate students at the London Business School, who were making a case study of her success. She told them she led her small company by staying close to the customer and responding rapidly to their needs, unencumbered by huge corporate infrastructure.

Staff selection has always been a priority for her. Delegation is a reflex. Empowering others has been her preoccupation. She doesn't like meetings and will avoid them, using fax and phone calls instead. She expects loyalty and commitment from her staff and believes in hard work. Before she bought Pineapple back from the group in 1988, she knew that she had the option of staying within the larger group and being financially comfortable for life. Instead she chose to rebuild the business she once founded and still deeply cared about. She knew that the road back to success would be difficult and filled with hard work.

'I am constantly being told how lucky I am, and, as former prime minister Margaret Thatcher is fond of quoting, "luck is only opportunity meeting readiness" – and I must admit the harder I work the luckier I become!'

Verity Lambert
Photograph courtesy of Graham Turner, *Guardian*

Verity Lambert, chief executive, Cinema Verity

British TV would be much poorer without Verity Lambert. Her credits as a TV programme producer include the legendary series of *Doctor Who*, *Widows*, *The Naked Civil Servant*, *Rock Follies*, *Minder*, *GBH*, *Eldorado* and detective series, *Jonathan Creek*. *The Cazalets* is her latest, lavishly produced six-part series for the BBC in collaboration with screen-writer Douglas Livingstone. Like most of Verity Lambert's work, this new series has received critical acclaim. For Boxing Day 2001 Verity Lambert produced a two-hour special *Jonathan Creek* programme.

For four decades she has made her diverse contributions in an aston-ishing career in TV that all began with an ill-suited secretarial job for a novice public relations officer at Granada. It was her people skills, a love of literature and drama and a sharp, exacting eye with scripts that made all the difference. Now 65, she simply does not seem to want to stop. 'It's fun and I enjoy it, and while you continue to enjoy something you may as well go on doing it. I do think it is very consuming. When you are working it is full stretch.'

She is not happy with much of the TV available today. She watches mostly news and documentaries. Low-cost gardening, DIY and cooking programmes are squeezing out drama on TV. 'I am not saying that the odd gardening or DIY or cooking programme would not be acceptable, but there are just too many of them. They have gone way beyond their entertainment value. When you felt something was truly boring, you used to say it was like watching grass grow or paint dry. Now that's all we see.'

But people do watch those TV programmes and they are cheap to pro-duce. Verity Lambert is at the other end of the market – the expensive end.

Forty years of successful programmes in the past is no guarantee of suc-cess in the future. Despite the excellent reviews and fine audience response it received, *The Cazalets* series was stopped after its sixth programme.

It is almost impossible to sell the series to another broadcaster. Because six hours have already gone out it is hard for someone else to take it over. Since it is a series, they would have to buy back from the BBC those first six programmes.

'But I have some projects in development, a couple of films and a television series – whether these will be made, who knows. To get one programme made you have to have more than one in development. I'm also developing a television series with a writer I admire. I do not see myself retiring because these projects are important to me.'

She won the Veuve Clicquot Business Woman of the Year Award for 1982, early on in her career, when she was chief executive of a small production company, Euston Films. 'Another award that thrilled me was the British Film Institute Award, which they don't give to many people. It's actually upstairs in my office', she said from her Holland Park terraced town house, which also serves as the headquarters of her production company Cinema Verity.

'It is a wonderful award, made out of the silver that has been reclaimed from old film; they take the silver nitrate out and make these awards out of the recycled silver. Obviously there are not that many of them. People like Hitchcock and Billy Wilder have received the award, and for me to have one is remarkable. I guess it is a sort of lifetime achievement thing.'

Growing up in wartime Hendon

'I was an only child born just before the Second World War, so my first few years were quite odd. During the blitz, aged 4, I was sent away to a boarding school until my mother was able to find somewhere to live. This was complicated by the fact that my father had TB and was there-fore not eligible for army service. [He actually went to volunteer for the submarine service, but was turned down.] His contribution to the war effort was to look after various factories, which meant that he had to be close to London. Because of that I was fortunate in that once we did find some-where I was with both my parents, which most children during the war were not.

'My mother did secretarial work for my father. I went to rather a good school, which still exists, in Cobham. I look back now and realize that I did very well at that school from the age of about 5 to 10.

'I was a fanatical reader. As an only child I was a real bookworm.'

The French connection

'My grandfather was French – from Rouen. He worked in the Gobelin carpet factory before he moved here. He designed carpets and painted flowers and decorations on ceilings. My stepmother has many of his paint-ings.

'At the age of 11 I went to Roedean, which I found difficult. Not diffi-cult academically – I was in the A-stream and I was a year younger than the average age – but difficult to fit in. English boarding schools like to mould you into a pattern and for some reason I could not conform to that pattern. Consequently, although I was quite bright, I left school at 16. My headmistress told my father that I could not possibly go to university, which was ridiculous. But I was 16 at the time and not very sensible and I didn't want to spend any more time at school with people trying to make me into something I wasn't. I transferred my feelings about authority to further education in general and took the opportunity of leaving school altogether. My father suggested that I go to the Sorbonne in Paris to learn French. It was wonderful and I loved it. I took eighteenth- to twentieth-century French literature, a history course and a politics course, and then in the evenings history of art.

'The only way you really learn to speak French is the way I did. I lived with a French family and they refused to speak English. I am quite garrulous. But I didn't open my mouth for three months. I was so afraid that they would laugh at me. By the time I started speaking I could understand everything. Once I realized that people wouldn't laugh at me I started to speak.' She studied French grammar in the afternoon at a place away from the Sorbonne with other English girls. 'I still speak French, but I don't speak it as well as I did because I don't have the practice even though I have a flat in the South of France.'

Early love of cinema

'I went to the cinema a lot as a girl, never imagining that I could work in films. I was just someone who went to movies because I loved them. I went three times a week.

'Our family didn't have a television immediately. When I was about 16 or 17, I had a boyfriend and his family had one. On Sunday nights there was always a play on the BBC. They used to line the chairs up as if you were watching in a cinema. So when people say to me "did you want to work in television", I really had not the faintest idea what it was. I was unmotivated. I left school at 16 because I was in a huff. I did want to be independent but I didn't really know what I wanted to do. After that wonderful year in Paris, I was probably thinking about getting married – nothing very serious.'

Short-lived secretarial career

'My mother insisted I take a secretarial course, which took me about eighteen months. I hated it. I studied double-entry bookkeeping and God knows what else. It is something I've never used. But I do use my shorthand and typing. I was just motivated enough to know that I did not want a boring job. I did some temporary work. My first job was as a temporary secretary at the Kensington De Vere Hotel. Because I'd been to Paris and spoke French, I was assigned to type the lunch and dinner menus, which of course were completely different from spoken French.

'I then got a job in a lawyer's office. I could not bear typing those endless contracts without any punctuation. I had been taught English very well at school and it's my natural instinct to put in the punctuation, and you are not allowed to do that.

'My first job in television was as a secretary to the press officer at Granada Television. The press officer knew about as much about running a press office as I knew about being a secretary, so it was a rather disastrous coupling. I was fired after about six months.

'But it had been an exciting six months, and I became very interested in television production. My first step was to get a job as a shorthand typist at ABC TV, which broadcasts at weekends in the Midlands and the North. I was working in the managing director, Howard Thomas's, office. As well as TV he ran AB-Pathé, making newsreels for the cinema. I worked there for about a year and a half, when there was a vacancy as secretary to Dennis Vance, ABC's head of drama. I had always loved reading and literature. I applied for the job and got it because someone had misread Roedean and thought I had been to RADA.'

Steps to becoming a television producer

Her next step into TV production was to become a production assistant. 'I left being a secretary and I became what is called a production assistant or PA. Of course, I wanted to stay with drama, everyone wants to work in drama, but they put me through a learning process where you do lots of things including quiz programmes.

'I started off working on a programme called *State Your Case*, to which people wrote in about appalling things that happened to them. Fortunately, I was then moved on to work on drama, which I did for two or three years with a director called Ted Kotcheff. But before getting stuck there, I decided to go and work in America for a year. I got a job with Talent Associates, then probably the biggest independent drama producer in New York.'

In New York she worked with David Suskind, who was famous for his work in drama. She was basically a secretary, but she did some stage managing.

'I had enjoyed being Dennis's secretary: it was stimulating and exciting. *Armchair Theatre*, a series of single plays transmitted every Sunday night, was just beginning. I did have a well-read background and I had been to the theatre and to the movies. I did have a feel for how to structure a script and that comes down to how I was taught English. My teacher never *told* you anything. She made *you* tell her what something was about. Even if you were wrong she would say "Why do you think that?" If you produced some idiotic reason, she would say, "That clearly is not right is it?" And you would go back and try to find out what was right.

'When I came back to England, I wanted to direct, but I couldn't make any headway because I was a woman. I went back to ABC as a production assistant, but I was bored and decided that if I couldn't move up some-where within a year, I would forget about television. But one day in 1963, Sidney Newman, who had been producer of *Armchair Theatre* and was now head of drama, rang me, "What do you know about children?" "Absolutely nothing", I said. Yet he asked me to work as a producer on a brand new children's series called *Doctor Who*.'

It was extraordinary to be offered that job. '*Doctor Who*, of course, became a monumental overnight success. It was supposed to run for a year but after the first three or four programmes the BBC lost confidence and asked me to prepare to abort the series after the first 13 weeks. However, the second serial we broadcast featured the Daleks and viewing figures went through the roof. I was remarkably lucky to get the job as producer and lucky that it was the great success that it was. I was learning on the job. Although I had watched people I hadn't done it myself before. It's a very different thing watching to having to do it yourself. Funnily enough, I think perhaps I learned less on *Doctor Who*, because it was successful, than I did on other shows, which had more difficulties. Then I had to focus on how to make things work.'

After 18 months as producer of *Doctor Who*, Verity Lambert moved on to another of Sidney Newman's projects, *Adam Adamant*. 'Then I made a series of detective stories, and two series of Somerset Maugham stories, working with a brilliant script editor, Andrew Brown, for which we received a BAFTA award.'

Career development away from the BBC

'Shortly after I got my BAFTA award, the man who ran the drama depart-ment called me in to tell me that there wasn't any work for me at the BBC. I was scared. All my life as a producer had been with the BBC. You had everything around you and you had the best facilities, a wonderful library and first-class back up. You could live your life at the BBC and never go out, and some people did!

'I was nervous about being thrown out into the world. I had never been out of work. However, it was the best thing that could have happened to me. I realized that I could survive without the BBC. At that stage in my career it was very important to know this. Everything I had achieved had been with the BBC and I thought I needed it as a prop. When you discover that you do not, it is a very liberating feeling. This enforced rest came to an end when I joined London Weekend to produce a series called *Budgie*, written by Keith Waterhouse and Willis Hall.

'ITV companies are considerably smaller than the BBC. It was different in that sense and there were commercial breaks, which you don't have in the BBC. Apart from that the problems of making drama were similar. I found working there as enjoyable as the BBC. Those were the days when you were given a job and you just went on and did it. If you didn't do it well enough, you got the boot. Today there is so much more at stake. There are focus groups and hundreds of people who have to make decisions and everyone wants to cast your drama.

'After London Weekend, I went back to the BBC to produce *Shoulder to Shoulder*, a series of plays about the suffragettes.

'In 1974 Jeremy Isaacs, controller at Thames TV, offered me a job as head of drama. It was a most productive and prolific part of my career. I commissioned *Rock Follies*, *Bill Brand*, *Edward and Mrs Simpson* and *The Naked Civil Servant*. Then in 1976 I went to Euston Films and made *Minder*, *The Flame Trees of Thika*, and *Reilly, Ace of Spies*. I also commissioned *Widows*, Lynda La Plante's first major television series. My relationship with her has gone from strength to strength.' It was at this time of her career that recognition from outside the industry came.

Veuve Clicquot Business Woman of the Year Award

Verity Lambert won the award for her role model managing at the head of Euston Films. 'It was for the year 1982 and I received it in April 1983. I feel very privileged and fortunate to have won. Some of the women who won later are so brilliant and admirable that I feel I was lucky to get it.'

Verity Lambert offered advice to other women keen to carve out careers. 'Almost every job I've ever had I have asked for', she said when she was presented with the Veuve Clicquot Business Woman of the Year Award. 'Women still have to be exceptional to get on.' She argued for a career structure to be created for women in the same way as one exists for men. When she received the award she was 46 and both the director of production at EMI Films and still chief executive of Euston Films.

Flirtation with films

'I was then asked, in 1983, to go to Thorn EMI as head of feature film production. Unfortunately, the person who hired me left, and his successor didn't want to produce films and didn't need me. I did manage to produce some films I was proud of: Dennis Potter's *Dreamchild* [about Alice in Wonderland when she grew up] and *Clockwise* with John Cleese [as a headmaster who ran his life with clockwork precision until one little slip turned his life into anarchy]. It was very tough and not a happy experience. I was there for three years and in the end I had had enough of corporate life and wanted to see what I could do as an independent. When I left they gave me an output deal and I made a movie with Meryl Streep called *A Cry in the Dark*.

Back to TV and the Beeb

'Then I went back to television and did *Coasting*, *A Class Act* and *May to December*, and in 1992 I got the contract to make *Eldorado*. We foolishly agreed to start in too short a time. That was the chief mistake and I take full responsibility for it – allowing it to be put on the air too quickly. There were other mistakes in the Euro-soap series.' She admitted that having people speak in their own languages was a serious blunder. There were also casting errors 'But I still think that it was a very good idea. It was about Europe and the difficulties people face when they leave their roots and settle elsewhere. I was sorry that the BBC cancelled it because I think we had started to turn it round.

'When I read a script, I first read it all the way through. Then I go back and look at it in a much more analytical way. I don't write, but of course I have a huge admiration for people who can put words on paper. I enjoy working with writers and will always give them the benefit of the doubt. But you can't just say "I don't understand this or that." Suppose I ask the writer "What do you want to say in this scene?" They will tell me what they intended and then sometimes I realize that I've missed the meaning. Or sometimes I don't think they have it quite right and I will make a suggestion, but it is imperative to be constructive.'

Not all writers appreciate her critical technique. Playwright Alan Bleasdale told how, when Verity Lambert was executive producer on his Channel 4 series *GBH*, she sat him down on a sofa and suggested 200 pages worth of script cuts. As she remembered it, 'All week he sat glaring at me, getting redder and redder in the face. Later he rang Peter Ansorge at Channel 4 in the middle of the night, saying, "I'm going to kill her." He told me later he'd really meant it.'

Writer Lynda La Plante has had a totally different reaction to Verity Lambert. 'Working with Verity was the best education in writing for television I could have had. Things she said then, I've never forgotten. Like: "Lynda, if you want a character to wink on that line, put it in because you're not going to do it by hypnotherapy. If it's not on the page, it won't be on the screen." We recently finished working together on *She's Out*, the sequel to *Widows*. It has been wonderful. Verity is an excellent editor who always knows exactly what she wants, and how to get it without destroying a writer's confidence . . . She's also someone who will admit to being wrong herself. That's rare.'

Personal meaning of success

Success in my opinion is being as excellent as possible in what you do. It is very nice to be mega rich, but I suppose the feeling that my peers admire my work and consider it to be good is probably the most important thing. Not just my peers: as I work in the communications field, other people matter too, the audience – the viewers – are also important. Occasionally, I receive letters from viewers that say they have watched my material and loved it. There are people out there who have watched what I made and actually enjoyed it. That's the first point of all my work.

'The second point is, of course, making money. Other people make money out of your creativity and that is quite galling. Many years ago, when I was doing *Doctor Who*, I was paid a pittance to produce the series for my first job as a producer. I had to fight to get as much money as I was earning as a production assistant. I used to share a flat with girls and on Saturdays we would treat ourselves to a long, expensive lunch. I was with a friend of mine in the George & Dragon, a Wheelers restaurant. It was late, the restaurant was empty except for ourselves and another table of four next to us. We started talking and this man introduced himself. His name was Walter Tuckwell. When I told him my name, he said to me "You made me a millionaire." I asked him what he meant and he said that he'd bought half the franchise for the toys for *Doctor Who* from the BBC. This was in 1963 and he had made millions. I never received a penny for *Doctor Who* except for my salary. So when one talks about money in this business, it is not that you are money grabbing, it is just that you know what can happen and you know how you can be exploited.'

She started her own company – Cinema Verity Ltd – in 1985, late in her career. 'Working for yourself is completely different. You think that you are free, but you're not. You are still beholden to other people making decisions. However, those years were terrifically enjoyable. You do feel that you are working for yourself as opposed to working for another organization. The only drawback is when you wake up in the middle of the night and think of all those salaries that have to be paid. It can sometimes be very demoralizing. I enjoy making *Jonathan Creek*, but I do that for the BBC. I have downsized my company but Cinema Verity still continues to make programmes.'

Today Verity Lambert tries to maintain a work/life balance using her flat in Antibes for holidays. 'You have to make time for holidays. The flat is built in the ramparts of the old town and there is nothing between it and the sea and no way anyone can build there. I think it has the most beautiful views in the South of France.'

Gender barriers to her career

To carve out a career in television production in Britain in the 1960s was very difficult for any woman. Verity Lambert actually broke down gender barriers when she was in her late twenties to become one of the first British women TV producers.

Things were better for her during the year she spent in New York, working in television there with producers like David Suskind, who employed many women and had women as colleagues. 'I suspect it was because he got them cheaper than men. But he did like women and was good to his employees.'

When she returned to England she immediately bumped into the gender barrier. It was in 1961, fourteen years before the Sex Discrimination Act became law in 1975. 'The one area where I came across obstacles because I am a women was when I came back from America and wanted to direct. I was told by ABC Television that they did not want women directors and were not going to interview them.

'I didn't even obtain an interview and that really depressed me. That is what made me say that I was going to give it a year and that if I didn't move somewhere I would give up television and find something completely different.'

When she herself became an employer, she hired mainly women. 'That was not a conscious decision on my part. It was because when women came along they seemed to be better. I have always employed people, even when I was at Thames, on the basis of how good they were and tried to be non-discriminatory about it. The reason I found I employed many women was that for women to succeed in television they had to be exceptional. There were times at Thames when I suppose I was discriminatory in that I did believe that if you are making programmes for the public you have to have a broad base. So I would try to achieve a gender balance of people in my department.

'When I started in television there were no references to a glass ceiling in organizations. As a woman I did have to work twice as hard. You really had to be good. When I went to the BBC I was the only woman producer and considerably younger than most of the other producers in the department. Meeting me was a shock to a lot of people. I would be introduced to someone and I could see horror flit across his face before he rearranged it into a sort of smile. People were amazed and I think that they thought that I was sleeping with the head of the department. I am sure they thought that, and people did ask me.'

Leadership and management style

'I did not go to a business school. I suppose I just learned to manage by watching other people. Most of my role models were men. There just were not many women in positions of leadership. Women do come to me and say you have been my role model and I find that quite worrying because one is not perfect by any means.

'I made a decision at a certain point when I left EMI. I was offered a job in corporate life and I decided instead that I wanted to form my own company. That was a conscious decision. Indeed, when I was still running my own company and it was big I was offered another corporate job, which I considered and decided not to take.'

She has straddled both worlds – that of the large broadcasting company or film-making firm and that of her small entrepreneurial company.

After experiencing the lack of communication in large organizations it is imperative for her to communicate with her employees. Anna Callaghan,[1] her PA at Cinema Verity in November 1997, took the job on the strength of Verity Lambert's contributions to television. 'Verity was in Australia setting up a series so I didn't meet her for several months . . . but I liked her immediately.'

Her testimony continued: 'I felt quite bitter during the hard times, when, having seen Verity work so hard and put so much into the project, the BBC axed *Eldorado*. She is a perfectionist and is also deeply honest, even the smallest white lie is beyond her. Nothing really fazes her. When a project is in production she has to write off the rest of her life, but she just gets on with it. I guess not having a family of her own makes it easier, but she thrives on working hard and playing hard.

'Verity took the office to Paris to celebrate the company's tenth anniversary.'

A project on permanent hold

When Verity Lambert and Sir David (now Lord) Putnam optioned the film rights to Vikram Seth's novel *A Suitable Boy*, they had high hopes of turning the love story, set in post-independence India and involving a vast panoramic exploration of a whole continent, into a stunning series. Under their powerful sponsorship, the project looked bound to succeed. They persuaded Channel 4 to buy the options to the rights and the broadcaster commissioned and paid for ten scripts and second drafts. 'David and I obtained some money from India and this had been going on about a year. We stayed in touch with Channel 4 all the time. Then Channel 4 just said they did not want to do it. Shame, isn't it? I loved that story but it was too ambitious a project to do on our own with just the Indian money. Eventually the option ran out. The last I heard Vikram tried to set it up with his sister who works in television in India and they were going to do it in Hindu. I do not think that has happened.

'It's becoming very difficult for independents. Television is now much more to do with ratings and money, and people don't have the leeway to take as many chances. There are certain things you have to say goodbye to. I was very sorry to say goodbye to *A Suitable Boy*.'

---

[1] 'I Work for Verity Lambert', interview by Katie Sampson, the *Independent* (London), 26 November 1997.

Ann Burdus

Ann Burdus, former chairman and chief executive, McCann and Company Group

Ann Burdus was never shy of taking on a challenge. In the fast lane of market research and advertising, she kept her career in overdrive. She liked the fun and excitement of it all – the exhilaration of doing demanding, pioneering work in market research. She drew on her background as a psychologist and created new ways of market research that revolutionized the advertising industry. Her work experiences, both in New York and London, and her growing reputation, competencies and skills, inevitably moved her upward into senior management and corporate leadership.

'As you become more senior, whether you like it or not you drift into many areas of management knowledge. The jump from just knowing about management matters to actually managing things yourself is not that big. I also had some enormously supportive people helping me.' But she never had the luxury to study management formally at business school and she later wished she had insisted on taking 'her turn' on the Harvard management course. She learned her management on the hoof and was very good at it.

As part of her own career development Ann Burdus went to the United States. 'I worked in the US twice. I was first working with McCann International at their headquarters and then I was seconded to McCann-Erickson US from 1978–79. This was a deliberate career choice because in advertising it is important to have US experience. I was recalled to the UK to become chairman and chief executive of McCann UK which consisted of three companies.'

Ann Burdus was the first woman to become chairman and chief executive of the McCann and Company Group. She won *The Times* Veuve Clicquot Business Woman of the Year Award for 1979. The award reflected her standing in the business world as a pioneer in market research and the development and scrutiny of advertising strategies. It celebrated her leadership at the head of a cutting-edge market research department that influenced the entire industry. She remained in the post for two years and left to gain broader experience of research into marketing and advertising in America on a second stay there.

She became director of strategic planning for Interpublic Group of Companies (IPG) in New York City. At that time IPG was the largest advertising company in the world. The experience broadened her understanding of the international advertising industry. It gave her a knowledge of the industry and its international networks that proved invaluable in her future career moves.

After this two-year stint with Interpublic she returned to the UK again. She became a director of AGB Research plc, Europe's largest market research group. She was responsible for pulling together many of the research companies AGB had bought on the international market, getting them to work smoothly with each other and with the parent company. AGB, a world expert on continuous market measurement and television audience measurement, decided to expand their US operations and made a bid to take over Nielsen. It overreached itself. The bid failed, leaving AGB itself vulnerable to takeover.

Robert Maxwell moved in and bought AGB. Ann Burdus had to write the copy informing everyone in the company of the new owner. 'I had met him several times, both before and after this episode. I came home and said to my husband that I had written the piece announcing Maxwell as the new owner, but that I could no longer be a director of a company that he owned. Everybody was shocked at my decision', she recalled.

Then came a stroke of good fortune and a new, different challenge for her at the age of 53. 'A friend of mine was an adviser to Olympia & York, the Canadian company that was developing Canary Wharf, and they were looking for a head of marketing and communications. So I went along to 10 Great George Street, off Parliament Square, where they had this amazing "marketing suite", on the top floor of the building.' The suite, with its mock-ups of the location, models of the buildings, plus scale simulations of the views from the top of Canary Warf Tower, captured her imagination. 'I just fell in love with Canary Wharf and entered into one of the most wonderful phases of my career. For most of my career I had been selling – selling advertising or selling market research. Now I was offered the opportunity to become a buyer. I could set up my own structures to decide what we were going to do, who we were going to communicate with and how we were going to do it. And I had this wonderful product, Canary Wharf.'

Meeting the famous three brothers, Albert, Paul and Ralph Reichmann, whose global financial empire was developing the Docklands project, was fascinating for her. 'The Reichmanns were amazing people to work for and amongst other things they believed that any intelligent person should have an opinion on anything. You would go in to see Paul Reichmann, for example, to discuss an advertising campaign and he would show you a model and ask you, "What do you think about this building?" Or he would show you pieces of marble and ask you, "Which one shall we have in the lobby?" I had been tipped off about this – he expected you to have an opinion on everything and to express it, otherwise he would think you were some kind of wimp. There were many oddities about the company. None of us had titles and so in order to communicate with the outside world you had to invent your own.'

She had joined Olympia & York Canary Wharf as Director of Communications and Marketing in April 1989. By the autumn of the following year she was in full flow trying to do her strategic marketing part to fill the Canary Wharf's 800-feet-high, 50-storey tower with clients by its completion date in May 1991. She needed to market 4.2 million square feet of office space immediately. A further 6.2 million square feet were planned for phases two and three of the development over a six-year period. It could not have been a more visible challenge. Failure would have been impossible to hide. It would have been as visible as a half-empty tower that could be seen from twenty miles. Canary Wharf was the tallest building in Europe.

She made use of the 'marketing suite' that transfixed her initially and drew her into taking the job. At the entrance, visitors were greeted with a statement of intent, lest they had doubts about the staying power of the Canadian-based financial investment firm: 'Throughout its history, this company has maintained a philosophy of never starting a project without seeing it through to completion.' The company had sunk £1 billion, partly its own money, partly loans, into Canary Wharf and they had employed Ann Burdus, one of the best-known professionals in the advertising/ marketing world, to market it successfully. The ultimate aim was to create a new business centre for London.

Part of her plan for Canary Wharf was to put thousands of executives through the 'marketing suite'. She mounted a marketing operation of a quality and scale that impressed even people in 'Ad-land', used to extravagance.

To make the challenge greater, the country was going through a recession at the time. The Canary Wharf development (compared with Central London locations) was seen as remote. (Much later the extension of the London Underground's Jubilee line into the Docklands diminished this remoteness.) It was the supreme challenge for all the advertising, marketing and management skills she had spent decades developing.

But before three years had passed Ann Burdus found her plans in ruins and her career in trouble through no fault of her own. Olympia & York went into administration. At 56, she could have considered early retirement had not Robert Maxwell secretly helped himself to the pension fund at the newly acquired AGB Research plc before his untimely death three months earlier. 'It dawned on people pretty quickly that something had happened to the pension fund. As I had a separate pension fund, I thought I was safe. To reassure myself, though, I rang the man running it. He said there was absolutely nothing to worry about. He said: "We are the trustees of your pension fund and Robert Maxwell could not have touched it without our knowing about it." Three days later one of his partners rang me to say that one of Maxwell's employees had transferred all the money out of our pension fund into three banks. My pension from the Interpublic Group of Companies in New York had also gone into the same Maxwell pot.' Her two pensions contributed towards the over £400 million Maxwell had siphoned from his companies' pension funds to hide his business failures.

There was no money for her to retire early on and in her late fifties she was not confident of finding another senior marketing position.

She remembered that a few months earlier a small company, Dawson International plc, had asked her to serve on their board as a non-executive director, but Olympia & York had refused them, saying that she was too busy. She phoned an intermediary and was offered the position immediately.

'To be a non-executive director of a plc company you must have been on a plc board before. I had been an executive director on AGB Research plc.

'Dawson was a respectable, middle-size Scottish company. At the same time I had contact with other people who wanted me to be either a non-executive director or a consultant in marketing research or promotion, and so on.

'I gradually built up this stable of non-executive directorships. I discovered that I really enjoyed doing things I had never done before.' She collected non-executive directorships with Safeway, Prudential and Next. She was an Advisory Director for Barclays Bank, London North West (1987–93). She served as part-time director of the Civil Aviation Authority, and was a committee member for the Automobile Association. When she ran into something she did not understand, she asked. 'When Dawson went through serious problems, I needed to understand the issues. So I asked. It was almost like having my own personal seminars from the City institutions. They took a wonderfully helpful approach: "If you do not understand how this works, sit down and we'll explain it to you." '

Today she continues to be a non-executive director for Prudential Corporation and Next plc. She is a trustee for Barts and the Royal London Charitable Foundation. 'As the positions begin to fall away, I am doing more charity work. I also see more of my friends.'

Family life and education

'I was born on 4 September 1933, in Alnwick, Northumberland, and therefore some of my childhood memories have to do with the Second World War.' Her maiden name was Julia Ann Beaty, she was a middle child with a sister four years older and a brother eighteen months younger. I was notorious for tagging along and wailing "Wait for me." We were very privileged because we lived in Northumberland. Newcastle, thirty-two miles away from where we lived, was bombed. We took in a constant stream of evacuees and it all added to the colour of life. Children were taken seriously. You had your own gas mask and you jolly well carried it. You collected silver tops off milk bottles, rosehips and old newspapers. You were an important part of society as a child, but, of course, we were still children. You roamed the fields and played with dogs and climbed trees. But you were also treated as part of the fabric of society, which is very different from nowadays.'

Her father, Gladstone Beaty, was a council surveyor and sanitary engineer and came home for lunch and for tea. He was there for her and she knew where to find him if she needed him. She credited her parents 'and the generally secure background' with giving her the confidence that stood her in good stead throughout her career. 'When I left Ogilvy my father wrote me a letter which I do wish I had kept. He said that these people had been good to me and had trained me and given me all these opportunities, are you sure you are doing the right thing in leaving them? It was a wonderful letter of its era – filled with old-fashioned values about loyalty to the company. I do think a lot of people became over-cautious about their careers in those times.'

She went to the University of Durham where she studied psychology and philosophy from 1952 to 1956. 'I was at St Mary's College at Durham. At that time everyone went into teaching, but I wanted something different.' She received a BA degree with honours in psychology.

A stint in clinical psychology

She enrolled on a clinical psychology training course at Winterton Hospital, a huge psychiatric hospital in County Durham, and practised as a clinical psychologist for four years. During this time she also did some part-time, freelance market research.

'I went into clinical psychology, but after a few years decided that it was not for me. By nature I'm not judgemental, and my time at the hospital confirmed that. Our reports always had to be couched in cautious language. We would never say, for example, "He's stark, raving mad!" But later, in the managerial world, I've subsequently had to take a strong line and speak directly. It took me some time to adjust to that change.

'On the other hand, the behavioural psychology from my university days has been very useful. Everything had to be boiled down to a testable proposition: good training for a market researcher.

'I enjoyed much of my time at the hospital. As a junior member of staff, I was well treated and well taught. I did psychological testing at other hospitals and the local approved school.

'At hospital I was sort of an apprentice to a man called Dr Hayward who was a very good theoretical psychologist. He left the hospital and they advertised the post of a senior psychologist for which I was not qualified. I nevertheless applied for it and then one of the chaps, who had been in my year at university, was actually appointed to be the senior psychologist. He had not even been working in clinical psychology. He was in educational psychology. So I quit and so did he, because without a knowledgeable number two he could not do the job.'

Research into marketing and advertising

'I went to a conference of the British Psychological Society and I was chatting to someone there and saying that I did not know what to do next. She suggested that I do in-depth interviewing in market research – something that I had been doing a little of to supplement my income. So I decided to change careers and I wanted to find out more about market research and psychology in market research. I was lucky, and it was incredibly good timing as it had suddenly become terribly fashionable. That was in 1960.

'I applied for a job and went for an interview in London. Five minutes into the interview, the man knew that I was the wrong sort of psychologist, but he wrote down a list of names and telephone numbers of people who he thought would like to meet me and interview me. That is how I got my first real job in market research.'

She joined the London advertising agency of Mather & Crowther Ltd (later Ogilvy and Mather) in their research department as a specialist in attitude and motivation research in 1961. She worked there until December 1966 and during her last year there was manager in charge of its advertising research unit. In the course of this work, she modified several measurement techniques from other branches of psychology for commercial use, and gave her first paper on the commercial use of psychology measurements at the 1964 annual conference of the European Society for Opinion and Market Research. She eventually became a council member of that organization and greatly valued this international experience. In 1965, she set up a special unit in the agency for using research to help the creative teams produce better advertising. This unit was unique at the time.

At the end of 1966 Ann Burdus left Ogilvy and Mather to join Compton UK Partners Ltd (later called Saatchi & Saatchi Compton Ltd) as a research director. She stayed with them for five years. Two years into her spell with the company she was appointed to its board of directors. One of her main achievements was producing a book on statistical forecasts of trends to the year 2000 entitled *If Present Trends Continue . . .* The book was published jointly by Compton UK Partners Ltd and the *Guardian*.

Recognition for her market research

It was a pattern she would apply throughout her career – breaking new ground in researching advertising and marketing and, if possible, publishing an account of it. In the spring of 1971 she joined McCann-Erickson

Advertising Ltd, a subsidiary of Interpublic, as research director and a member of the board of directors. Two years later she became a member of its executive committee and eighteen months later was made vice-chairman and director for advertising development. Later in the same year she became executive research director of the European region of the McCann-Erickson International agency system. Throughout her career with the Research Department of McCann-Erickson in London, Ann Burdus actively encouraged experimentation with new ways of data collection and data handling. Under her leadership the agency developed some advanced models of consumer purchasing behaviour. By building current purchase habits and attitudes towards brands into computer models, she was able to predict the likely response to changes in marketing activities.

In 1973 Ann Burdus won the company's Harrison K. McCann Award for professional research leadership, and in 1976 she received the parent corporation's Robert E. Healy Award for unusual contributions to Interpublic and its clients. (A cash prize of $5,000 came with the latter.) Although both awards were available only to employees of the company, they were widely recognized throughout the advertising agency business.

In 1977, under Ann Burdus's leadership and supervision, McCann-Erickson Advertising Ltd produced the McCann-Erickson Middle East Media Study, a widely acclaimed study of media habits and purchasing patterns in the Middle East. The following year she transferred to the company's New York office to serve as director of research and strategic planning. On the two-year tour of duty in the United States she worked on several important projects. One was a study of the attitudes and behaviour of young people in twenty-five countries around the world, which was published by the company in a book entitled *Youth in Europe*.

She returned to London to take charge of the McCann-Erickson company as chairman and chief executive officer. It was quite an honour as the London agency was the company's second largest agency in the world with about 550 employees. During her tenure she grew the business in terms of advertising revenue. (In 1980 it prepared and placed $184 million advertising revenue for its clients, who included General Motors, Exxon, Unilever, Nestlé, Martini & Rossi and The Coca-Cola Company.) As the head of the company she put new management in place and changed the way the company was run.

She then became *The Times* Veuve Clicquot Business Woman of the Year for 1979. In addition to acknowledging her high visibility as a chairman and chief executive of a leading advertising agency, the award singled out her unique contributions to the science of market research. The award also acknowledged a social dimension to her work. She was advising the World Health Organization on advertising and control systems. She was also one of five advisers at the time examining the marketing of British agricultural products for the Minister of Agriculture. She was also on the Council of the Institute of Practitioners in Advertising.

She has appeared as a speaker at conferences and seminars across the world. She has lectured on a variety of training courses and spoken to student groups. For five years she was a visiting lecturer at Ashridge Management College, lecturing managers on the use of market research in marketing and advertising. She spoke to management students at the University of Chicago. She has spoken to special audiences about the McCann-Erickson Youth Study, its interpretation and significance. She has appeared on many television and radio programmes around the world as a spokesperson for the marketing and advertising agencies on the role of advertising in society. Her involvement with relevant professional organizations continued throughout her career. In those organizations she often held positions of leadership and influence. For example, she served on committees establishing standards for advertising agencies.

Ann Burdus returned to New York to the Department for Strategic Planning at Interpublic's worldwide headquarters. By September 1981, she was heading the new department and applying to the USA government for permanent residency in the States. She was a highly visible senior director in the Interpublic group of companies at a time when it was the largest advertising company in the world, setting up a new department in strategy; but after two years she was needed back in London.

She returned to London in 1983 to AGB Research plc. She joined as a director of Audits of Great Britain Ltd and became a director of AGB Research plc in 1986, resigning her executive directorship only after the purchase of the agency by Robert Maxwell in 1989.

From 1987–90, she served as deputy (and then vice-) chairman of the Health Education Authority. In her post with the Health Education Authority, Ann Burdus took charge of the anti-AIDS programme. As a director of AGB, Europe's biggest market research firm, she was uniquely placed to help government ministers spend the vast amounts they designated for AIDS education. Her work in the US also added to her knowledge of AIDS awareness and strategies for dealing with it.

At the time she thought being a woman helped her with the AIDS work. She had seen the enormous involvement by women in America in the campaign to counteract AIDS. 'Maybe it is that we can take a more neutral view of this problem', she speculated. 'It could be that when it comes to AIDS, women are able to take a much less emotional view than very many men.'

Private and public bodies continued to make demands on her. She was a council member of the Royal Society for the Encouragement of Arts, Manufacturers and Commerce (RSA) 1992–94. She served on the Senior Salaries Review Board 1991–94. She served as a member of the Advisory Committee on Business and the Environment from 1994–96. She was appointed to the Company Law Review, Working Group G: Corporate Governance in 1999.

Personal meaning of career success

Her personal meaning of success has stayed constant throughout her career. Her career anchor has always been 'autonomy'. As she explained: 'I have no idea why, but at some point in my life, it became terribly important to me to be in charge of my own life and that included to have enough money to live comfortably. My definition of career success had nothing to do with the pecking order of the top executives in large companies, who have to be earning an extra 'X' million compared with someone else. For me it is simply knowing that I have created a situation whereby I am in control of my life.'

Another part of career success for her was making a contribution to the field of research where she has spent her life. As she explained, 'A friend of mine e-mailed me from New York a week or so ago and said that she had a friend who was in London and that maybe I would like to have dinner with her. So one night a complete stranger came here to my home for dinner and we got very quickly on to the topic of careers for some reason. I told her a little bit about the creative research I did in the early sixties and she said: "Yes, I read some of the things you wrote then." And I had an inner glow about that. I was thrilled about the contributions that I had made to the business – something which, at the time, was revolutionary.

'When I think about what I did wrong in my career, it all has to do with not taking my career seriously enough. There were certain turning points where I should have stood my ground. I was just not thinking enough in terms of a career. I was thinking in terms of doing a job and having fun. When I say "having fun", this is a special definition of the words. Having fun could include working incredible hours and all weekend, and it did not matter because you were getting the job done. And that was quite important to me and I was lucky enough to be able to do it. I do realize that if people have other responsibilities it is not so easy. Nevertheless, I never measured my commitment to what I was doing in terms of hours and days, it just had to be done. I still quite often read board papers at five o'clock in the morning. Why not?

'I probably would have gone a lot further if I had taken my career more seriously at certain points. Being in the right place at the right time was important for me. I joined market research in the advertising business when it was taking off. Being a psychologist when psychology was fashionable, definitely helped. Oddly enough, I think that not being scared also played a large part in my success. I think that quite a lot of women don't speak out or do not take a stand or do not move on to something else because they are scared. I wasn't scared. Even when my world was falling about me in the late eighties and early nineties, I was not really scared. I was once talking to my sister – and we are totally different and have had totally different careers. I said to her that I always felt that if the worst came to worst I could always wash glasses in a bar. We had this attitude that we were going to survive and we are survivors.'

Women on the board

Ann Burdus has distinguished herself as a woman who has served on many corporate boards. Her thoughts about why it is so difficult for women to obtain boardroom posts reflect the realities of business. They also highlight a 'Catch 22' that serves as a serious barrier for women who want to become executive and non-executive directors. 'I said earlier that you can't be on the board of a plc unless you have been on a board of a plc. I challenged a chairman about that one day and what he said was quite interesting. He said: "You know how to behave." In other words, you know how a board is run. Of course, he was not talking about me personally, he was saying that there is a code of behaviour on boards and it is really pretty boring if you've got someone who does not understand that code of behaviour.

'You can be enormously effective on the board, but you have to do it in the right way. I think people are at times suspicious. For a woman to have got to a very senior position, she has to be a pretty strong personality. Some of them are less than tactful about expressing themselves, less heedful than they might be.

'It is not just women. I have sat at a board meeting for thirty people, where one man had spoken for three minutes twice and you multiply that by thirty and wonder how long you are going to be sitting there? So you learn to apply common sense – men and women both – to manage your contributions.

'I think it is possible that "headhunters" get a bit nervous if you have a strong, forthright woman: is she going to actually understand how to operate within a formal board structure? The same is true of some men.

'The problem is getting women as executives on to boards. Once they've had that experience then they become much more useful as non-executive directors elsewhere.

'When I was in New York at Interpublic, seventeen women in the corporation came to me one day and said, "We are going backwards!" And I said, "What do you mean?" They said that twenty years ago there were more senior women in the company than there were now and they wanted to know from me what they were doing wrong.

'So we had a really close look at it and the answer was that they were climbing all the wrong trees. They were heads of departments that were not natural routes to the main board. I'm afraid that still happens today. If you asked all middle management women to stay at home one day, industry would grind to a stop, because they run call centres and they run IT centres and they run HR and they run huge sections of industry. But these women are not moving up natural routes to the board in most cases.

'Natural routes to the board have to do with the core of whatever the business is and it is less so now than I would think then when I was coming up. There was a tendency for women to rise to the top of departments where their performances were measurable. I think that is why women have done quite well in the City. Their performances are measurable; you have either sold the bonds or you have not sold the bonds. If you think about medicine, the women doctors do splendidly until they get to a level where people are making a qualitative judgement not a quantitative one – a qualitative judgement about should this woman be a consultant or not.

'If you want to be at the top of the company you have to be in the core of what the company is about. Most boards that I have sat on do actively look for women and want women on the board.

'Stepping back from the woman's issue for the moment, there is another thing happening about board membership. There is the idea that nobody should be a non-executive director over the age of 70. If you take the normal pattern of two stages of three years, you are now down to 63 years old, which is the maximum age at which you will appoint someone. What you really target for is somebody in his or her mid-fifties.

'A lot of companies will release a board director to serve on other boards – remember we have not got that many executive directors anyway. So they will release an executive director for *one* non-executive appointment. That is fairly common and banks and other companies will do it. Some of them expect the fees to come back to the parent companies.

'Now when you consider that the women we are talking about probably have overcome more problems than a lot of men and are still running complicated lives by the time they are in their early fifties, for them the idea of taking on yet another responsibility is an onerous idea.

'I have a little hobby horse. There are so-called family-friendly firms, but they are really child-friendly firms. And many women in their fifties have family commitments and problems to deal with that have nothing to do with children and therefore few support systems provided for their use. So in addition to all this, you are now asking them to fight the battles of being a lone executive director and to fight the family battles with little or no support and now in addition to take on a non-executive directorship as well. Sorry if this sounds sexist, but if women take on non-executive directorships they will do it properly, which means that they will spend most of Sunday reading the papers for next week's board meeting.'

Was it really different in America? 'At one time, people used to say that there were so many more women on boards in America, which was true, but two things had to be considered. Firstly, that quite a lot of them had inherited the company, either from their father or from their husband. So the statistics were slightly skewed. Nevertheless, because of that you had an acceptance of women in various senior positions. Secondly, there is this question of confidence that the Americans in particular exude.

No one has told them they cannot do it. In fact, I would say that there is a huge pressure there for women to succeed.

'The European women are a bit more of an enigma to me because they do not have that American thrust. There is a certain acceptance of the entrepreneurial women. We have always had entrepreneurial women and that has always been accepted throughout Europe.

'So personally I would not put Europe and the United States in the same bag. I think they are quite different and I think that the pressure on the American women is very strong. Women here have a much easier role in a way. We can choose. Still no one says: "Why aren't you more successful?" Rather they say: "Haven't you done well?" Whereas in America, it would be: "Your should be striving to be CEO, what are you doing sitting around?"'

International experience

'International experience is important to develop your breadth as an individual and your standing and so on. But it has to be *true* international experience. I have met people who have travelled the world and they might as well have stayed at home.

'One of the super things about my experience at McCann was that I was usually going in somewhere to help them with a problem, so I was part of a team. I used to say that at the end of the day, if they took you to an international hotel for dinner, you had failed. If they took you to their local restaurant, around the corner, you had won because you were part of the team.

'One of the most rewarding things of my life – more important to me than where I have reached in terms of status – is the amazing experience of working with people all round the world. I think one of the things that you do know is that it has nothing to do with being a non-executive director or anything else. You learn that there are different ways of doing things that are going to succeed and so your mind is a little more open. That is even more so if you have lived in another country, because then you learn that there are different relationships between people and the government and there are different ways of buying insurance and all sorts of things. You learn that there are so many, many different ways of doing things. That is a mind-opening experience.'

Åse Aulie Michelet

Åse Aulie Michelet, president of Amersham Health, Norway

Åse Aulie Michelet won the Veuve Clicquot Business Woman of the Year Award for 2000 in Norway, wearing two hats at once. She is both president of Amersham Health AS in Norway and she is executive vice-president of the manufacturing and supply chain for Amersham Health globally. She has grown quite used to doing two jobs at the same time. As a medical researcher starting her career in pharmaceuticals over twenty years ago, her goal was simply to do research that resulted in 'something good for people'. She completed a Masters Degree in Pharmacy at the University of Oslo, having started her studies at ETH (Eidgenössische Technische Hochschule) in Zürich. Initially she became a researcher at the University of Oslo and later at Nycomed, a family-owned pharmaceutical company at the time.

'Starting out in Nycomed as a scientist in the labs, I soon got a group of people to manage, followed later by a department. After a few years I could look back at a number of different positions in Research and Development.'

She loved scientific medical research and was totally dedicated to it. At one point in her career as a researcher, her husband went off to INSEAD, a top European Business School in Fontainbleau, France, to give himself a greater understanding of corporate business. She was not even tempted to join him.

Soon, however, she found that her product knowledge as a medical researcher was required in another function of the company – marketing. Rather than try to bring a marketing person up to speed in science by putting her into Research and Development, the company took Åse Aulie Michelet out of R&D and taught her what she needed to know about marketing. Fortunately, she had as much flair for marketing as she did for research.

At that time the company had just developed the second generation of the world's first non-ionic X-ray contrast medium – Omnipaque – for which there was a global market.

'The demand for Omnipaque grew much faster than we predicted. Within two years it was the tenth biggest pharmaceutical product in the world and it is still on the market today. It is a patient-friendly and safe product injected to get enhanced X-ray pictures of body organs like the brain or the liver for better medical diagnostics.'

Today, every five seconds a patient somewhere is injected with the product for medical diagnostic imaging purposes. If one includes the full range of the company's diagnostic products, a patient is injected every two seconds.

Åse Aulie Michelet not only exploited her product knowledge and her scientific experience to learn how to market drug products globally, she became involved in strategic planning, which led her into designing manufacturing plant. Strategic planning also took her into leadership roles in mergers and acquisitions and joint ventures at an international level.

'About twelve years ago I left R&D for strategic planning. I knew the product. I understood the field. I started to build up project management and strategic marketing departments. I made new connections between R&D and sales. I had clinical development and other areas of the business reporting to me, so I was able to see the big picture. About three years later we saw the need to invest in new manufacturing capacity to meet the global demand for our imaging products.'

The newest manufacturing plant she helped design and build is in Lindesnes, Norway. It opened in September 2001 and provides employment for 300 people. The project is special to her. The production plant for basic substance (bulk) for the company's medical diagnostic imaging products is built with terraces cut into the mountainside. Raw materials enter from the top of the terraces and finished products emerge from the bottom. Storage tanks are built into the rock faces. The administration buildings are built like boathouses at the base.

It was not her first venture into manufacturing. Earlier, before Norway became a member of the European Economic Area (EEA), her company decided to open up manufacturing capability in Ireland as a pre-emptive action. When the project ran into trouble she was called in with her project management skills to put it right.

'I was pleased to be of help to the manufacturing people, but I didn't want to stay there and even made sure the company put it in writing that my assignment would end in two years. Being involved with manufacturing added the third dimension to my own understanding of our business.'

She accepted the challenge of sorting out a 'very difficult plant in Puerto Rico' and then took a small team to China to negotiate a joint venture.

No sooner was one challenge over than another began. She had an important senior role in her company's merger with Amersham in 1997 to form Nycomed Amersham and then simply Amersham Health. Surviving a merger with a big English company with its headquarters in the United Kingdom is not easy for a Norwegian senior manager.

'I survived because I showed results. I was happy to be in operations at the time of the merger, where it is easy to see if a manager is delivering or not. My team was delivering the products every day all over the globe. The new top management team looked at the quality of the products we produced against delivery times within the designated productions costs – all that was easy to measure – and they were pleased. So I stayed.'

The joint venture in China progressed from the relationship-building stage to plant building to the start-up of manufacturing operations in Shanghai. 'Today we have eighty to ninety people in the plant and several sales offices across China. The pharmaceutical industry is strictly regulated and the products you produce in Oslo, China, Ireland or Puerto Rico must be exactly the same, manufactured to the same rigorous standards.'

Meanwhile a different set of standards – management and leadership standards – were being applied to her personally as a nominee for the Veuve Clicquot Business Woman of the Year Award for 2000 in Norway. The criteria used for selecting the winner are to judge if 'she has led her enterprise to further growth', and to decide if 'the candidate is determined, innovative and dynamic'. In addition, she needs to have achieved long-term results. Åse Aulie Michelet, 48, met the criteria on all counts and is an exemplary winner of the award that was established for Norway only in 1991.

Family background

Åse Aulie Michelet was born in Oslo to a financial manager father in the dairy industry. Her mother worked as a secretary in the same industry. Åse was the youngest of four children. It was boy–girl–boy–girl. Not only was she the youngest, her closest sibling was a brother seven years older. There came a time, when she was a teenager, she started feeling like an only child, living alone with her parents. Growing up in Oslo, but away from the city centre, had its advantages for her. She did a lot of cross-country skiing, starting the sport when she was 4 years old and even skiing to school. As a schoolgirl during the summer months she found a job in the dairy industry, working in the labs.

'I tested ice cream for bacteria. I was into biology and wanted to see how things worked in the laboratories.'

She now lives close to where she grew up with the husband she met as a student playing in the same 'Glenn Miller type' big band. She played trumpet and he played saxophone and keyboard. Her husband has become a senior partner in a large legal firm that acts for many of the big global oil and gas companies involved in the North Sea. They have two daughters, one 14 and one 18, both still in school, both musical like their parents.

The older daughter is still uncertain what to study at university. She is good at languages and psychology, but does not share her mother's passion for science. The younger girl is into dancing and the performing arts.

Like most mothers who also are executives, she needed a support system – a nanny to help her look after her two girls, an sympathetic husband who did his fair share with the children, and an emergency backup which is still provided today by her 88-year-old mother.

'Even before my father died nineteen years ago, mother was always phoning me to ask if she could help out with the children. In an emergency she would be there within half an hour.'

Personal meaning of success

'It's extremely important for me to get things done and when I see that something is done I feel successful. If I have a vision as to where we should go, then it's urgent that we get there.'

Achieving goals and delivering on targets drives her, and there is a global dimension to most of her goals. There is also a team aspect to them. 'It is very much a team effort most of the time.'

Leadership for her is giving clear directions and setting very clear, measurable goals, especially at the operational level. 'I believed I was very technical and scientific, but I have found that I am also very people-oriented. Recently, I pushed one of my people up the promotion ladder because he had such strong potential – even though it caused us difficulties to lose him.'

She is not bothered about taking credit or making sure her initiatives are recognized as hers. 'We are building a new production line, making huge investments in our plant in the southern part of Norway. What is important is not that it is my idea but that the decision is right. The results from this project are already positive and very promising.'

Focus on the future

Logically, her new career goal must be to win a position on the main board of Amersham Health, where there are no women board members. Today she is on the level just beneath the main board. As a result of receiving the Veuve Clicquot Business Woman of the Year Award 2000, she has gained much higher visibility within her own company, both in the UK and in Norway. As part of raising her profile outside her own company, she now sits on the board of Orkla, the food and drinks giant and one of Norway's largest corporations. She is a non-executive officer and the first woman on Orkla's main board. It was not her first appointment to the board of a company. She served on the boards of middle-sized and small companies before, but nothing as big and prestigious as Orkla, a company which is quoted on the Oslo Stock Exchange.

'I have had many mentors in my career and they have been important to my progress. It is always best to have a mature older man as a mentor, not someone close to your own age who might be in competition with you for promotion. The mentor suggests what directions you should move in to progress your career, based on his or her many years of experience and intimate knowledge of the formal and informal workings of an organization.'

Women today are learning more about impression management – how to make sure that their bosses and other senior managers in the company become aware of their achievements. It is something that does not come naturally to Åse Aulie Michelet, but she is learning.

Shortly after she had been privately informed that she had won the Veuve Clicquot Award, she had an appraisal meeting with her own British boss, a dedicated and methodical man. They went through the dozen key items on her appraisal form one by one. Most of the items were measurable goals that both she and her boss could see she was achieving or even surpassing. These objectives had to do with unit costs and investments and deadlines. As they came to the final point, dealing with her own exposure as a manager and responsibilities for raising the company's image in the community as well as her own profile, things were harder to quantify. She said, and he agreed, that it was more difficult to measure how well she was doing in this area. She told him she tried to be 'out there in the wider community, making speeches whenever she could and to be more involved with the business associations and all that, but I do not know how you measure it'.

The Veuve Clicquot Business Woman of the Year Award 2000 for Norway so raised her profile that a group of fifteen women scientists, at the middle-management level, invited her to a luncheon without telling her what it was for. At the lunch these women gave her some drawings and a private prize for being such a good role model for them in the company. There was the usual splash of publicity in the Norwegian press about her winning the award – all positive, as was the feedback from the readers, except for a few reactionary responses saying that: 'This is exactly the kind of woman we do not want leading our companies. She should be at home looking after her children.'

Actually the children have been well cared for. Having a supportive husband is key to getting the work/life balance right.

'We are really a dual career family. My husband has been very successful with his career. In an English publication for lawyers, he was named one of the fifty top commercial lawyers in Europe. I can discuss some of my business problems with him because he is a business lawyer. He sees things from a legal point of view or a financial angle. I see them from more of a technical perspective. We do not compete with each other, we complement each other. He tries to add value and be helpful. He has never been afraid of my success.'

Marianne Nilson

Marianne Nilson, managing director, Atlet, a family-owned truck manufacturer, Sweden

Marianne Nilson, 40, is managing director of Atlet, a family-owned fork-lift truck producer. For seven years she has been at the head of the company of which she is part-owner with her father, Knut Jacobsson, and her four sisters. Her entry into the business since she left her first profession as a pharmacist and her first job as pharmaceutical salesperson has added value continually to the family firm. She has helped take the fork-lift truck manufacturers and suppliers for indoor material handling to a record turnover. Since 1994, Atlet has increased its revenue from SEK 751 million to SEK 1,235 million in 2000 and to SEK 1,440 million today. The increase came partly by organic growth and partly by acquisition. Atlet employs a thousand people, almost half of whom work outside Sweden. The head offices and one production plant are located in Mölnlycke in Sweden. The other production plant is in Oberhausen, Germany. The group has wholly owned sales subsidiaries in Sweden, Norway, England, Holland/Belgium, Germany, France and the USA. Atlet also sells its products and services through independent distributors in Europe, the Middle East, Asia and South Africa.

Marianne Nilson's decision to enter the family business surprised and pleased her father, who had given up hope of any of his five daughters joining him. He tried to persuade each one and failed. He involved them in the business as girls by giving them each a sixth share in the ownership and a rotating position on the board. The sisters took turns, two at a time, to be on the board as a learning experience to see how the business operated. But the nature of the business – engineering – did not appeal to them. Their father's excessive dedication to it, expressed in workaholic hours away from the family, alienated them from the company. The fact that their father wanted them to study engineering was in itself reason enough for the rebellious daughters to do otherwise. Each daughter went her own way into a separate profession, becoming a dentist, doctor, pharmacist, psychologist and kindergarten teacher.

Then Marianne Nilson had a change of heart. She was weary of her chosen career. 'In January 1987 I was working as a medical representative selling medical products across a huge district of Sweden. I was spending hours on the road to reach my customers and waiting for hours for doctors who sometimes never showed up. I was working very hard at the job and I realized that I could not change the world, but had to adapt to the situation. When I start to do something I want to do it right. I was working flat out and I suddenly realized that I might as well work for myself. After all, I owned one-sixth of Atlet. I called my father and asked him if he had anything that I could do at Atlet.'

The only experience she had of managing anything was running a student organization at the University of Uppsala, where she spent four years studying for her pharmaceutical exam. There was a big gap between her knowledge as a pharmacist and that required of a manager manufacturing fork-lift trucks. She decided, while she worked part-time in the family firm, to study business administration at Gothenburg University, from where she earned a B.Sc. in economics in 1992.

Since arriving at Atlet, Marianne Nilson has involved herself at all levels in the company and in nearly all aspects of its business. At first she worked in marketing to call on the same selling skills she had been using for a pharmaceutical company. She became export manager for England and the USA after completing a production project on component supplies. A year later she became marketing manager.

Meanwhile her father had started to think about succession in his own company. He and his wife attended an International Institute for Management Development (IMD) seminar on succession planning for family-owned companies in Lausanne in 1991. 'It enabled him to see how other Swedish family-owned companies, including IKEA and Tetra Pak, handled the issue', Marianne Nilson said.

In 1994 her responsibilities were increased to cover the entire Swedish operation, including product development, production, sales on the Swedish market, and administration.

In 1995 the chairman of Atlet retired and her father, already 72 himself, replaced him as chairman, leaving the post of managing director to Marianne. She was only 33. The matter had to be negotiated with both the external board members and with the trade union leaders who had vetoed the idea a few months earlier. By springtime, though, everyone was in agreement with her appointment. Although there had been inquiries from outsiders interested in the top job, Atlet did not seriously consider an external appointment. Knut Jacobsson and his five daughters still formed a family council and the four sisters supported Marianne's promotion. In the seven years since then she has gone on to prove that those who supported her appointment were right to do so.

The old adage 'like father, like son', applied to the daughter. Like her father she over-invested time in the company and made long hours a normal routine. 'It was tough and a lot of work. I did not have time for anything else. I think that was part of the reason I divorced my husband in January 1996 – not the whole reason, but definitely part.'

She was not nervous about taking on the top job. 'I am not a nervous person', she said, 'I knew I had the support of my parents, who think I can do anything. The fact that I did not have the initial support of some of the board members made me work all the harder. Certainly the staff supported me. They thought it was good to keep the leadership of the company in the family.'

The staff also liked her leadership style, which is in sharp contrast to her father's more autocratic style. Her style was empowering, supportive, richly communicative, sharing in responsibilities, but also insisting on accountability and performance measurement. She pushed the decision-making down to the appropriate lower levels in the company. She reorganized. Some of the staff of varying lengths of service did not like the changes and could not keep up so they were asked to leave the company.

'Knut is a person with great authority. If he says: "Let's do it", everyone does it without questioning. With me they could say: "I don't believe we should be doing this or that", and give their reasons. And I would listen to them carefully. We had more communications and I had a better inter-personal style, which I get from my mother who is a very sociable person.'

It was a softer style than they had been used to but she was no less determined to achieve clear objectives. She was prepared to discuss every-thing even though it took time. Apart from a woman finance officer and herself, the company was still dominated by men. But everyone grew to respect her strong leadership. 'When I said something like: "I think you should look into that", and no more, the men managers knew what I meant.' An Englishman appeared on the management team and attended the monthly management meeting. He was quickly put in the picture by the human resources manager, who told him, 'When she says, "I think you should look into that", she is saying, "You'd better have that report here by Monday, or you needn't show up at all."'

'I am more into discussing things with others', said Marianne. 'I listen to people's arguments. I don't interfere in too much detail. My father knows all about the trucks. But he also knows all about the company and a lot about other companies. In the beginning, I made mistakes because – I would not say that people were lying to me – people were giving me only part of the truth not the whole truth, and I made decisions based on information that was wrong or misleading or incomplete. But my father, when he talks with people, can immediately link things up and say, "Well what about this or that", and he gets more information and better infor-mation and can make better decisions based on better data. I think that comes with experience.'

In a fiercely competitive but expanding market, with tremendous scope to innovate and make use of new technology to help customers improve profitability and efficiencies by offering them user-oriented material handling equipment, Atlet has captured fourth place in the fork-lift truck market in Europe and is constantly improving its products

Marianne Nilson has gained high visibility at the head of Atlet. For one thing there are not that many top women managers in Sweden, especially in engineering companies. A newspaper announced that she was the ninth most powerful woman in Sweden, which she took with a grain of salt. When asked by a journalist how it felt to be so powerful, she replied, 'Well I do not actually get up in the morning, look in the mirror while I brush my teeth and think how powerful I am. I do not feel powerful.'

She was named the Veuve Clicquot Business Woman of the Year for 2001 and it meant a great deal to her. In addition to helping her self-esteem, the award triggered much favourable publicity for her company and gave her leadership a boost, increasing her authority everywhere in the company but especially among those who doubted her abilities to head the company at such a young age. 'The ceremony for the award was in Stockholm with a lot of journalists and the previous winners, those on the short list with me, and the judges attending the midday event. In Sweden the award was given every other year, at the same time, but will now be awarded every year. You're in the spotlight and have to answer everybody's questions.

'The recognition for work well done is one good thing about the award. As the top manager in the company I hear about all the problems and all the mistakes made – and I certainly made many mistakes myself through lack of experience or not reading people well when they were only giving me part of the truth about a situation. You never hear, "Marianne, you have done a great job!" Remember my boss is also my father and he is a brilliant engineer, but he is very, very poor at giving compliments. He never says that something is well done. He just never does, so I do not expect it. So it was gratifying to receive that award. I met a lot of people at the ceremony and gave many interviews. But one of the best things is the new network it created for me. You can become isolated in a family business, so the network of new woman managers is wonderful.'

Family life and early education

Marianne Ingrid Nilson was born in 1961 to Knut and Ragnvi Jacobsson. Three years earlier her parents had founded the 100 per cent family-owned corporation Atlet. To start with they had no capital, products or organization. But Knut Jacobsson was a talented engineer with the drive to start his own manufacturing business. He purchased his first components with money his wife had saved to buy a scooter. He saw that the large counterbalance trucks and pedestrian stackers which were prevalent in the 1950s were slow and ponderous. So he decided to create a company that took a completely new approach to goods handling, one that was rational, inventive and cost-effective. The company started to produce an inexpensive rider stacker that was an immediate success.

'I was number three of five girls. My parents always wanted a boy. They tried and tried and didn't succeed. Then after five I suppose they gave up. We used to joke that even the dog in our family was female.

'We hardly saw our father. The day we started school my eldest sister asked my mother, "Everyone has their dad with them, don't I have a dad?" All my sisters and I were very ambitious at school and we got high grades.

'I was always interested in science, maths, physics, biology, chemistry, those kinds of subjects. I studied them in high school. My father graduated from one of the best engineering schools in Sweden, Chalmers Technical University, and he wanted me and my sisters to study engineering there. I decided to do chemistry, not engineering, at Chalmers Technical University. It was that teenage thing where you do the opposite of what your father wants you to do. I took a gap year and worked between high school and university. For some reason – I don't know why – I ended up studying to be a pharmacist. I began my studies in January 1983. Today it is a five-year-course, but then it was only four years. The four years whizzed by and all of a sudden I was standing there with my diploma in hand. I was very active in student organizations, part of the steering committee and so on.'

Since 1996 Atlet has been a member of an organization called the Family Business Network, started by Barbara Dunn, who had conducted research into family-owned businesses at the University of Edinburgh. Marianne Nilson and her sisters attend the conferences of the Family Business Network in various locations across Europe.

Personal meaning of success

The first thing that comes into Marianne Nilson's mind when she defines her personal meaning of success is reaching her targets. She is results-driven and restless in the pursuit of what she sets out to do. She is focused. 'I have a motor inside me that keeps me from leaving something unfinished. I jump into everything, like plunging into a lake only to realize that it is a bit too chilly to swim, but I must carry on. I throw myself into my work and forget everything else.'

Her strengths are based on communication, organization and team-orientation rather than the technical, detailed knowledge that her father is famous for in the business. 'Success for me is also success for the business which in turn is success for me.'

Her advice for senior women managers who wish to lead their organizations includes:

- Define the company's strategy as clearly as possible.
- Communicate with the board of directors regularly, particularly the chairman of the board, if you are the MD.
- Communicate with customers and key people in the company.
- Follow up, follow up, follow up!

Ideal maternity leave

For the board of directors' meeting at the end of June 2001, Marianne Nilson included an important item under 'any other business'. 'I told the board of directors I was pregnant – already in my fifth month. They congratulated me, of course, but then said, "What do we do now? We are not used to this kind of problem." The solution was exemplary. She took ten months off work to have her baby and settle it in. A board member with several years' experience on the board, Peter Kaschner, was designated temporary managing director to replace her. She will be away from her post until August 2002. 'Ten months may seem a long time from a UK perspective, but it is very short for Sweden where mothers are normally away from their jobs for a year to a year and a half.'

Will she return to full-time work in August? Her partner's company is in the south of Sweden and working out how they will live together has been difficult. 'I've been thinking about this a lot. It would be great to work only four days a week but I do not think that it is realistic. It has to do with discipline and organization and also how much responsibility I give other people. It also has to do with how much longer Knut will want to continue as chairman of the board. [He is 79.] We could have another person on the board with more executive, operational duties. It is not a "must" that a managing director or CEO comes from our family. But it is very difficult for a person to go into a family business where the chairman is very active and the owner.'

Monique Moullé-Zetterström

Monique Moullé-Zetterström, managing director, Orange mobile phones, Denmark

Monique Moullé-Zetterström is French by birth. She single-handledly set up the Danish operations for Mobilix A/S, which is now part of Orange, the UK mobile phone operator owned by France Telecom. She won the Veuve Clicquot's Business Woman of the Year Award for 2001 for Denmark on the basis of her outstanding business achievement.

The mobile phone sector of telecommunications is a tough business. Purchasing the licences to operate in each country in auction sales run by the governments costs millions. Building the network and starting a mobile phone service is astronomically expensive. She knows the business better than most because she has built up Orange in Denmark from a one-woman operation to an organization with 1,400 employees within three years. It is a remarkable achievement.

'I came to Copenhagen in March 1997. I thought I was going to be there for three or four months maximum. But it was fascinating to work again to build the mobile phone business from nothing. It was a big challenge. This time I was creating the network and infrastructure for a big mobile phone company. While I was looking for a general manager for the company, I was also negotiating for a partner to invest capital in the venture. The Danish railway company became the partner. I needed to find a good candidate for the job of general manager who had to be approved of, not only by my company France Telecom but also by our railway company partner. Four times my company approved a candidate for the post, who was then vetoed by the railway company partner. After the fourth veto, my boss himself finally called the railway company directors and asked them if they had their own candidate for job. And they admitted yes, they did have their own candidate and that it was me.'

It was very flattering for her. The railway company bosses insisted on her becoming the general manager of the mobile phone organization as a condition of their investing capital in the venture. They wanted a guarantee that she would hold the top position for a minimum of three years until the year 2000.

'So I was offered the job of general manager for Denmark in Copenhagen. I was very happy but my Swedish husband in Stockholm was furious. He said that it looked like the end of our life together. Of course, I was sad about my husband's reaction. But I was very interested in the position. In fact, I was already doing the job. It was quite impossible for me to say, "no" and walk away from it. I was already totally engaged and in love with what I was doing. I had further discussions with my husband and explained all this and very reluctantly and after some time he understood and I stayed on as general manager.'

In the beginning she spent every weekend in Sweden to compromise as her husband would not go to Copenhagen. 'Gradually he realized I had made a good choice and he could see how happy I was in the job. We found a new balance. Now it's more like two weekends in Copenhagen and one in Sweden and, when we can manage it, a trip to France.'

The start-up was tremendously demanding. 'I was working every day from early morning till eleven at night. Had my husband been there, he would have strangled me.'

When she started working with France Telecom in Denmark the company was called Mobilix. In May 2000 France Telecom bought the UK mobile phone company Orange and changed all their mobile phone companies, starting with the one in Denmark, to the brand name Orange. 'Our company in Denmark was the closest to the Orange strategy anyway so it was fitting. The strategy was innovative and successful.'

The Danes have taken to the diminutive Frenchwoman's leadership. The Mobilix ad-campaign slogan, 'Talking is understanding', was very successful in helping win the company market share in the fiercely competitive mobile phone business. 'Talking is understanding' became a catchphrase throughout Denmark. She saw turnover rise to DKr 1.2 billion. Her easygoing yet dynamic management style contributed greatly to the company's success.

Success is tempered by the enormous costs of creating a mobile phone company. But she predicted that the company would break even by the end of 2001 and thereafter start to show a profit.

Monique Moullé-Zetterström was appointed Chevalier de l'Ordre du Mérite in 1997. Under her leadership, Mobilix A/S received the 1997 Danish-French Export Prize. In 1999 she was appointed Chevalier de la Legion d'Honneur.

Today her company Orange has obtained a licence to set up a mobile phone operation in Sweden and has been building the network from a base in Malmö. She is thinking of merging the two companies – the Danish one and the Swedish one – to achieve greater synergy and strength.

Flashback to a Swedish start-up

She had done it all before in Sweden. She brought telecoms operations from France Telecom to Sweden in 1992, starting, as she was to do again later in Denmark, as a one-woman band. She had been working in the

GSM group for France Telecom and had asked her boss a year earlier to let her go to Sweden to represent the company there. She had both a business and a personal agenda. Her new husband was Swedish and they wanted to live together in Stockholm.

Her boss at France Telecom, who was in charge of international telecommunications, shocked her by saying that there "was nothing to do in Sweden". But she is nothing if not persistent. She kept trying to explain to him what was happening in Sweden in telecommunications. Eventually, after ten months, he agreed to let her test things out in Sweden from 1 January 1992 for a six-month trial. 'So I went to Sweden as an expatriate, on my own, with no help at all. I had a computer and a telephone and nothing else. I had to find my own way. I used the guest room at home as my office. I worked in Stockholm trying to find the potential business for mobile phones. No leads, no contacts, just possibilities.'

She became director of France Telecom Nordic. She did get moral support from her husband, Yngve Zetterström, a Swedish telecommunications engineer, whom she married the same year – 1992. In September 1994, France Telecom Sweden received the Prix de l'Entreprise Française from the CCFS, presented by the King of Sweden. The number of employees of her telecommunications start-up had grown from one (herself) in 1992 to 13 in 1993, to 50 in 1994 and to 200 by 1997.

Family background and early education

Monique Moullé-Zetterström was born in Orléans into a large family. There were seven children in all – six girls and one boy. She was the third daughter. 'My family lived modestly and, with seven children, my mother stayed at home. As I had two older sisters to help my mother, I didn't have to help raise the rest of the children.

'My father was a technician in a big electronics company named Thompson. He had been brought up on a farm and was expected to take over the family farm.

'So when he was young, his father refused to send him to the lycée high school. It was an impossible situation for him, but he had no choice but to accept his fate. Without formal education later, the best he could become was a technician. All his life he regretted not having the chance to study and he made sure that his children would have excellent educational opportunities. All seven children went to the lycée. Some of us, like me, were very good in school, others less good but OK. I found school easy and my father was quite proud of me. It was enough for me to read something once and I would remember it in detail.

'We were a close-knit, loving, quite happy, devout Catholic family, quite happy. Today I continue to have a strong bond with my mother and father and with my sisters and my brother.'

At 18 she left school, much to her father's disappointment and anger.

'He was furious, but could do nothing about it. It was my decision to work. I thought it was stupid to stay in school, and besides I was more interested in boys.' By 19 she was married, by 21 she had two daughters of her own. She also began a lifetime career with France Telecom. The company financed her further studies and she agreed to work for them in return.

She took lots of tests and her cleverness got her admitted to the 'Adopt Programme'. 'We were sent to university. We gave half of our time to our company and drew a salary and half the other to our university studies. I decided to do psychology and sociology. I was living in Paris. It was a very busy time. At the same time my personal life was not so good. My husband was not supporting me or our two girls. By the time they were 5 and 6 years old we decided to divorce.'

She was still going to university and working half the time for France Telecom and looking after the two young children, who had just begun school themselves. 'My daughters became latchkey children. It was tough, but it taught me very quickly about priorities – which things were nice to do, which ones were necessary. Fortunately, I had a good relationship with my neighbours. Sometimes they helped me out with my children and sometimes I helped them.'

Career commitment with France Telecom

After ten years with France Telecom she was free to go to another company, but she stayed. Deregulation had just taken place, privatizations were starting and many exciting technical breakthroughs were happening in telecommunications. 'It was not boring to be in the same company. There was no need to change companies because the telecommunications world was changing all around us.'

She was also grateful to the company for helping her obtain academic credentials against the odds. She earned her first degree in sociopsychology from the University of Paris and a second degree in the sociology of organizations from the French Institut d'Études Politiques. While she studied she moved steadily upwards in her company. By 1987 she was working in France Telecom's sociology and organization department. The following year – 1988 – she became department director at France Telecom Mobiles Division. She was like an entrepreneur, but working within a big company, using the company's massive assets to do something in mobile phones where huge outlays of corporate funds were required.

While working in Paris with the GSM group of France Telecom, she met her second husband, a Swedish telecommunications engineer. 'He had been married twice before and had two young boys who were 5 and 8 in addition to two older children about the same ages as my daughters. When we decided to live together it was clear that he could not leave

Sweden, so I would have to go and work in Sweden. At that time he was working for Telia, the Swedish operator. Now he works for Ericsson.'

Gender barriers to success

Monique Moullé-Zetterström enjoys being French and feminine. 'In Scandinavia very often to be successful women have to copy men. Swedish businesswomen particularly are very masculine in their manners and dress. They shy away from makeup and fine feminine clothes. I refuse to comply with that. For me to be a woman is a pleasure. The fact that I am also a businesswoman does not make me stop being a woman. I am always very feminine. I simply refuse to try to look masculine or behave in masculine ways. In Sweden I was a bit of a shock for people. I remember one day I came to a meeting of businesswomen. It was winter. I had very feminine shoes with high heels that went click, click, click on the floor. The other women said: "We knew it was you, Monique, when we heard your heels." I looked round and they were all wearing big boots. They haven't been a barrier for me because both the Danes and the Swedes forgive me, saying "she's French". They see me first as French and then as a woman. Because I am French I can do some things they cannot do.

'It is always more difficult, though, for a woman in business. You have no right to make mistakes and to be truly successful you have to do more than a man. Your performance has to be better.'

She attended a business meeting in London for Orange. Afterwards there was a Christmas party. 'I met many young women who came up to me for a chat and who directly told me that I was their role model in the company.'

Veuve Clicquot Business Woman of the Year Award

'The award was a total shock for me as it came out of the blue. It really did. I never expected it. I am a foreigner and when I speak Danish, my Danish is imperfect. I speak it with a strong French accent. Sometimes at meetings I've had this feeling that I am not totally accepted – mostly because of the language. The award then was very good for me and dispelled any feeling of non-acceptance.

'There was a great amount of publicity about me and the company because I am well known to the journalists and they like me. There are few businesswomen in Denmark, especially in telecommunications. I know a good deal about telecommunications and many journalists phone me and talk to me about new developments in the field when they need expert information. So I'm in the newspapers nearly every day about something. But this award was special!'

Her speciality is marketing, but she knows enough about the complex technology in telecommunications. 'I know enough about most things to talk with the press and they like that. I can speak about marketing and technology and human resources. If it is a high-level technical question I simply refer it to my technical director. I have an overall view of the business.'

Her personal meaning of success today and throughout her career is doing interesting work. 'I am not a career woman. I do what I like to do. If one day I find that what I am doing is no longer interesting, I will give it up immediately.

'I am asked sometimes to be on boards of other companies. Unfortunately, I have to say "No, thank you." Maybe later when the merged company is established, I'll have time for appointments to outside boards. For now, merging the two companies in Denmark and Sweden is my goal.'

Monique Moullé-Zetterström wants to stay in Scandinavia. She does not miss France. She keeps a house in Provence. Her girls are both living in Paris. One of them has two children, making her a grandmother.

The future

What about the future? (One would expect a company answer from such a committed company person.) 'The future is bright! Yes, the future is Orange. But long term I would like to do something totally different. Two things, actually. I would like to write', she said, 'and I would like to do some deeply human service or charity. I do not know exactly what. But a good friend of mine who was working with me one day said he would leave France Telecom to do something more important. He sent me an e-mail six months later saying he was studying to be a priest. He is now helping children in Vietnam. I admire what he is doing.'

She was looking forward to a big reunion of all the children – her children (and grandchildren) and her husband's children (and grandchildren) – over Christmas at their house in Provence, where it was held the year before. She is not a woman who does everyday cooking. 'I am not the kind of woman doing hamburgers or things like that. I refuse to cook every day, so if I do a dinner it is great.'

Part III
The commentary

Making it to the top

The profiles in Part II of this book suggest strongly that, given the oppor-
tunity, women are capable of performing to the highest standard in any
top managerial job. The Veuve Clicquot Business Woman of the Year
Award winners have run organizations across the whole spectrum of busi-
ness and commerce from telecommunications to software design, from
publishing to retail trade, from health to advertising, from television
production to transport. In this chapter we look at women and their career
development. We restrict our sample to the six women in corporate/public
sector life who have had to advance to their top positions in career moves.
We exclude the ten entrepreneurs who owned the companies.

There is not one study in managerial research that suggests that women
are less suited to managerial careers than men (Powell, 1990). However,
the literature on gender suggests that the process of career development
may be different for males and females. Women managers tend to occupy
different types of managerial jobs from male managers. They tend to hold
'specialist' support roles, such as personnel and marketing, rather than
'generalist' line-management roles which generally enjoy higher status than
support roles. Furthermore, women managers in the UK are clustered in
certain business areas, such as the public sector, which are distinguished
by lower pay than the private sector, and service organizations, such as
retailing (Davidson and Cooper, 1992).

Some initiatives have been taken to address this imbalance. A Hansard
Society Commission was set up in 1989 which reported on what it saw as
'formidable barriers' for women at the top in 1990 and again five and ten
years later (McRae, 1995; Ross, 2000). Good progress had been made in
some areas, and some progress in most areas, towards getting more women
into positions of power and influence. But only 2 per cent of British executive directors of the FTSE 100 were women in 2001. One of the Commission's outcomes was Opportunity 2000 (Opportunity Now), launched in
1991, under the direction of Britain's top business leaders. Organizations which joined showed a doubling of women directors from 8 per cent
to 16 per cent by 1995 (McRae, 1995). In 2001, women made up 30 per

cent of all British managers and 16 per cent of functional heads, but only 9.9 per cent of directors. Where women were board members they tended to be non-executive directors (Equal Opportunities Commission, 2002). Research published by the Cranfield Centre for Developing Women Business Leaders (Singh and Vinnicombe, 2001) shows that there are fewer women on the boards of the FTSE 100 companies than ever and only one woman CEO, Dame Marjorie Scardino of Pearson plc. British women managers still fail to reach top management in numbers similar to their male peers. Yet the profiles of corporate women in this book show that these women have achieved top-level positions and fulfilled their career ambitions within company structures.

Career development theory

There has always been a male bias in the literature about careers. Theorists such as Super (1957) and Schein (1971) assume that a career is a life-long, uninterrupted experience of work, which can be divided up into neat stages of development, starting with initial ideas about working and ending with retirement. There is no allowance for any variation from the norms they establish.

However, the patterns of women's career development are frequently affected by family as well as workplace commitments and responsibilities, unlike those of men (although this may well be changing in the early twenty-first century). Therefore Astin (1984) proposed that career development theory should describe women's careers separately from men's careers. Her model of career development is based upon four constructs which she believes shape women's career development. They are: work motivation, work expectations, sex-role socialization, and structure of opportunity, which includes factors such as sex-role stereotyping, distribution of jobs and discrimination.

Larwood and Gutek (1987) concluded that any theory of women's career development must take account of five factors:

1   Career preparation, or how females are brought up to view the idea of a career and whether they believe they will have one or not.
2   Availability of opportunities should be taken into consideration, and whether they are limited for women, compared with men.
3   Marriage, viewed as neutral for men but harmful to the careers of women.
4   Similarly, pregnancy and having children inevitably cause women to take some kind of career break.
5   Timing and age, as career breaks and family relocations often mean that women's careers do not follow the same chronological patterns as those of men.

Powell and Mainiero (1992) claimed that women have two overriding concerns in their lives, for their career and for others (e.g. family and friends). Their model, therefore, incorporates the influence of personal, organizational and societal factors to describe the balance between work and non-work aspects of life which most women strive to achieve. They develop the concept of 'emphasis on career' versus 'emphasis on relationships with others', which they claim dominates the choices women make about their careers. A woman may change to emphasize one or the other at various points in her life. The model portrays these as opposite banks of 'the river of time'. Powell and Mainiero's model differs further from classic models of career development in that it does not assume straightforward linear progression throughout the career.

The process of career development

From such career models, it is evident that women's careers are influenced by several factors which do not affect men's careers to anywhere near the same extent. In particular, the process of career development appears to be very different for female managers, compared with male managers. In a study of the influences which lead to women and men's managerial advancement, Tharenou *et al.* (1994) tested situational and individual influence models and found that whilst training was of advantage to both men and women it had a greater influence for men than women. Moreover, women received less encouragement from their seniors to undertake training. Women's advancement was hindered by having dependants at home, while for men having a spouse at home was a contributory factor to career progression. But career encouragement had a greater effect on women's advancement, and organizations were advised of the benefits of fast-tracking women's careers, or talent-spotting women, encouraging female managers, mentoring, and providing opportunities for training and development for them.

Women have to learn to manage themselves as well as others. They have to develop strategies to deal with being different from male managers, being different from many of the women around them, having few same-gender role models to emulate, and being treated differently from men in the organization.

Women with mentors do better, because the mentors provide reflected power, feedback, resources and access to the power structure (Ragins and Sundstrom, 1989; Turban and Dougherty, 1994; Vinnicombe and Colwill, 1995). The mentoring relationship can provide training in corporate politics, and access to information sources that otherwise might not be available. However, as there are so few senior women, female managers usually have to seek cross-gender mentor relationships, which bring fear of exploitation and gossip. Women at times may not want to approach males for mentorship in case the approach is construed as a sexual overture (Ragins and Cotton, 1991). Senior males may not consider women to be appropriate as protégés for future senior management. Schein's 'think manager, think male' survey of corporate managers, which she undertook fifteen years previously and repeated in the mid-1990s, still elicited the same stereotypical attitudes to women in management (Schein *et al.*, 1996). The study revealed that male managers still thought of 'men as being more qualified than women to be managers'. Women may seek out female mentors, but they are often less powerful and may not be able to deliver many of the benefits of being mentored in a male-dominated organization.

There is evidence that women are less adept than men at handling informal networks to manage their careers and, as a result, respond better than men to formal organizational career management. Pazy (1987) reported that the more women managers perceived that the organization had formal mechanisms to develop their careers, the less willing they were to use informal mechanisms.

The distinguishing features of successful careers

So what are the distinguishing features of the careers of successful women managers? Some of the key ones appear to be early challenge, a chance to prove oneself and gain confidence early on, a wide range of experience and finding a mentor (Stamp, 1986; Ragins and Sundstrom, 1989).

Early challenge is thought to be a key factor for later success for managers (Hall, 1976). When examining the work histories of their sample of 'successful' women, White *et al.* (1992) found that they generally included early challenge, success generating success.

Mainiero (1994) proposed four key stages through which women managers must pass en route to becoming senior executives. Political *naïveté* leads to awareness that outspokenness and honesty must be tempered with an understanding and awareness of the corporate culture. She must build credibility with her superiors, peers and subordinates, and begin to form alliances and interpersonal networks. Refining a style means learning to be tough as well as direct. Finally, shouldering responsibilities as the sole woman at the top means taking responsibility for mentoring others.

Likewise, Morrison *et al.* (1992) pointed to four paradoxes, which they claimed women managers must contend with if they wished for successful organizational careers. They must take risks but remain consistently outstanding, be tough but not macho, be ambitious but not expect equal treatment, and take responsibility but follow others' advice.

This brief review of the literature has highlighted several models of career development processes for women. Table 1 sets these out by date. We now turn to the Veuve Clicquot winners who worked their way up to the top corporate jobs: Dame Marjorie Scardino, Dianne Thompson, Ann Burdus, Mair Barnes, Patricia Vaz and, from the public sector, Phyllis Cunningham.

Table 1 Some models of career development

Astin (1984)	Larwood and Gutek (1987)	Mainiero (1994)	Ragins, Townsend and Mattis (1998)
• Work motivation • Work expectations • Sex-role socialization • Structured opportunities	• Career preparation • Available opportunities • Marriage and pregnancy • Timing and age	• Assignment to high visibility projects • Demonstration of critical skills • Top level support • Entrepreneurial initiative • Accurately identifying what company values	• Consistently exceeding performance • Developing style with which males were comfortable • Seeking challenging assignments • Having influential mentors

The key factors for corporate success

Many men who reach the top of organizations have been to the 'right' private schools and prestigious universities like Oxford or Cambridge, Harvard or Yale. This is commonly referred to as the 'Old Boy Network'. There is no female equivalent. None of these corporate women went to private school, and only four went to university – Manchester, Durham, Bangor and Baylor (Texas, USA).

Even more non-stereotypical of the male model of success, of the six women only Phyllis Cunningham seemed to have had any idea of a career plan at the outset. 'I had always had a bent for business and organization. I handled money well and I organized well. So I got a Business Studies Diploma and sought out a hospital environment straight from college.'

Even then she felt she only had a very basic career plan. 'I have never said I am here now and I want to be there in five years and there in ten years.'

The others expressed no idea of a career, or no career preference:

'I had no idea what I wanted to do except that I did not want to teach. I fell into marketing by accident' (Dianne Thompson).

'When you are 18, as I was then, if you are at all curious, it is hard to focus on what you want to study. I had no career plan' (Dame Marjorie Scardino).

Once in management it is increasingly popular to take an MBA to accelerate one's career. None of the six women followed this route. Dianne Thompson did obtain her Institute of Marketing Diploma and Phyllis Cunningham had her Diploma in Business Studies. The others did not invest in any significant management development for themselves. When Dame Marjorie Scardino was running the *Georgia Gazette* with her husband it did cross her mind to do a course at Harvard Business School, but her friend, a dean there, said, 'You are learning so much more having your own business . . . You would just be bored.'

Her sceptical attitude towards business education has stayed with her. 'We try to find people at Pearson who have had unusual careers or haven't just got out of university or business school. Business schools tend to teach people conformity in the way they think and we want just the opposite – creativity and asymmetrical ways of approaching problems.'

If these six high-powered corporate businesswomen launched their careers in a somewhat haphazard way, what catapulted them to success? Ten factors come through their personal stories (see Figure 1):

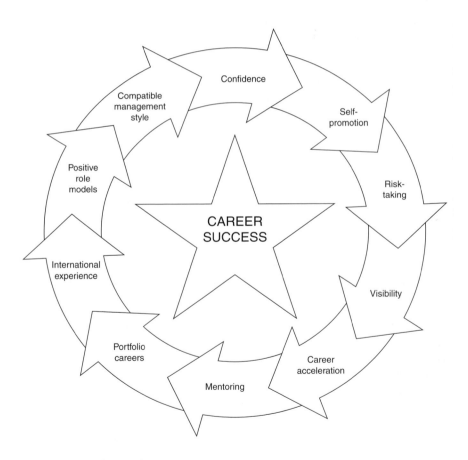

Figure 1 Key factors for career success

1 Confidence
2 Self-promotion
3 Risk-taking
4 Visibility
5 Career acceleration
6 Mentoring
7 Portfolio careers
8 International experience
9 Role models
10 A management style compatible with that of male colleagues

Let us examine each of these factors more closely.

Confidence

The key quality that these six corporate women possess is self-confidence. Every one of them commented on it.

> 'I was fortunate enough to have parents who did not think that there were any limits to what you could do. No one told me that girls didn't do this, that or the other' (Dame Marjorie Scardino).

> 'I was a problem child. I was one of the hundreds of people that failed the eleven-plus and looking back on it now they [her parents] did their best, giving me extra lessons and that sort of thing. They were never condemnatory, they were always encouraging' (Ann Burdus).

> 'My mother said women could do anything a man could do and I was determined to prove she was right' (Patricia Vaz).

Confidence was the bedrock of success for all six women. Despite the fact that they had no career strategies, no formal business education and no high-powered networks developed at school or university, they expected to have successful careers. They would not have settled for less.

Confidence is key to self-esteem and putting oneself forward for promotion. In all the studies on sex stereotyping of managerial attributes women constantly rate themselves lower on confidence than men. This lack of confidence leads to self-doubt, questioning one's competence, feeling isolated and limiting one's career potential. Many organizational cultures give little support to women. Not surprisingly many women get stuck in their organizations, while others drop out of organizational life (see Marshall, 1995). When women are confident they are more resilient in handling the 'barriers' facing women. In fact they go further by seemingly programming themselves not to see barriers. None of these corporate women focused on barriers. Dame Marjorie Scardino recalled being sent home from the office once when she wore trousers to work. She brushed aside the incident as 'ridiculous'.

The only woman who did meet a real obstacle was Phyllis Cunningham, who entered the Withington Hospital in Manchester as a secretary with a view to settling into the training programme for administration. She observed that all the places were given to men. 'In the end I decided there was no way to advance, so I left the hospital service and got a job at Geigy Pharmaceuticals.'

Dianne Thompson also recalled gender bias in her work experience. 'ICI was the worst place and when I was actually interviewed for the job they said to me that to be treated equally I had to be at least 10 per cent better than men . . . At the time I said "that it is OK because I am 15 per cent better so there is no problem." That was absolutely false bravado. It just came out. I was thinking "O my God, you know I will never be able to do this." You felt you were under the microscope to prove yourself, really hard. The irony is that once you do the job and you prove you have some ability then you get judged on your own.'

Patricia Vaz summed up her experience: 'You must put your head above the parapet and you often get bruised.'

Perhaps the greatest example of confidence and resilience was demonstrated by Ann Burdus. At 56 she was made redundant by Olympia & York and at the same time discovered that her entire life pension had been lost through Maxwell's fraudulent behaviour in AGB. 'Even when my world was falling about me in the late eighties and early nineties I was not really scared . . . I said that I have always felt that if the worst came to the worst I could always wash glasses in a bar. We had this attitude that we were going to survive and we are survivors.'

Self-promotion

A second key personal quality of the six women was being self-promoting – not being afraid of putting themselves forward.

> 'Running *The Economist* was great for me. It was very brave of them to hire somebody who had run just a little newspaper in Georgia. But their aim at that time was to grow and to make some transformations and I said, "I know how to do that!" And the guy who was CEO of *The Economist* in London at that point said – "Why not?" ' (Dame Marjorie Scardino).

> 'In BT, switching from personnel to networks was something that was never done. My manager at the time, a woman, called me in and said "this is a big mistake. You do realize that the only place where women will get on in this company is Personnel" ' (Patrician Vaz).

When Dianne Thompson was appointed marketing director at Sterling Roncraft, her predecessor became MD: 'For the first three or four months my MD interfered all the time, so we had to have one grown-up conversation that said if you want to do my job do it but I will go somewhere else. So he backed off and after that he was fine.'

Mair Barnes joined Woolworths in 1985 as director of the Books and Toys business unit. She told chairman Geoff Mulcahy that she was unhappy with the company's direction and where she felt it had come off the rails. He agreed with her analysis and made her managing director in 1987.

A problem that many women have is that they focus all their energies on their jobs and assume that this will get them promoted. It is essential to manage upwards, to build good relationships and to let senior managers know about your success and your ambitions. As Gowler and Legge (1989: 447) say, 'The "successful" manager is the one who manages the good opinions of others.'

Risk-taking

It is not possible to be a CEO/MD without taking risks. Dianne Thompson's job as marketing director at Signet, formerly Ratners, after Gerald Ratner's infamous speech leading to the rapid decline of the jewellers, was a risky choice. In three years she rebuilt the business and it made £27 million profit the year she left. Her next risky project was renewing Camelot's licence to run the lottery. She rose to the challenge and won.

Patricia Vaz took on a challenging promotion in 1990 as director of BT's payphone operations. The payphones – 130,000 of them – were a great source of embarrassment to BT, as well as losing £70 million per annum. Patricia Vaz won the Veuve Clicquot Business Woman of the Year Award for 1994 in the wake of the payphone success for turning around the loss-making division into an independent and profitable part of BT.

Ann Burdus resigned from AGB when Maxwell took over the company. She was 50 and had no job. She joined Olympia & York marketing Canary Wharf. This was a completely new experience for her. The company went into administration within three years and, having discovered that she had lost her entire pension in AGB due to Maxwell's fraudulent behaviour, she was once again in the job market. Most women/men would despair at such a position. Not Ann. She remembered being contacted recently by Dawson International plc to take on a non-executive director (NED) post. She took the post and hasn't looked back. She has sat on at least six boards, as well has having held a number of other public appointments.

Dame Marjorie Scardino is a pragmatist when it comes to risk: 'One thing that having a business that completely failed gives you is the lack of the fear of failure. I had totally failed and that turned into a great advantage – I was not at all that frightened.'

Visibility

Visibility gives individuals' careers a boost. There are several notable incidents of visibility amongst the six corporate Veuve Clicquot winners. Dame Marjorie Scardino is still called 'The First Lady of the Footsie' since she is the only female chief executive amongst the FTSE 100 companies. When her appointment was announced, the City responded by shooting Pearson's share price sky high. Experts estimated that a quarter of the multi-billion pound company's value was attributable to her. When Ann Burdus was at Mather & Crowther she set up a special unit for using research to help the creative teams produce better advertising. The unit was unique at the time and captured the industry's attention. Mair Barnes became a very visible managing director at Woolworths. She was appointed in 1987 and in a year she turned a £5 million loss into a £45 million profit. Dianne Thompson's public fight to renew Camelot's licence in 2000 catapulted her into the spotlight. Winning the case and the licence brought rich rewards – CEO at Camelot and national recognition.

In each of these cases visibility enhanced the individual's reputation enormously, leading to further career success and public endorsement through the Veuve Clicquot Business Woman of the Year Award. It is not incidental that many of these award winners in the UK have gone on to gain further public recognition for their good work. Five of the sixteen UK women featured in this book have subsequently received OBEs or CBEs. In 2002 Marjorie Scardino became a Dame of the British Empire.

Career acceleration

Knowing how to pace a career is critical to success. Too many women (and men) get stuck in jobs where their careers do not progress. All these women showed a careful management of pace in their careers. When they had exploited the learning and development from a job, they realized it was time to move on.

Patricia Vaz saw this as an important element of career managing early on in BT. 'When I joined BT as a clerical officer, I moved up the organization by having a vision of where I wanted to be. There were twenty-nine males between me and the top. So I set a goal which was roughly five years ahead and I worked back from that goal to see what I had to do to get there in the five years. At each stage I would reinvent my dream.'

Patricia Vaz and Mair Barnes moved through a series of jobs spanning over twenty years in their respective organizations (BT and Fraser) to reach director level. Clearly, if women can get themselves into 'talent pools' or fast-tracks in large organizations they can progress their careers quickly. The other four women worked in a number of organizations before winning the Veuve Clicquot award: Dianne Thompson (9), Ann Burdus (4), Phyllis Cunningham (5), Marjorie Scardino (4). This kind of career is now referred to as 'the Protean career'. It is interesting to note that when Dianne worked in ICI (her second job) the organization wanted to fast-track her, along with several other women managers. This would have entailed a move out of marketing. Dianne objected and left the company. Dianne's moves into Signet and Camelot, and Marjorie's key move into *The Economist* in New York, were all facilitated by headhunters. Headhunters are often able to cast a fresh eye over the job role and see potential candidates in innovative ways. From the individual's point of view headhunters can jump-start a career.

Mentoring

A surprise finding in this small sample of corporate women was the lack of mentoring. It is well known that mentoring is closely associated with female managers' success.

The only corporate woman who mentioned a mentor was Phyllis Cunningham. 'I worked for the medical director. He gave me all sorts of developmental things to do, like running the double blind trials on new drugs and things like that. I was about 23 at the time. He mentored me – although we never called it that.'

This mentor suggested that she should seek international experience in health care, which is what influenced her to go the United States. Later on, when she returned from America, she met her mentor again and as a result went back into the NHS in London.

Dianne Thompson paid tribute to the help and encouragement she received from Sir James Hann. When she was holding a board dinner to celebrate Camelot's success, she invited Sir James along and acknowledged publicly to her team the support she had received from him. He was very surprised: 'Men will not admit to having mentors – they are too macho to admit it; they feel "I can do this on my own." '

Whilst Dame Marjorie Scardino made no direct reference to a mentor, Dennis Stevenson, Chairman of Pearson, has clearly always been a keen sponsor of hers.

Networking proved to be valuable, particularly for Dianne Thompson and Ann Burdus. For example, Ann Burdus went into market research after chatting to someone at a British Psychological Society conference. Dianne Thompson heard about the marketing director job at Ronseal from an ex-student of hers at a DIY Week awards lunch.

Portfolio careers

When you are unsure about career direction, portfolio careers are a useful way of combining different roles. Whilst Dianne Thompson was a marketing lecturer she ran an advertising agency, carried out consultancy assignments and tutored at the Open University. She refers to this period in her life as 'plate spinning'. Ann Burdus did part-time marketing research alongside her clinical psychology job. The part-time work proved to be the catalyst in redirecting her career.

Dame Marjorie Scardino did start off in journalism after graduating, but then qualified in law and became a partner in a law firm for nine years. During that time she helped to run the *Georgia Gazette* with her husband and gave birth to her two eldest children. In 1985 she was headhunted for *The Economist* in New York. At 38 she left law and committed herself to a career in publishing. Her rise to CEO of Pearson in 1997 has been meteoric and a true inspiration to young women (and men) who have no clear career strategy after graduating. Many CEO and chairmen of large plcs believe that to get onto a corporate board it is essential to have general management experience. Dianne Thompson, Dame Marjorie Scardino and Ann Burdus defy that belief.

The remaining three factors – international experience, role models, compatible management style – were mentioned less often by the six women.

International experience

Ann Burdus, Dame Marjorie Scardino and Phyllis Cunningham all had work experience in the US. Dame Marjorie Scardino is American.

In 2001 five of the top ten women voted most influential in European business by the *Wall Street Journal Europe* either came from the US or spent formative years there. Theories abound as to the reason: that women reared or educated in America have an edge here because they are more assertive, or that they know more about technology, or that they have more experience dealing directly with powerful men. The US has a greater proportion of women at executive level than any other country and it probably has an easier time accepting them in such positions (*Wall Street Journal*, 2001).

Role models

Women managers who are ambitious inevitably look to the top of their organizations to check for the presence of other women in leadership positions. The Institute of Management survey of women managers (2001) indicated that women managers are more optimistic about promotion where they see women directors in their organizations than where they do not see them. Hence the presence of women at director level sends out a powerful message to other women managers about positive opportunities for their career development. A high-profile woman manager such as Patricia Vaz, with a position on the Retail Board at BT, sends a signal to women throughout BT that it is possible to advance to the summit of the telecommunications structure, and that has a positive effect.

But role models are not always positive and women can unwittingly be negative role models. Certain women at the top of their organizations, who conform to male models of behaviour rather than demonstrate different female ways of leading, may serve as negative role models for other women. As such these negative models can produce negative reactions among women who refuse to compromise their femininity at work. Certainly, it is difficult for a woman, or anyone for that matter, to introduce an entirely different style of leading in an organization that has already established a mould of male leadership.

Phyllis Cunningham saw many women in senior positions in the New York hospitals. 'This struck me as a huge difference from current practice at that time in the UK.'

A management style compatible with that of male colleagues

Mair Barnes took a personal mission in making men feel comfortable with senior female managers. Significantly, this is a key strategy reported by women managers today for progressing their careers. Whilst it is good to be sensitive to the styles of others, it is rather sad that women managers feel that they have to adjust their styles to fit in.

Emerging women entrepreneurs

'People often ask me to explain Microsoft's success. They want to know the secret of getting from a two-man, shoestring operation to a company with more than 21,000 employees and more than $8 billion a year in sales. Of course, there's no simple answer and luck has played a role, but I think the most important element was our original vision.'[1]

Bill Gates's vision was of the ubiquitous power of cheap computers and the new software that would be needed to exploit it. 'We got there first and our early success gave us the chance to hire more and more smart people', Gates wrote. 'We built up a world-wide sales force and used the revenue it generated to fund new products. But from the beginning, we set off down a road that was headed in the right direction.'[2]

The 'original vision' of an entrepreneur is obviously as important for women entrepreneurs as it was for the two male founders of Microsoft. Anita Roddick's vision of beauty products that did not exploit women with inflated prices due to exquisite packaging, excessive advertising and corporate greed has revolutionized the entire industry. Imitators of The Body Shop have sprung up across the world. The high-street stores could not ignore what she had done. They created a range of 'me too' products to compete. The original vision may be as dominant for women as for men entrepreneurs. But many other factors may be different for women entrepreneurs, such as their motivation to go into business for themselves and their ways of operating the businesses. It is these gender-specific elements that we explore in this chapter.

Most of the winners of the Veuve Clicquot Business Woman of the Year Award are entrepreneurs. Ten out of our sample of sixteen British winners are entrepreneurs. Perhaps that simply reflects the career of the woman the award celebrates, Madame Clicquot, who was herself an astonishingly successful female entrepreneur. Or it may be a modern fascination with the excitement that surrounds the role of a woman entrepreneur. Take someone like Anita Roddick who, on the strength of her global success

[1] Bill Gates, *Road Ahead*, London, Penguin Books, 1996, p. 19.
[2] Ibid., p. 20.

with The Body Shop over the last twenty-seven years, has dared to challenge 'the system' to recognize its social responsibilities, as well as to follow her example and undertake best-practice business ethics. Just as Anita Roddick begins to withdraw from the running of The Body Shop, a new generation of female entrepreneurs comes forward to take her place. The press pulsates with positive articles about Go's CEO Barbara Cassani just three years after setting up her business and leading it successfully in a management buy-out. At 41, she is the new inspirational businesswoman with a caring concern for her 750 staff that spills over to the customers of her low-cost airline.

In 1997 almost a third of new British businesses were started by women (Gracie, 1998). That level of participation by women is predicted to increase as women acquire greater access to capital and new opportunities open to them.

To define 'entrepreneur' in the words of Peter Drucker (1985) as 'one who drastically upgrades the yield of resources and creates a new market and a new customer' is to narrow the definition whilst elevating it to a level only a few entrepreneurs reach. Not every entrepreneur can be a Bill Gates or an Anita Roddick, a James Dyson or an Ann Gloag.

The US government, for example, until 1966 classified all business owners under the category 'sole proprietor'. The US Small Business Administration's Office of Women Business Owners defined women-owned as '51 per cent owned, operated or controlled by a woman or women'. The National Foundation for Women Business Owners (NFWBO) formerly used the '51 per cent or more' of the shares in their companies to indicate ownership in its definition, but has altered it to include women with a plurality of shares in their businesses so as to reflect the growing costs of business start-ups, especially in the technology and bio-medical fields.

Rosabeth Moss Kanter (1990) resisted the temptation to restrict entrepreneurship to an independent business venture. For her entrepreneurship is any activity that produces something, or adds value or capacity to an organization. Such a wide definition has led to the concept of 'intrapreneurship', where managers act like entrepreneurs within corporations, as Arthur Fry did at 3M when he created the Post-it note and turned it into a global product.

Elizabeth Chell (2001) proposes two definitions of an entrepreneur: (1) *the capitalist* who owns the means of production and is able to marshal resources successfully, assuming the risk for the sake of profit, and (2) *the opportunist* who is able to recognize and pursue opportunities for business development and growth and is confident that the resourcing of these ventures is possible. Building on Chell's two definitions, we suggest that *an entrepreneur is an opportunist who founds a business, or comes to own and control it, to provide the customer with products or services at a profit to the company and a benefit to the community.*

Performance and the 'Veuve Clicquot curse'

The media enjoy celebrating the success of British entrepreneurs, if only to be the first to bring them down to earth when their performance is less brilliant or when they fail. Journalists have invented the so-called 'Veuve Clicquot curse', which they ascribe to women who have won the award and who later see their corporate or entrepreneurial businesses decline. Journalists called Nikki Beckett one of Britain's 'techno-babes' as her company NSB became more global and successful and her personal wealth soared. When her retail software company's share price began to slide (along with the shares in other high tech companies worldwide), the same journalists were swift to announce how much her personal, paper wealth had shrunk. They claimed that she, like other winners of the award, had fallen under the 'Veuve Clicquot curse'.

The fact that profits for Anne Wood's production company Ragdoll fell in 2001 to £4 million from £10.4 million the year before is not a sign of the 'Veuve Clicquot curse' but rather of the maturing of a global product – *Teletubbies* – from the spectacular, universal response to its first 365 programmes. That she took a director's salary of £478,535 instead of her previous year's salary of £1 million is the consequence of extra costs incurred in research and development and the rising cost of testing new technologies for the children's films she produces. It does not indicate a failing enterprise.

Of the sixteen women in our British sample of award winners only one – Sophie Mirman – saw her business fail. Two years after she received the award for the year 1987, Sock Shop went into administration. She has recovered from that setback to create a smaller-scale, thriving retail business with Trotters. 'It was a bruising experience [seeing the business with over 100 shops go into administration]. I don't have any need to do it again by expanding Trotters', Sophie Mirman said.

The so-called 'curse' was supposedly visited upon Dianne Thompson when Camelot reassessed its target of £15 billion revenue in five years – a target that was identical to its rival's target for running the national lottery, Richard Branson's The People's Lottery.[3] At the time both targets were set Lord Burns, head of the Lottery Commission, cautioned that they were too ambitious and would have to be reduced. So prudent reassessment is mistakenly viewed in the press as failure due to the curse.

Barbara Cassani's airline Go, despite its early solid successes under her leadership and profit gains of £4 million in its first report period since its break from British Airways, remains a risky business financially. She sank most of her own personal £4 million share in the business back into Go. 'To be honest, it was a moral question', Barbara Cassani said. 'I wanted

---

[3] Tom McGhie, 'Is Dianne Thompson of Camelot about to fall victim to the curse of Veuve Clicquot?', *Financial Mail on Sunday*, 20 May 2001.

to show my commitment and I put nearly all of that money back into the airline.' But acknowledging the risks inherent in the business she's in, she added: 'I don't want them [her employees] mortgaging their houses to buy up stock. I saw what happened in the US with People Express[4] and, whatever you say, airlines are risky financial business.'

At best, the so-called 'Veuve Clicquot curse' is simply an invention of the media to draw attention to the inevitable fluctuations that occur in business performance because of product life cycles and changes in the economic climate. At worst, it is a form of slander against courageous business people who should receive support from the media rather than unwarranted criticism.

The amazing growth of women entrepreneurs

The spectacular rise in the number of women entrepreneurs over the last three decades – particularly in the USA – conveniently parallels the timeframe of this book, the three decades in which the Veuve Clicquot Business Woman of the Year Award has been in existence in Britain. By 1990 one out of every ten American women over the age of 35 was involved in an entrepreneurial business (Divine, 1994). These entrepreneurial enterprises are altering the economic landscape of the country. Between 1967 and 1996 employment in these women-owned businesses tripled and sales more than tripled. Today one in every four American company workers is employed by a woman entrepreneur. The economic contribution from women-owned businesses to the national economy is about $2.3 trillion annually (National Foundation for Women Business Owners, 1997).

Before 1978, almost nothing was known about women entrepreneurs in terms of scientific research (Stevenson, 1986). Between 1975 and 1990, the number of women entrepreneurs more than doubled. The numbers of women who were self-employed increased by 63 per cent as women started their own businesses twice as fast as men (Murphy, 1992).

From the mid-1980s on, there has been a marked rise in the number of women entrepreneurs and heightened attention has been paid to them (Mattis, 2000) Business articles cite three main reasons for this growth in female entrepreneurs:

1   pay inequalities for women;
2   career frustration due to the glass ceilings or glass walls in American corporations that hindered women's advancement;

---

[4] People Express was a low-cost airline created by Don Burr with employee ownership at its core. It had over a hundred jets operating in January 1985 when it acquired Frontier Airline in Denver to become the world's third largest airline in only five years, but went bust six months later.

3   the flexibility afforded by entrepreneurial activities in dealing with the demands of dependent relationships such as children, the handicapped or older parents.

These new-style women entrepreneurs were referred to as the 'Second Generation'(Gregg, 1985). The earlier generation of female entrepreneurs fitted a narrow profile. They were, according to Moore and Buttner (1997), 'primary sole proprietors with similar educational backgrounds (usually liberal arts graduates) and a basic interest in extending home skills into the marketplace'.

The new female class of entrepreneurs came from corporations often armed with MBA degrees and filled with the knowledge and skills of state-of-the-art technology and management science. They also had networks to help them in their enterprises and access to capital. Audaciously, they moved into business areas previously reserved to men, such as finance, insurance, manufacturing and construction.

Landmark research on women entrepreneurs

Three US organizations came together in 1997 to conduct landmark research about women entrepreneurs. The organizations were:

1   *Catalyst*, a not-for-profit research organization with its national head-quarters in Wall Street in New York City, advises companies and the professions on how to get the most out of women's talent. It is an advocacy agency committed to the advancement of women.
2   *The Committee of 200* (C200) is a professional organization of eminent businesswomen who promote entrepreneurship and corporate leadership among women. It has about 400 members.
3   *The National Federation for Women Business Owners* (NFWBO) has a global reputation for being the best source of information about women entrepreneurs. By research and sharing information NFWBO strengthens women-owned enterprises whilst providing a support network for the entrepreneurs themselves.

These three organizations won funding from Salomon Smith Barney, Inc. to conduct a study of the motivation of women entrepreneurs and the avenues they have taken to founding their own businesses. The results were published by Catalyst in 1998. Three cohorts of female entrepreneurs were studied: First Generation Women Entrepreneurs who have been in business twenty or more years; Second Generation Women Entrepreneurs who have owned their businesses for ten to nineteen years; Third Generation Women Entrepreneurs who have been in business less than ten years.

The research was based on a randomly drawn sample of 800 US business owners – 650 women and 150 men. Using a full range of data-collection techniques from focus groups to develop the interview protocol to structured telephone interviews, the data were derived from the following questions:

- What motivates women to start up their own businesses?
- What work experiences have the women had before undertaking the start-up?
- Do these motivations and work experiences differ from men's experiences, and, if so, how?
- Has the glass ceiling or downsizing played a part in their motivation to go into business for themselves?
- What, if anything, would be needed to get them to return to their original organizations?

The main findings of the study that relate to our purposes have to do with motivation to move into ownership.

The women entrepreneurs left their private sector organizations for the following reasons:

- flexibility (51 per cent)
- glass ceiling (29 per cent)
- unhappy with work environment (28 per cent)
- unchallenged (22 per cent)

There was a marked difference between the three cohorts when it came to starting up their businesses with an entrepreneurial idea. Fifty-one per cent of the women from the First Generation (twenty years plus) started up with an entrepreneurial idea, whereas among the Second Generation (ten to nineteen years) 48 per cent began with an entrepreneurial idea; of the Third Generation (the newcomers with less than ten years' experience) only 35 per cent started their business with an entrepreneurial idea.

The women who decided set up their own business did not limit their choices to their past employment or career experiences. They were just as likely to start a business that was totally unrelated to their previous jobs (42 per cent) as they were to create a business closely related to previous work experience (41 per cent).

For men there was a much closer link between the businesses they established and the work they were doing just before taking the entrepreneurial route (59 per cent).

Research in the UK on women entrepreneurs has not yet had the scope, rigour or the resources employed in the US.

There is already evidence that dissatisfaction at what organizations have to offer is playing a part in women's decisions to leave work in search of more meaningful self-employment (Fierman, 1990; Rosin and Korabik, 1992, 1995; Brett and Stroh, 1994; Marshall, 1995; Mallon and Cohen 2001)

In their findings as to why women move from organizational careers to self-employment Mallon and Cohen (2001) identify two separate categories of women. 'Entrepreneurs in waiting' are the women who pounced upon an opportunity to break loose from organizational constraints to grow their careers in a different direction. The second category, which was much larger than the first, were those for whom the career change was triggered by their dissatisfaction and disillusionment with their organizations. These women were being pushed out. 'These women's stories were characterised by an urgent desire to leave an organisational situation that was causing them much personal and/or professional pain' (Mallon and Cohen, 2001: 227).

Until more insightful, comparable research is done on women entrepreneurs in the UK we can only speculate as to whether the same motivational forces are at work for women in both countries. Given the rise in the numbers of women in middle management in Britain, there is great scope for them to be as discouraged by the glass walls and glass ceilings still in place as their American counterparts.

The thousands of women downsized out of UK telecommunications, banks and other financial services may contribute to a rise in reluctant entrepreneurs. The growing number of women achieving MBAs and other business qualifications will, we suspect, spill over into the start-up of more women-owned enterprises.

Types of entrepreneur

For the purpose of clarity we have developed a typology showing five categories of entrepreneur, as follows:

1   Reluctant entrepreneurs.
2   Born-to-be entrepreneurs.
3   'Corporate incubator' entrepreneurs.
4   Entrepreneurs through family connections or inheritance.
5   Dual-career couple entrepreneurs.

Some of the entrepreneurs among the award-winners are what we call *reluctant entrepreneurs.* These are women who have suddenly found themselves outside organizations they have been working for because of downsizing or corporate collapse or mergers, or mismanagement by men who have blocked their career advancement through the whole range of glass ceiling experiences.

These women have gone into business because they had to survive or to prove their own worth. This category is written large in the literature. A desire for increased responsibility and recognition were the main reasons for leaving their company for 27 per cent of the sample (Moore and Buttner, 1997). The study was in keeping with a recent study (Catalyst, 1998) in which components of the glass ceiling most frequently cited by respondents were: failure to have their contributions recognized (47 per cent of women out of the private sector), and not being taken seriously (27 per cent). Women spoke of feeling isolated in their organizations (29 per cent) and seeing others promoted ahead of themselves (27 per cent). Reluctant entrepreneurs set up their own businesses out of self-defence or reaction to intolerable conditions at work.

TV producer Anne Wood was a freelance film producer who described herself as a reluctant entrepreneur. She was told by a senior manager of a television broadcaster that he could no longer deal with her in her freelance capacity – she had to turn herself into a production company to obtain further work. Her response was to set up a company, Ragdoll Productions, and to learn rather quickly the rudiments of running a business.

For similar reasons – the demands of the broadcasters – Verity Lambert moved from being a freelance director of television productions, to creating her own small production company, then back again to working as a one-person operation.

Born-to-be entrepreneurs are business owners who have entrepreneurial instincts 'encoded in their DNA' as Anita Roddick puts it. (In the American research only 2 per cent among the women and 4 per cent among men described themselves as 'born to be' entrepreneurs. [Catalyst, 1998].) These business owners grow up with the idea of being their own boss, running their own show. For some the passion to create their own business is so strong that they are almost unfit to work for anyone other than themselves. This category is referred to in the literature as 'intentional entrepreneurs'.

Anita Roddick was born into an Italian immigrant family where to be in business for oneself was natural. Her immediate family ran a restaurant. Her other relatives ran their own restaurants. Her father set up a restaurant in Littlehampton, modelled after an American diner. Her widowed mother sold her restaurant to buy a nightclub. Although she went to college and studied to be a teacher, Anita Roddick stayed less than a year in the profession, leaving to travel and work abroad. When she returned to Littlehampton it was to set up a bed-and-breakfast hotel with her partner Gordon Roddick. She came into her own as an entrepreneur when Gordon Roddick left to travel for a year and she needed a small business to run to support herself and their two daughters. She started the first outlet of The Body Shop in Brighton, which grew in twenty-seven years into an international chain with 2,000 shops. Her daughter, Sam, has opened her own retail shop in Covent Garden, continuing the family tradition of entrepreneurship.

'I'm a natural trader. I like everything about trading. I always have. Most of us were entrepreneurs who, with the zeal of a convert, say that business wasn't just financial science, where profit was the sole arbitrator, it was more about participating in political social activism; using products as emissaries for social change or stores for leveraging our customers on social action,' Anita Roddick said, adding the social dimension to entrepreneurship.

'Corporate incubator' entrepreneurs come out of large corporations where they have acquired the management skills, knowledge and often even the technology and contacts to set up businesses for themselves. This is the fastest growing category and is well identified in the literature.

Nikki Beckett provided an outstanding example of this type of entrepreneur. She stayed with IBM for a decade and a half to be fast-tracked in many management jobs, educated at the local university at IBM's expense and then groomed for a series of positions and placements in business strategy for IBM, culminating in a secondment with a software operation in retailing. That last assignment led to her breaking away from IBM to set up (with IBM's blessing and support) her own company, NSB, in the identical area of software applications to retail businesses, using some of IBM's contacts for funding and business leads.

'IBM was very good to me. They said to me, "why do you want to go away to university?" . . . they persuaded me that the most flexible way forward for me was with them. They invested in me and for seven years I went to college whilst I was working with IBM and enjoying the management training.'

She went into IBM's business development department and enjoyed a variety of business experiences, some of which involved working abroad. When she tried to resign from the company after nearly fifteen years with the firm, 'I was persuaded to stay on and run one of the small companies IBM had taken an investment in. That gave me small company experience without risk.'

Sophie Mirman also fits into this category, as she learned all about the retail trade from Marks & Spencer for many years before she was let loose in entrepreneurial ventures, first the Tie Rack and then her own Sock Shop chain of retail outlets, and now the two Trotters shops. She was fortunate to have a year's experience managing another entrepreneur's venture (the Tie Rack) before launching her own idea (the Sock Shop).

But the most spectacular example of corporate-led new business creation is the case of Barbara Cassani and Go Airlines. The idea for the new business – a low-cost airline to compete with several others that had just started up – came from Bob Ayling, the CEO of British Airways itself, where Barbara Cassani was a senior manager. She had joined BA in 1987, the year it was privatized, and had ten years of managerial experience with the company. She was thinking of leaving BA in May 1997 when Bob Ayling asked her to study the idea of BA setting up a low-cost airline that would contribute to its profits and fend off some of the competition from Ryanair and easyJet. BA gave her £25 million in November 1997 and the directive to start up Go Airlines within six months. She did. In June 2001, after BA put Go Airlines on the market, Barbara Cassani talked with her staff and led a £110 million buy-out of the business with the backing of the venture-capital firm 3i. Her personal stakeholding in the new airline was £4 million. She became Go's CEO.

Entrepreneurs through family connections or inheritance. Some women become entrepreneurs by virtue of a family connection or inheritance. In the United States three-quarters of all corporations are family-owned or family-controlled. These companies employ half of the US workforce and generate half of the gross national product.

Increasingly, women from these entrepreneurial families, whose firms were started by male family members, are coming into the businesses. Figures for the UK reveal a similar pattern, where family-owned companies are choosing women from the families to run the companies. Research into this category includes work done by Barbara Dunn at the University of Edinburgh, which led to her formation of the Family Business Network (FBN).

None of the Veuve Clicquot Business Woman of the Year Award winners in our UK sample have come to entrepreneurship by this family connection or inheritance route. However, the Veuve Clicquot winner for 1996, Nicola Falston, and Janet Holmes à Court, award winner for 1995 as chairman of Stoll Moss Theatres & Heytesbury Holdings, an international company with a varied portfolio, both fit this category. Nicola Falston inherited her father's business, Brands Hatch Leisure, plc, the largest organizer and promoter of motor sport in Europe, and continued its success. Janet Holmes à Court also inherited the family business and continued its development. Sweden's Marianne Nilson (see pp. 221–226) illustrates the family connection route.

Women in our sample, nevertheless, acknowledge the role models their parents were for owning their own businesses. Anita Roddick attributes learning much about the hard work it takes to be an entrepreneur to participating as a family member with her parents and other relatives, who all worked in their small businesses. 'My mother was the cook and my grandfather peeled the potatoes in the garden at the back. As soon as we were old enough, all of us children were expected to help in the café after school and at weekends taking orders, clearing tables, washing up, buttering endless slices of bread, operating the till.'

The same can be said for Patsy Bloom whose parents ran a small chain of sweet shops in London. 'My parents had three sweet shops called Tommy Frost's and were working seven days a week to run them. I worked in the shops as a kid . . . Small talk in our house was about other people's businesses.'

Sophie Mirman learned about quality retail products from her mother, who was a famous designer of hats. 'I was brought up in an environment where I always saw both my parents work. Half of the house was for their business use and the rest was where we lived . . . My mother could fiddle with a hat and turn it into an extraordinary creation. She made all the hats for the Christian Dior shows. I used to deliver hats in beautiful black boxes, with white trim around them, to earn pocket money. I was the main hat deliverer.'

Ann Gloag owed a debt of gratitude to her bus-driver father for teaching her about deal-making on a very small scale in the used car market. 'My father was a bus driver and he used to buy and sell used cars. He would go to the car market and buy a car and bring it home and clean it up and sell it on. He would take us off school. We would go with him to Glasgow and look round at all the cars . . . As we got older, and he bought a car on the market, he occasionally would say: "You can have a share in the sale if you want; have you got any money?" We did have a bit of money from fruit picking and potato picking and we would take a share in a deal, maybe putting in a few pounds. He would give us a pro rata return on what we invested against the profit made. I always look back and think that I learned a lot about dealing and negotiations from those trips with my father from a very young age.'

Dual-career couple entrepreneurs are those couples that form an entrepreneurial business together. In *Working Woman* magazine's top fifty women-owned companies (Bamford, 1995), there are nine women CEOs who share ownership with their husbands and six more women owners who employ their husbands full-time. Dual-career couple entrepreneurs form a sizeable and growing category of entrepreneurs in the UK that is well represented in our sample.

The enduring wife-and-husband partnerships among the award winners in our sample included Anita and Gordon Roddick, The Body Shop; Sophie Mirman and Richard Ross, Sock Shop and Trotters; Prue Leith and Rayne Kruger, Leith's cooking enterprises; Marjorie and Albert Scardino, the *Georgia Gazette*, a weekly newspaper, founded by the couple, whose editorials won Albert Scardino a Pulitzer Prize. A year later the newspaper failed as a business. The failure spurred Marjorie into a corporate career, in part to pay off debts. Since the collapse of the newspaper they have pursued separate careers – he in journalism and she in corporate life – with equal shared care of their three children.

Wife-and-husband partnerships that broke up in divorce during the lifetime of the business in our sample included Debbie Moore and Norris Masters, Pineapple; Nikki and Geoff Beckett, NSB; Ann and Robin Gloag, Stagecoach. (Ann Gloag's partnership with her brother Brian Souter carried on without the ex-husband.)

Although she does not fit into this category, Patsy Bloom had a unique attitude to having a male business partner. She remained unmarried during the launch and twenty-year development of Pet Plan. Yet she attributed part of the success of her enterprise to having a male business partner, David Simpson, who was neither a romantic partner nor a spouse. At first she just used his financial knowledge as a silent partner in the business, but as Pet Plan grew she wanted a man in the company full-time. She felt that a male figure in the business was 'necessary to be taken seriously'.

'But after two years or so, I said to David that we had to sit down and talk about the business. We had about eleven staff at the time and I told David that, if we wanted to go further, either he had to go full-time or we had to hire someone to take on his role. So he came on full-time.'

Achieving a better work/life balance

The image of the entrepreneur pursuing goals to the exclusion of all else, a rampant workaholic, is out of place amongst those women who chose entrepreneurship to have more control over their work lives, a better balance. Flexibility is one of the main reasons women cite for going into their own businesses in America. The flexibility is needed to look after their own children or a handicapped child or parent. If you are your own boss, you decide your hours of work and time off and the allocation of resources.

Debbie Moore needed both the flexibility and the liberal use of the money she earned from her own company, Pineapple, to look after her daughter Lara, who had several bouts of a rare disease that required – during certain periods of her growing up – continual maternal care and expensive medical treatment.

'Money can't buy happiness, but if I hadn't had my own business I could never had contemplated taking Lara to New York. There are people who say that the children of mothers with careers are deprived, but in this instance it was only because I worked that I was able to do the best for Lara.'

To be the first woman chief executive of an airline must be a demanding job. As the newest winner of the Veuve Clicquot Business Woman of the Year Award for 2001, presented in April 2002, Barbara Cassani is the holder of that challenging job in a financially high-risk business.

She has a dual-career couple relationship. Her husband, a merchant banker, is not part of her business. As the mother of their two growing children, Barbara Cassani tries to be at home each evening to read her children bedtime stories. She celebrated the £110 million management buy-out of her airline by hurrying home to play Monopoly with her children. 'I played with the kids last weekend for the first time in ages', she said at the time. 'I wasn't able to spend much time with them while we were putting the deal together.' If, as she plans, Go is floated in 2004, and the flotation matches easyJet's, her £4 million share in the airline could have her playing Monopoly for real.

Personal definitions of success

Before exploring the personal meanings of success for the award-winning women in our sample, it is important to examine the context of success in terms of the research into women in management. Women's experience of management is often significantly different from men's because of the particular roles they fill both at work and within life in general. This is likely to affect their definitions of success. At work they often find themselves stuck in supportive roles. At home they do most of the domestic work and, where there are children in their families, they spend more time and energy in rearing the children than their male partners.

In 2001 the proportion of women engaged in managerial work was 30 per cent, up from 7.9 per cent in 1990 (Equal Opportunities Commission, 2002). The higher the level in management, the more glaring is the gender gap in terms of sheer numbers. Entry into management has neither assured British women access to top jobs nor has it guaranteed them equal pay. In the UK in 2001 the average earnings of male and female managers in the National Management Salary Survey were £40,289 and £34,789 per year respectively. These pay inequalities between men and women are generally shrinking. But there is a new growing gender polarization in the economy between part-timers and full-timers: 75 per cent of part-time managers are female. The pay inequality for women managers takes two forms. Part-time women managers are frequently restricted to lower grades (and salary scales) and often their official work hours do not reflect the long hours which they invest in their jobs.

The nature of women's career paths themselves can block their progress up the organization. At junior and middle levels, women are often in staff functions, such as personnel or training, public relations or customer care, rather than in operating or commercial functions. Once women perform well in these support roles it is often difficult for them to negotiate moves into other functions. Such functional barriers at work are referred to as 'glass walls' (McRae, 1995).

A woman manager's situation is exacerbated by the fact that many of them do not network with senior managers who might facilitate transfers into more central roles in the company (Ibarra, 1992). Such networking is difficult for female managers since the networks are almost exclusively male. Women managers' own attitudes also hold them back as many do not positively value networking and politicking at work (Mainiero, 1994).

Long working hours make it very stressful for women to combine careers and family responsibilities. Surveys continually show that women take the greater share of activities related to child rearing and running a household. In the UK, 73 per cent of women still do 'nearly all the housework' and men with working partners have an average of six hours more spare time at weekends than their partners do (Cooper and Lewis, 1999). Not surprisingly, many women see a conflict between family and career and hence decide not to have children or to work part-time.

In a recent survey of male and female managers about long working hours, Simpson (1998) discusses how women are doubly disadvantaged. They may be unable or unwilling to put in the long hours, so they are not seen as fully committed. As a result of their exclusion from late informal meetings, they do not have the same access as male managers to information. At the same time it is often difficult for women to challenge the issue of long hours because of their vulnerable position. According to Simpson (1997) few women managers have families at home, in contrast to male managers.

These essentially different male and female experiences of being a manager influence personal definitions of career success. The traditional model of career success in organizations has emphasized the external criteria of hierarchical position and pay. Yet there is evidence from women that they do not define their own career success primarily in terms of position and pay at all.

A qualitative study (Sturges, 1999) which investigated how male and female managers saw their own career success indicated four types of manager:

1   The *climber* sees career success chiefly in terms of the level of organizational seniority and pay achieved, is status conscious and competitive, but often wants to combine material success with enjoyment at work.

2   The *expert* defines career success as being good at what they do and receiving personal recognition for this accomplishment, is not particularly goal-oriented, and values the content of a job more than its status.

3   The *influencer* associates career success with the degree of organizational influence they achieve and may seek hierarchical advancement to gain greater influence but does not value status *per se*.

4   The *self-realizer* defines success in terms of achievement at a very personal level, which usually involves personal challenges and self-development, and sees having the ability to balance their work and personal life as an integral part of career success.

Of the thirty-six managers interviewed for Sturges's research, women were more likely to be *experts* or *self-realizers* and less likely to be *climbers*. Men were more likely to be *climbers* or *influencers* than *experts* or *self-realizers*. This suggests that external criteria for career success such as pay and hierarchical position may be far more central to men's conceptions of career success, whereas women define their own career success much more in terms of internal criteria such as accomplishment and achievement, and subjective criteria such as influence, personal recognition and respect (Sturges, 1999). These differences have implications for how women act as managers and how they communicate their ambitions to senior managers. How are these differences constructed?

The psychology of gendered development

Psychologists who write about gender are not surprised by these differences in career success criteria. Women and men arrive in organizations with a differently constructed sense of self as a result of the ways girls and boys are brought up. If, as many writers have suggested (e.g. Gilligan, 1982; Asplund, 1988), organizational practices build on the individual's sense of identity, the fact that the attitudes developed in men are more likely to be rewarded at work (since many organizations are male dominated) is more likely to create tensions for women as they struggle to establish themselves as managers.

Chodorow (1978) provides an important interpretation of how gender differences arise. She suggests that it is the social system of mothering that creates different patterns of behaviour between boys and girls. She shows how women, as mothers, produce daughters with mothering capacities and the desire to mother. The mother–daughter relationship itself builds up these capacities and needs. Boys are cared for by a primary caregiver of the other gender. As boys develop a sense of identity, it is as separate from and other than the mother. Girls, in contrast, cared for by a same gender caregiver, separate later and grow up to value closeness to others and to experience care and dependence as less anxiety-inducing than do boys. Girls, however, are more likely to be anxious in situations where independence is called for. In this way men are prepared for a more distant family role and to engage in the impersonal world of work and public life. Chodorow argues that, to the extent that females and males experience different interpersonal environments as they grow up, feminine and masculine personality will develop differently and be preoccupied with different issues.

The structure of the family and family practices creates different relational needs and capacities in men and women that reflect themselves in the roles enacted in adulthood, including the managerial role. Undoubtedly, there is a spectrum of behaviour among both sexes. There are some men who are far more nurturing than some women, and women who are more distant than some men. Social structures are created through the interaction of individuals, whose responses are likely to vary. Some girls identify with their fathers and not all boys develop independence. But on the whole there is a continuum in which some behaviour is more typical of one gender than of the other.

Evidence supporting this account is provided by a number of studies that show differences in the way people perceive and present themselves in the world. Among them are the work of psychologists such as Gilligan (1982), who identified differences in girls' moral approach to the world; Belenky *et al.* (1986), who presented evidence for women's different ways of learning and knowing; and Levinson (1978, 1996), who charted the differences between the ways men and women develop their adult lives. Gilligan extended the psychoanalytic work of Chodorow to demonstrate how, by showing life as a web of relationships and stressing continuity, women portray autonomy rather than attachment as illusory and even risky. In her work, based on studies encompassing all age groups, Gilligan explored concepts of self and morality, and experiences of conflict and choice.

Personal definitions of success

Using Sturges's definitions of success fifteen interviews were analysed to identify success themes. This analysis, summarized in Table 2, was not straightforward. Many women discussed how their definitions have changed over time. For Ann Gloag at first it was earning money through the caravan business to help make ends meet on a nurse's salary. Then it shifted to not losing her father's redundancy money that was invested in setting up her bus business. Then the concern was protecting her house that was collateral for the business. Next came beating the competition and going global. Now she is a non-executive director and her mission is raising money to finish the hospital ship, *Africa Mercy*.

It is unlikely that any of the women would now be classified as *climbers*, since they are all at the top. We have, however, classified three of the

Table 2 Categories into which the award winners fall

Climbers	Experts	Influencers	Self-realizers
Patricia Vaz	Ann Burdus	Marjorie Scardino	Debbie Moore
Dianne Thompson	Sophie Mirman	Dianne Thompson	
Mair Barnes	Anne Wood	Mair Barnes	
	Patsy Bloom	Nikki Beckett	
	Verity Lambert	Anita Roddick	
		Ann Gloag	
		Prue Leith	
		Phyllis Cunningham	
		Patricia Vaz	

women as *climbers,* since they were always focused on moving up to the next job, setting themselves challenging targets and clearly being very competitive. Now the three women frame success more in terms of leaving their mark on the organization.

Only one woman, Debbie Moore, comes out as a *self-realizer.* She was the only one to be truly tested on the work/life balance issue through her daughter's illness, but her response was confident and consistent over the years.

Influencers

The *influencers'* view of success is being able to do things at work that have tangible and positive effects on the organization. Their organizational status is only important in terms of giving them the opportunity to exert influence. The *influencers'* definition of success is set in making an impact or leaving a mark on the business. Nine women were *influencers.*

> 'They said that it [the job] was with Camelot and my perspective of Camelot was that everything was fine and this was a company that was doing incredibly well and had a fantastic start and I could not see what I could do to make a difference really. What I don't enjoy doing is coming in and doing a maintenance job. I like to get stuck in and make changes, not for change sake but to improve things' (Dianne Thompson).

> 'We are one of the three largest companies in our niche in the retail sector . . . If I go back to my 1995 business plan, I had identified all the prime competitors or potential competitors in the market in the UK and I either had an acquisition strategy for them or a kill plan . . . Everyone who joins your company is acknowledging that he or she believes in you personally, because they are placing their careers in your hands. I have always thought of that as a huge responsibility' (Nikki Beckett).

The influence these women exert is not always just on their organizations. For Ann Gloag and Anita Roddick the mission extended to contributing to social justice on a global scale:

> 'I don't really know the moment . . . I knew I had become "the million-airess". So there was no instant elation . . . It was some time in 1987 . . . my definition of success right now is to find a way to raise the £12 million more to finish the [Mercy] ship. Writing the cheque myself wouldn't be a success. I only want to be in partnership. It is only successful when other independently wealthy people come along and share our vision and wish for the ship' (Ann Gloag).

'My personal definition of success does move. In business you are measured by this unimaginative band called profit and loss, or the financial bottom line. I demand that the financial bottom line include human rights and social justice and community development' (Anita Roddick).

Experts

Five women were identified as *experts*. Experts describe success in terms of achieving a high level of competency at their job and being recognized personally for being good at what they do, be it in terms of being seen to be an expert or winning the respect of the people they work for. Ann Burdus was renowned for the psychological perspective she brought to marketing research, Sophie Mirman for her expertise in clothes retailing, Anne Wood for her production of educational programmes for very young children, Patsy Bloom for animal health insurance, and Verity Lambert for her production of adult drama.

'I set up a business so I could go on doing the work that I loved to do. People can be quite scathing. They say: "For someone who never intended to make money, you've made quite a lot." I say, yes, but it's all going back into the company and it does not have any reality for me' (Anne Wood).

'I told her a little bit about the creative research I did in the early sixties and she said "Yes, I read some of the things you wrote then." And I had an inner glow about that. I was thrilled about the contributions that I had made to the business – something, at the time, which was revolutionary' (Ann Burdus).

Climbers

The *climbers* traditionally describe success in terms of job title and progression through promotion and reward, especially pay. Status is very important to them. In this sample we would have to amend this definition as Patricia Vaz, Dianne Thompson and Mair Barnes were clearly competitive and keen to be promoted regularly, but none of them spoke about status or money. They were all passionate about their work.

'My key to success is I have worked hard all my life and I am a driven person. I have not always got the balance right between home and work and if I have a regret it is . . . that I am absolutely passionate about what I do and I have been very fortunate to be able to choose the jobs I have done. I have never had a career plan. I have just fallen into jobs and had a call from a headhunter and thought that sounds all right. I will have a look at that one. The main characteristics [of the jobs] have been that they have been marketing-led, dealing with consumers and in the main the brand leader in the market', Dianne Thompson said.

Interestingly, Dianne Thompson decided in 1992 that she needed to provide a stable base for her daughter after her divorce, and hence refused to move house until her daughter had finished school. Her salary during that time had moved up to about £1 million a year. Dianne has announced publicly that she wants to take on the issue of fat-cat salaries in Camelot. She has always been sensitive of top executives' pay. She was critical of Gerald Ratner for his millionaire lifestyle – a gym in his offices and a personal helicopter, while working conditions at the company's functions in Birmingham were squalid.

Patricia Vaz's attitude to promotion is typical of a *climber*. 'When I joined BT as a clerical officer, I moved up the organization by having a vision of where I wanted to be. There were twenty-nine males between me and the top. So I set a goal which was roughly five years ahead and I worked back from that goal to see what I had to do to get there in the five years.'

Self-realizers

Career success for *self-realizers* is described as an internal concept, based on the idea of achievement at a very personal level. They might cherish personal recognition or influence but the desire to achieve on their own terms dominates their definition of success. A vital part of the self-realizer's life is achieving a balance between work and home; it matters that they succeed in both spheres.

Debbie Moore is the only woman in this category. She is an impressive example of a woman who has balanced running a significant business with nursing her daughter. 'Lara's illness became like a parallel career: I'd find all the best people to talk to, and read every medical journal. That was my life, and it still is. I had a brilliant assistant at the office. Whoever called me, she'd say I was in a meeting – but in fact I'd be at home with Lara.'

Debbie Moore is not blind to how the balance she struck in life was to affect her business success. '*Womenswear Daily* did a big write-up about my revolution in desk-to-dinner dressing with component parts. That's how Donna Karan got her inspiration and of course she's global now . . . That's probably where Pineapple would have been by now, if I had been able to devote myself entirely to the business.'

Pulling together these results, our Veuve Clicquot sample demonstrates that most of the women are *influencers,* not *experts* and *self-realizers* as expected. The majority of these women want to leave their mark on the business. Anita Roddick and Ann Gloag insist on using their corporate influence to have a positive impact on the global causes of social justice. Dianne Thompson, Mair Barnes and Patricia Vaz did not agree that all the criteria associated with *climbers* were important. Table 3 redefines the four personal definitions of success.

Table 3 Characteristics of categories

Climbers	Experts	Influencers	Self-realizers
• Organizational level	• Being good at what they do	• Degree of organizational influence	• Achievement at personal level
• Movement up the organization	• Getting personal recognition	• Extending influence beyond organization	• Involves personal challenges and self-development
• Competitive	• Valuing content of job rather than status		• Balance work and personal life
• Passionate			

Although only one woman was a *self-realizer*, family played an important role in all the women's lives. Out of fifteen women, only two had been single throughout their careers: Phyllis Cunningham and Patsy Bloom (now married). Of the remaining thirteen, ten had children of their own (as opposed to stepchildren). In each case a husband or other member of the family was involved with the wife's career:

Patricia Vaz	Husband also in BT
Nikki Beckett	Ex-husband set up business with her
Anne Wood	Son on the board of Ragdoll and husband an adviser to business
Marjorie Scardino	Husband is a journalist. They ran the *Georgia Gazette* together. He is a freelance journalist in London
Prue Leith	Husband was chairman of her company
Ann Gloag	Brother was partner in Stagecoach
Sophie Mirman	Husband business partner
Anita Roddick	Husband business partner
Debbie Moore	Ex-husband was partner in Pineapple
Dianne Thompson	Ex-husband had parallel career in early days at University of Manchester

Perhaps what this pattern tells us is that these women high-flyers are choosing to manage the work/life balance by negotiating with their families rather than negotiating with their organizations. Of course, 70 per cent of these mothers are entrepreneurs so they own their organizations. But, of greater interest, all the corporate mothers have partners linked into their careers. So the adage that 'women can't have it all' isn't true. They can have it all as long as they have partners who are prepared actively to support those careers. Richard Ross (Sophie Mirman's husband) sums it up, 'Behind every successful businesswoman there's a man without a chip on his shoulder!'

It doesn't always work out. Five of the Veuve Clicquot winners interviewed are divorced. Dianne Thompson was the only one to discuss her divorce and claims that her regular trips abroad did upset the equilibrium at home. Interestingly, in the last ten years of being a single mother, Dianne's negotiations over the work/life balance are with her daughter. In 1992 she promised her daughter that she would keep her at the same school. As a result Dianne has not changed house in ten years, despite changing companies three times and increasing her salary considerably. That work/life decision has clearly shaped, but by no means limited, Dianne Thompson's spectacular rise to become CEO of Camelot.

Leadership with a difference

Leadership is probably the most researched subject in the field of management. Traditionally, however, the research has focused on male leaders managing male subordinates. The whole topic of gender and leadership is relatively new. Rosener (1990) sparked a debate that argued that women do have a different style of managing. Rosener argued that women, now making it to the top, were not adopting the styles that had proved successful to men, but were drawing on the skills and attitudes they developed from their shared experiences as women. In contrast to the short-term, hard, command and control style associated with men ('transactional' style), women were more likely to use a 'transformational' style. This involves actively encouraging participation, sharing power and information, enhancing the self-worth of others and stimulating enthusiasm about work (Rosener, 1990). Subsequently, Sally Helgesen developed this thinking further, calling it 'the female advantage' (Helgesen, 1990), and Amanda Sinclair (1998) encapsulated it in *Doing Leadership Differently*.

In male-dominated industries women managers lead in ways that are more similar than different to the men in those industries. This is consistent with Kanter's work on tokenism; where women are in the minority, they alter their management style to reduce their visibility or to lessen perceived differences and stereotyping by men. Given these studies we intend to analyse the leadership styles of the six women in the big corporate organizations separately before moving on to the ten entrepreneurs.

Since these women all work in large male-dominated organizations, and to a greater or lesser degree had to work their ways to the top, we might expect their leadership styles to be more masculine. This situation was more the case for Phyllis Cunningham, Ann Burdus, Dame Marjorie Scardino and Patricia Vaz. It was less so for Dianne Thompson and Mair Barnes who were headhunted at director level into Camelot and Woolworths. Patricia Vaz, though, is critical of the research which demonstrates that women leaders behave like male leaders: 'I do not like the parody of women having to claim to behave like a man, to be able to mix with the men and to get on with the men. I never went in much for drinking with the boys. I had a house to go to and meals to cook.'

Worked hard to achieve good results

All six women worked extremely hard:

> 'I will work incredibly hard – give of my all – I will do the best I can' (Dianne Thompson).

> 'I never measured my commitment to what I was doing in terms of hours and days, it just had to be done. I still quite often read board papers at five o'clock in the morning. Why not?' (Ann Burdus).

> 'To achieve a leadership position in any organization you need tenacity – you must keep going and keep trying' (Patricia Vaz).

The long working hours of BT were always a problem to Patricia, particularly in the early days: 'I had a son to look after and a house to run. I had a childminder to look after my son only to a certain time. I needed to catch a 5.30 train every night. So I had to use my negotiating skills. I'd go to my manager and say: "Look, I'll do a deal with you. If you do not hold meetings at 4.30 in the afternoon when you know I can't stay and participate effectively long enough, I'll take work home and do these specific things in my own time." And I would list all the things I was prepared to offer if they did not make my life impossible.'

These women worked to achieve results. They were always goal-oriented.

'People had been working in their own little part of Pearson and did not know what each other did. They did not take advantage of the fact that they were part of a larger company. They were also not too oriented toward performance. Sure they cared about what they did – and that's important – but they were not attuned to the financial measures ... I wanted to change that!' said Dame Marjorie Scardino.

As managing director of Woolworths, in three years Mair Barnes turned a loss of £5 million into a profit of £45 million in 1988. She also reduced the number of suppliers from 8,000 to 1,000.

Patricia Vaz was renowned for her 'handbag' style of managing. This meant staying focused on two or three dimensions of performance. 'I invented what I call a handbag report that keeps track of these key indicators. Each month I ask my people to provide me with a handbag report. I want only enough indicators to give me a hold over my business that I can fit into my handbag. I don't want great stacks of statistics ... I would rather be vigilant about these few critical success factors – the ones I carry around with me in my handbag.'

Patricia Vaz stressed another aspect of achieving results – clarity of thought: 'You know how you get to the first stage of the goal and then the second stage of the goal ... It does not seem to matter what particular part of the organization I am involved in or how big the challenges facing me – you need to define the desired state, understand the gap and then break it down to get from where you are to the goal.'

Power and authority

Working long hours, setting goals and being results-driven are key characteristics of many male corporate executives too. However – and this is the key difference between male and female leadership – these women's styles are based on personal respect, openness, consultation, recognition of the contribution of team members, and the development of staff. This is called the 'transformational style' of leading. The traditional 'transactional' style, preferred by men, relies on power position and formal authority. Several of the women leaders talk about their attitudes towards power and authority:

> 'I've always had a very open policy. I like to talk with people to get their views. But I am very careful not to usurp the authority of my directors or managers. Part of my management style was to be always approachable . . . I did recognize that the buck stopped with me. There were many hard times during my stay at Marsden. As everyone knows, it is lonely at the top. But I never abused my status or stood on ceremony' (Phyllis Cunningham).

> 'I never went to conferences for the sake of going, to seek the limelight or centre stage' (Phyllis Cunningham).

> 'I liked to surround myself with people who were good at those things I was not good at. I enjoyed building a diverse team that was dynamic and full of brain power. I did not have a big ego' (Mair Barnes).

Similarly Ann Burdus talks about the importance of good colleagues: 'One of the most rewarding things of my life – much more important to me than where I have reached in terms of status – is the amazing experience of working with people all round the world.'

Dame Marjorie Scardino works closely with David Bell, Director for People in Pearson. For two years they have been trying to simplify how they choose people to hire: 'We've tried to think of some criteria. One of them should be "Be able to suffer fools gladly, because we are all inherently foolish".'

She reflects on her own style of leadership: 'I hate talking about myself or pontificating. One of the things I do not like about some businessmen is that they appear to know all the answers. They know how to do things. They have been terribly successful in their jobs because they are so clever. They go on to tell the rest of the world how they should behave in business.

I think that is ridiculous. Everyone does it differently. Some of us succeed and some of us fail and some of us do both.'

On her success, she remarked: '[I]t is always good to see someone else succeed and to say "Gosh, that person looks ordinary. Maybe I can do that too." I guess I see myself that way too, as ordinary.'

Dianne Thompson similarly reflects on her limitations as leader: 'My style of leadership has always been that I am only human ... In the end, you get what you see, and I think that in many ways that sort of openness has held me in good stead.'

Let us now look at these women's transformational styles of leading in more detail.

Openness

All the women talked about the importance of an open style, that involved listening, empathizing and managing conflict.

'If there is one huge difference between men and women – and there are many – it is that women tend to be more open. From my experience throughout my career I know that women talk more openly about what they can do and what they can't do and the problems they have', said Dianne Thompson.

When Dame Marjorie Scardino was appointed CEO in 1997 she sent an e-mail to everyone in the company: 'I described the kind of company I would like to work for and I got a fair number of responses. I began to use e-mail every time we had an important announcement. I realized that as we added more Americans I got a lot more e-mails back. Then it caught on. That was the best thing I did, because it gave me intimacy with 28,000 people.'

Mair Barnes believed in employee participation at all levels in the company. Ann Burdus feels that one of the qualities required of a NED is acknowledging your lack of understanding and being prepared to ask questions: 'When Dawson went through serious problems, I needed to understand the issues. So I asked. It was almost like having my own personal seminars from the City institutions.'

Phyllis Cunningham spoke about the need to consult before making a decision in the NHS. 'I have never been frightened to tackle things, but I'm not someone who starts off confident and brash. I generally buckle down and I will find out. I am not frightened; if I don't know things I'll ask people ... I have always had a very open policy. I like to talk to people to get their views.' In talking to trade unions Phyllis refers to their 'full and frank discussions'.

Working in the NHS involved a political dimension in decision-making not present in the other five corporates. 'Because we did not run our hospital through a district authority, I had direct relationships with under-secretaries and permanent secretaries. I developed a political nous due to these contacts and was able to analyse political currents in the Health Service.'

Patricia Vaz is the most articulate of the six women leaders on the values that underpin her style: '[Integrity] is one of my hot buttons. I cannot abide people who are not honest and open enough to acknowledge the real situation.'

Patricia reflects on her first experiences on being on a BT board – how overwhelming it was and how she got little support from the chairman: 'I've never forgotten that and I try to listen to people and note their body language and where they are uncomfortable and draw them into conversations at meetings before problems arise. It's a form of empathy and empathy is something women are particularly good at.'

Conflict resolution is another aspect of Patricia's open style: 'I do inject an element of conflict resolution among the people I lead. It's the same sort of thing I've been doing at home in the family – it comes naturally to me. I've done it all my life. I find it easy to say, "well you are being hurtful here" or "someone has a problem here, let's address it". Women often have a different perspective on conflict resolution because our level of experience is different and our lives are different.'

Team player

The six women leaders, particularly Dame Marjorie Scardino, emphasized the importance of teamwork and recognizing individual contributions in the business. Mair Barnes enabled people to run with projects aimed at increasing profitability while achieving career success.

Of the six women leaders, Dame Marjorie Scardino emerges as the most conspicuous team player of them all. She consistently attributes all her success to her team. When Dame Marjorie Scardino worked for *The Economist* in New York the circulation trebled under her leadership. 'The circulation did grow a lot and everybody attributes that to me. But it was due to a team of people who knew what they were doing. The only smart thing I did was to keep them on. They were the ones who did it, and I made sure they had food and water.'

When the company results are announced she always demands that her finance director, John Makinson, is with her. She tries to put an arm round him in any photo call to make sure he is included in the newspaper photos. She complains when the press still manages to cut him out of the photographs and credits her with success as if it were purely her work. 'It's annoying. It makes me look as if I think I am the only one who is doing all the work, and it is completely untrue. I get all the attention because I am the chief executive and partly because I am a woman – sort of a novelty, you know, like the only blonde-haired person in the whole of the FTSE. But I completely rely on the people who run the different businesses within Pearson.'

Share options for employees are as much part of her commitment to her staff as sharing credit. Under her leadership the percentage of Pearson employees owning stock has moved from 20 per cent in 1996 to 96 per cent in 2001.

Care, development of staff and diversity

The last aspect of transformational leadership is caring for the staff and developing them. This theme came through most strongly with Mair Barnes, Phyllis Cunningham, Dame Marjorie Scardino and Patricia Vaz.

When Mair Barnes won the Veuve Clicquot prize in 1989 a key aspect of her leadership style was identified as reforming the training programmes for many of the 30,000 staff in Woolworths. Interestingly, she had personally hired Dianne Thompson to Woolworths as a marketing manager and helped her develop her talents and skills. Dianne went on to be promoted in Woolworths before moving to Signet Jewellers.

Phyllis Cunningham was always aware of the lack of women in management in the NHS before 1974. 'I have never been a feminist *per se*. But I have encouraged many of my women staff members to seek goals that they may not have thought they were able to achieve. I have never believed in the token woman and I still believe fervently in the best person for the job.'

Dame Marjorie Scardino refers to the Pearson 'family'. The most publicized example of her care of employees came in her e-mail of 12 September 2001 to her 28,000 employees. 'Dear everyone, I want to make sure you know that our priority is that you are safe and sound in body and mind. Be guided by what you and your families need right now. There is no meeting you have to go to and no plane you have to get on if you don't feel comfortable doing it. For now look to yourselves and to your families, and to Pearson to help you any way we can.'

Dame Marjorie Scardino is embarrassed by the publicity her famous e-mail has attracted. But it is a tribute to her extraordinary leadership style – a style in which she can spontaneously find the right words and the right way to talk to 28,000 people in a truly caring and intimate way.

Patricia Vaz is a role model both inside and outside BT for women in management. She actively champions diversity. 'I look every single year at all the performance indicators of all my people. I strip out the females and the people from ethnic minorities to see if their performance rankings are in any way out of line with the males or the majority of the workforce . . . I watch every year when the salary reviews take place to make sure that we are not allowing people to be disadvantaged because of where they come from or who they are . . . I have also produced a set of personal values over the years – these value statements are a sort of scaffolding around the way you expect the people in your unit to work and the way you expect your people to behave. For example, my values around harassment call for zero tolerance. The people in my unit know that. If you

disregard this value, you'll be fired ... [Y]ou have to create an environment where people are treated positively and not undermined.'

Entrepreneurs as social activists

Being an entrepreneur means by definition that you are the leader of the
business. There are no constraining pressures as with the corporate or
public sector leaders to lead in a particular way. There is no need to 'fit
in'. The ten entrepreneurial women thus provide an interesting stage on
which we can see leadership played out in their own individual ways; they
define the roles and write their own scripts.

In general, the ten entrepreneurial women are more similar than different
to the six corporate/public sector women. They work exceedingly hard and
are goal-oriented, yet all of this is carried out in a transformational leadership way. The difference between the two sets of women leaders is the
extent to which a number of the women entrepreneurs have committed
money and energy to helping the underprivileged in society, by way of
ethical trading practices, charity work and pursuing causes involving social
justice. The most notable role models in this respect are Anita Roddick,
Ann Gloag, Prue Leith, Anne Wood and Patsy Bloom.

Without doubt Anita Roddick has publicized the need for business to
incorporate ethics more so than any other business leader, male or female,
in the world. 'Leaders in world business are the first true global citizens.
We have world-wide capability and responsibility. Our domains transcend
national boundaries. Our decisions affect not just economics but societies;
not just the direct concerns of business but world problems of poverty,
environment and security.

'Open up a typical management book and you will find it hard to avoid
words like leadership, team-building, company culture or customer service.
However, you will be lucky to find words like community, social justice,
human rights, dignity, love or spirituality – the emerging language of
business.'

She sums up her experience of business as a vehicle of social change.
'Many of us in this movement [for social responsibility] would rather have
slit our wrists in the sixties than ever be seen as corporate leaders. Most
of us were entrepreneurs who, with the zeal of the convert, say that business wasn't just financial science, where profit was the sole arbitrator, it
was more about participating in political social activism; using products
as emissaries for social change or stores for leveraging our customers on
social action. In short it is about bringing your activism to work.'

Anita Roddick's successes as an activist are many – three books, a new
business journal and many campaigns like saving the rain forests in Brazil.
No other business leader can compete with her accomplishments. However,
four other women entrepreneur winners have clearly demonstrated how
they too 'bring their activism to work'.

Anne Wood has a trust to support charities and her own personal charities, and an arrangement with Save the Children to investigate child labour and other issues of exploitation. When companies in other countries bid to make toys and other merchandise for Ragdoll she has Save the Children check on them. Similarly, Patsy Bloom has set up a Pet Plan Charitable Trust, and since selling her business spends time with the activities.

Prue Leith became chairman of RSA's Education Advisory Group in January 2001. She feels passionately about education. She is quick to help charities and initiate community service projects particularly to do with schools. Two projects take up most of Prue Leith's time now: The Big Bowl and The Great British Kitchen. The Big Bowl is due to open late in 2002. It is an initiative of training for life, a charity dedicated to helping disadvantaged young people into work. The Great British Kitchen will be the National Centre for the Culinary Arts, a £40 million development in Stafford devoted to the promotion of good food to the public. It will be open in 2004. The scheme will incorporate cultural and charitable initiatives run by the British Food Trust, promoters of the scheme.

Ann Gloag has invested many millions in her acts of charity. Her main project is a £4 million Danish ferry which she is turning into a floating hospital to be used off the coast of Africa. She set up a burns clinic in Malawi and an orphanage in Kenya. She set up the Balcraig Foundation to spend £1 million of her own money on good causes each year. She is trustee of the Princess Royal Trust for Carers.

These women entrepreneurs have extended the role of leadership beyond the recently much talked about 'transformational' leader to those whose acts of leadership go far beyond their employees and customers to effect social change, on a global scale.

Breaking into the corporate boardroom

Only four of our sixteen UK Veuve Clicquot winners sit on FTSE corporate boards, Dame Marjorie Scardino, Ann Burdus, Mair Barnes and Prue Leith. Three are from the corporate sector, while Prue Leith is the only entrepreneur by background. Her move into corporate boards was triggered by an invitation from Sir Peter Parker, who used to frequent her restaurant, to join Traveller's Fare, a subsidiary of British Rail. She later moved on to British Rail's main board. This led to over a dozen directorships, from food and retail businesses like Safeway and Woolworths to banks and building societies like the Leeds Building Society, which merged with the Halifax. Her current board appointments include Whitbread, Woolworths, and a venture capital company Tri Ven – an arm of Matrix Securities. Prue Leith demonstrates two classic characteristics of being a non-executive director (NED):

- A personal relationship with the chairman/CEO is often the key to the invitation to become a NED. Sir Peter Parker recognized Prue Leith's talent, despite her lack of corporate experience.
- Once an individual has demonstrated success as a NED, other NEDs often follow.

Mair Barnes and Ann Burdus have made second careers out of NED posts over the past ten years. Penny Hughes (ex-CEO of Coca-Cola UK), while not part of our sample, is a younger example of a woman who had traded on her CEO experience to design a new career by acquiring a portfolio of NED posts (Vodafone, Mirror Group and The Body Shop) that gave her flexibility for her family – something she found not possible as a full-time CEO of Coca-Cola UK.

The selection process

Dame Marjorie Scardino is the only one of our sample who is involved with interviewing prospective NEDs. She says: 'We've tried very hard and Dennis [Lord Stevenson] has worked hard to get more women on our board and more Europeans as well. What you need out of a board is people with a range of experience who can help you make good decisions.'

She does not believe that all board members should have plc experience, but they must have experience of a relevant area. For example, Lord Burns on the Pearson Board draws on his experience of the economy as Permanent Secretary to the Treasury.

In her experience women could do more to make themselves compatible with boardroom behaviours and the environment: 'Many of the decisions about who goes on are determined by the chemistry of the new prospective member of the board and the board itself. I have been involved in interviews in which the women felt that they had to be serious and they intellectualized too many things that are not really intellectual. They just did not let themselves be who they were. It led the chief executive to fear that this person was going to be a bore on the board – too serious, and in a way too aggressive. At least twice I have seen a person rejected because of that fear. Women need to work hard at not taking themselves too seriously.'

What Dame Majorie Scardino raises here is the 'comfort fit' concept. This concept is repeatedly discussed in the leadership literature as a key barrier for women moving into senior management. In a Catalyst/ Opportunity Now Survey (2000), 'developing a management style with which my male colleagues are comfortable' is the primary career strategy for women who wish to advance their careers. In another Catalyst study in the US (1998) female directors say the main reason there are not more women on the corporate boards is 'male stereotyping or bias'. So Dame Marjorie Scardino raises a paradox for women aspiring to be NEDs. They must both 'fit in' and be more natural.

The business case for gender diversity

> Diversity on boards is said to provide better corporate governance through the sharing of a broader and different range of experiences and diverse decision-making processes. However, most boards of large companies are homogeneously constituted, by white, middle-class, middle-aged males with similar educational and professional backgrounds. There are few female directors, and even fewer female executive directors. Only one woman, Dame Marjorie Scardino of Pearson, is a CEO in the FTSE 100 list, and she was the only woman in the recent list of FTSE 100 directors paid more than £1 million in 1999.
>
> (*Guardian*, 2000: 27)

Bilimoria (2000) makes a strong business case for gender diversity on corporate boards. In the *Fortune* 500 listed companies she found that financial status was higher in the most profitable 50 of the 500 companies that also had female directors. It could be that the presence of female directors was linked to financial status, but it might simply be that when the largest companies became more profitable they were more open to diverse appointments. Bilimoria noted that females were often appointed as additional rather than replacement directors. Corporate reputations were enhanced by the visible presence of women on the board, and some major investors (such as pension funds) showed a preference to invest in firms demonstrating diversity in board appointments (Kuczynski, 1999).

Bilimoria (2000) argues that women directors do influence board decision-making, with fresh and often well-informed views on market, environmental and ethical issues. A classic example of this was the suggestion by a female director of Nike that they should introduce sports shoes designed especially for women. This created a whole new market as women's sports footwear became fashionable and colour-coordinated, as well as better suited to the structure and shape of women's feet.

Fondas and Sassalos (2000) suggested that women were more able to influence corporate governance because of their broader experiences and different 'voice', and that boards with even just one woman director would be less likely to rubber-stamp CEO decisions. Women's presence in the boardroom is said to lead to more civilized behaviour and sensitivity to other perspectives, as well as a more interactive and transformational board management style (Rosener, 1990). A male board member of a large furniture company recognized the contribution of the first woman appointed to the board and damned her ecological concerns with faint praise. 'I guess she's alright', he said. 'If only she wouldn't keep going on about the *trees*!'

The presence of women at such senior levels also encourages women lower down in the management hierarchy. Research by the Institute of Management in 2001 showed that women managers in UK organizations with women on the board are more optimistic about promotion than women managers in organizations with no women on the board.

Women directors: international research comparisons

Given increasing numbers of women in managerial positions, there should be a pool of women with the potential to attain board positions, leading to more heterogeneous board composition. However, although the number of women in management has increased in the UK since the launch of the Opportunity 2000 initiative in 1991, few females have yet reached the very top levels of the largest corporations (Holton, 2000). In North America, the glass ceiling of the 1980s has simply shifted up through the organization to the uppermost echelons (Burke and Mattis, 2000). Daily *et al.* (1999) showed there was a significant lack of women on Canadian and US corporate boards, and noted that even when women were appointed to US boards it was almost always as outside directors (equivalent to UK non-executive positions).

Burke (1997) reports that the chief reason for lack of progress is uncertainty by senior directors about female executives' ability to perform at this level due to lack of business and corporate experience. The most common ways for women's names to be brought to the CEO's attention were recommendations from board members and being known personally to the CEO. They (CEOs) believed that there were extremely few women who met the criteria for appointment, and had difficulty in finding appropriate candidates. Similar findings are reported by Ragins *et al.* (1998). These reasons imply need for better upward networking by women, who tend to be less instrumental than men in initiating and maintaining upwards relationships (Ibarra, 1992; Vinnicombe *et al.*, 2000).

FTSE 100 companies with female directors

In 2001, fifty-seven companies had at least one female director (Singh and Vinnicombe, 2001). This is one less than in 2000. Thus forty-three companies had no females on their board. There is still only one female CEO, Dame Marjorie Scardino of Pearson, who topped the female directors index in 2000 with two females on their board. There is one female deputy MD, Marie Melnyk of Morrison Supermarkets (see Table 5).

There are now five companies with at least 20 per cent female board representation, compared to only one last year (see Table 4). The number of companies with over 10 per cent female directors has increased, while the numbers with between 1 per cent and 9 per cent have dropped. Women are achieving board-level positions, although progress is still slow. Importantly, it is almost all the firms who already have women directors, with some of those who had one female board member last year, which are appointing others this year.

FTSE 100 companies with female executive directors

Only two companies have two female executive directors, Marks & Spencer, and Celltech, which has Dr Melanie Lee, Director of Discovery, and Dr Ursula Ney, Development Director (see Table 5). Six more companies have one female executive director. These are Legal & General, Kingfisher, Morrison Supermarkets, Pearson, Invensys and Abbey National.

Table 4 Companies and their female director representation (%)

Number of companies with	2000	2001
20–25% female board members	1	5
10–19% female board members	22	27
1–9% female board members	35	25
No female directors	42	43

Table 5 The 10 FTSE 100 female executive directors, 2001

Woman executive directors	Age	Job title	Qualifications	Company	Females on board (%)	Joined company	Appointed director	Background (from biogs in annual reports and websites, and from national press)
Kate Avery	41	Group Director	MBA FCM	Legal & General Group plc	23	1996	2001	Was MD of Barclays Stockbrokers Ltd & Barclays Bank Trust. Joined L&G as Sales and Marketing Director before promotion to main board. Married, no children, works 12-hour days.
Yasmin Jetha	48	IT & Infrastructure Director		Abbey National plc	6	1998	2001	Held several director positions with Abbey National before appointment to main board. Also Director of First National Bank.
Dr Melanie G. Lee	43	Director of Discovery	Ph.D. NIMR	Celltech Group plc	15	1998	1998	Specialist in cancer research, formerly at Glaxo. The UK's highest female executive earner last year (£1.14m) according to the *Guardian*. Married with three children, 13-hour days, but makes time for family. Leads team of 400 scientists. Strong focus on results. Reputation for making uncompromising decisions. Described as intelligent, charming and friendly.[1]
Marie Margaret Melnyk	43	Deputy Managing Director		Morrison (Wm) Supermarkets plc	14	1975	1997	Also in top earners list (£332,000). Unbroken service of 26 years in same company, a historic family supermarket chain with no NEDs.

[1] From *Daily Mail*, 30 August 2001.

Table 5 (continued)

Woman executive directors	Age	Job title	Qualifications	Company	Females on board (%)	Joined company	Appointed director	Background (from biogs in annual reports and websites, and from national press)
Dr Ursula M. Ney	No data	Development Director	Ph.D.	Celltech Group plc	15	1998	2000	Also in top earners list (£228,000). Started career in pharmacology. Reputation in asthma research in UK and Switzerland. Responsible for all Celltech development programmes from start to product registration.
Kathleen O'Donovan	44	Chief Financial Officer	B.Sc. ACA	Invensys plc	10	1991	1999	Joined Invensys in 1991 as Finance Director. Former partner at Ernst & Young. NED of EMI plc, and a Director of the Bank of England. Also in top earners list (£424,000). Reputed to put in 13-hour days.
Laurel Powers-Freeling	44	Director, Financial Services	Degrees from Columbia and MIT	Marks & Spencer plc	25	2001	2001	American, worked at McKinsey and Prudential, then Lloyds TSB where she headed Wealth Management. Joined M&S in 2001, hired to develop financial services at M&S and reinvigorate the loyalty card scheme. Guaranteed £520,000 p.a. plus bonuses up to £300,000. She has two children. Her chairman said 'Her successful track record in developing financial services and retail banking will be a huge asset to us.'

Table 5 (continued)

Woman executive directors	Age	Job title	Qualifications	Company	Females on board (%)	Joined company	Appointed director	Background (from biogs in annual reports and websites, and from national press)
Alison Reed	44	Finance Director	CA	Marks & Spencer plc	25	1987	2001	Was accountant at Touche Ross, joined M&S, was talent-spotted and became executive assistant to chairman/CEO, gaining visibility to board. Appointed as Finance Director UK Retail before promotion to main board. Friend said she would have St Michael engraved on her heart. She got a reputation for turning round two key departments. NED at HSBC Bank plc since 1996.
Marjorie Scardino	54	Chief Executive		Pearson plc	13	1997	1997	American. Second in top earners list (£883,000). Trained as lawyer; was CEO of *The Economist* before appointment to Pearson, later becoming CEO. She reportedly gave the company new focus, took it into the Internet, expanded in the US, and saw the share price rise. She is married with three children.
Helen Weir	38	Group Finance Director		Kingfisher plc	17	1995	2000	Also in top earners list (£185,000). Previously finance chief for B&Q. Also worked for McKinsey.

FTSE 100 directorships held by women

Executive directorships

The total number of female executive directorships has fallen slightly, from thirteen in 1999 to ten in 2001, but the percentage remains at 2 per cent of all executive directorships, indicative that the number of executive directorships has dropped from 547 in 2000 to 498 in 2001.

Non-executive directorships

Female non-executive directorships have slightly increased in 2001, to 9.6 per cent of all NED posts compared with 9.13 per cent in 2000, not quite catching up with the 10.82 per cent held by females in 1999. This may be explained by the fact that there was a large increase in appointments of women following the 1997 General Election, when there was a strong political will to increase the representation of women to senior levels in politics, the civil service, local government and business.

Age of directors

The average age of the female executive director is 44.3 years, and 89 per cent of them are under 50. The average age of the female NED is 54 years, and 20 per cent of them are over 60. This is significantly different from the female executive directors. Further research is being undertaken to ascertain the age of all the male directors, to see whether women are being appointed at similar ages to their male peers.

Other board appointments held by female directors

In their brief biographies, only one (10 per cent) of the female executive directors is reported to hold a public appointment, although 44 per cent of them do sit on other corporate boards. Of the NEDs, 42 per cent hold public appointments, and 73 per cent other corporate directorships. This indicates that, like their male counterparts, successful women belong to networks of interlocking directorships in both the public and private sectors, and that the older NEDs are most likely to be active in this way.

Women directors from other countries

There are several American and other non-British women who have achieved directorships in the UK's top companies. From brief biographies in annual reports, and from press cuttings, we identified twelve women from America, three from France, two from Sweden, and one each from Australia, Hong Kong and Spain. Sam Parkhouse (2001) comments on this phenomenon in his recent book, *Powerful Women: Dancing on the Glass Ceiling*, asking why American women have managed to break through the 'glass ceiling' in the UK top firms. Given that over a quarter of the women succeeding in the FTSE 100 are from abroad, we need to examine their backgrounds to see what it is that prompted appointing committees to offer them directorships. A quick glance through their biographies indicates high-quality education (e.g. Harvard, Stanford), and high-profile political and corporate roles, sometimes in more than one country. For example, before taking a job with British Airways, American Barbara Cassani, with a Master's degree from Princeton, had work experience as a management consultant.

Sometimes the women had undertaken European responsibility for US companies before being appointed as NEDs in the UK. They had high-level corporate experience, often entrepreneurial talents, and clearly demonstrated the ability to succeed and deliver in a variety of environments.

Backgrounds of female directors

We examined the backgrounds of the women holding these seventy-five directorships, and found a vast amount of corporate experience. Most had corporate backgrounds, often with experience as chief executive officers of other firms, not in the FTSE 100 list but still companies of significant size such as FI Group, Yahoo Europe and BUPA. Many had directorships in large companies, and many had started their careers in the big management consulting/accounting companies/investment banks such as McKinsey, KPMG, Goldman Sachs, and Touche Ross, often reaching partner level before branching out. A number of the women directors had chaired or been directors on boards of public sector bodies such as the National Consumer Council and the BBC, as well as, famously, the first female head of MI5 (Stella Rimington). Others had held directorships of the London Stock Exchange and the Bank of England, as well as the US Securities Commission. Some were senior academics, in the UK and elsewhere, and some reported periods at leading universities such as Harvard and Stanford. Women directors in the technical companies had been on government scientific committees, and there were a number who had political backgrounds, as ministers (including Minister of State at the Foreign Office, as well as a former French Minister of Health), ex-members of Parliament, or political and economic advisers to their governments.

'Back door to the board'

The opportunities and increasing responsibilities of company secretary jobs, many of which are held by women, are being referred to as the 'back door to the board'. A number of companies are now listing their top management teams as well as corporate boards in annual reports and company websites. Sixty-four out of the 437 additional senior executives identified were female, making 14.65 per cent of the total. This is an encouraging figure, as it indicates that there is a considerable number of female potential executive directors in this pool. Given that currently only 2 per cent of executive directors are female, there is some evidence of likely progress in the future. Where job titles of these top female executives were listed, there were eleven company secretaries, seven directors, eight function heads/managers/senior vice-presidents, and one financial controller. Nine had titles relating to corporate communications and PR, three titles related to investor relations, whilst unexpectedly there was only one human resources director.

When are women going to break through?

An Institute of Management study (2001) found that nearly half of the 1,500 women managers surveyed felt that women still meet discrimination over promotion, and a third of them felt the same about pay. In addition, 41 per cent of the senior women saw the 'Old Boy Network' as a significant obstacle. This is a finding replicated in many other countries. What is especially interesting is that 33 per cent of the women were aiming to achieve a directorship, even if it meant moving companies. This belies the myth that women are not sufficiently ambitious or committed to their careers.

Progress

Despite the slight drop in the number of FTSE 100 firms with women directors, women do seem to be making progress in companies where there are already women in the boardroom. This is an encouraging sign. It means that the pioneer women have done well, so that there should be fewer concerns about whether women can do the 'top jobs'. We have found evidence of a large number of capable female directors with significant corporate experience behind them. We hope that they, as role models for the women in their companies, will act as catalysts to change residual male stereotyping, so that the playing field is more even for women. Not all women want the top jobs – nor do all the men. But until executive women feel that they have an opportunity to reach director level in their own companies, their organizations run the risk of losing them at wherever the glass ceiling is. Although only sixty-eight females have been appointed as directors to seventy-five seats, it is interesting to compare the patterns of their recruitment with those of male directors. A higher percentage of the women directors (16 per cent of female board seats) were appointed in 2001 than the men, whose 2001 appointments had actually fallen to 10 per cent of male seats. There was a slight increase on 2000 figures for female appointments. No current female directors were appointed before

1981, whereas the longest-standing male board members were appointed in the 1960s and 1970s.

Advice for NEDs

The advice of Mair Barnes and Ann Burdus, who between them have sat on numerous boards over the past decade, is relevant here:

1   It's important to learn what that particular board expects of its NEDs – it is not the same with every board.
2   It's essential to know the difference between being a NED and being a consultant.
3   It's vital to have a proper induction; if it's not offered, ask for it.
4   Initially, observe and listen to how the board works (this may take several months). Remember that it may be more effective to have a chat with the chairman than to make a contribution at a board meeting until you have learned that board's ways of operating. In fact, develop a good relationship with the chairman.
5   Make the other board members feel comfortable to have you there. 'No doubt behaviour around the board is still male-dominated. It can be aggressive, where the loudest voice prevails, in which case I'd have no chance at all. Trying to be assertive as the fellows I was never going to win. I had to find other ways of engaging them and being in command. I used humour at times to lighten the stuffiness of the board. You know the issues are serious, but I would find a way to engage them on issues and sometimes I'd be flippant. It is a sign of a healthy board if the members are relaxed with one another and can even joke with each other' (Mair Barnes).
6   Follow up on issues that come before the board later outside the boardroom. 'You have to get yourself about outside the boardroom to talk with people about the issues they are facing. There is much work that non-executives can do away from the board' (Mair Barnes). Mair Barnes does a lot of mentoring, particularly with the female managers in the organizations where she is on the board.
7   Serving on the board is a learning experience. Boards are different sizes and operate differently, therefore it is important to be open and flexible.
8   Work to get more diversity on the board. 'Most British boards have no experience of diversity. I mean true diversity, not just having someone there in a skirt. When you've got people with widely differing points of view coalescing around the right decision – that is diversity in action. I have had my eyes opened to the different approaches people have towards issues and boardroom dilemmas. Quite often I read a board paper and say to myself that is quite obvious and that is exactly what we should do. Then during the boardroom debate someone puts

a totally different point of view that actually changes my opinion on the topic. It is intriguing to have inputs from diverse people from totally different walks of life' (Mair Barnes).

Conclusion

Anita Roddick predictably has her own explanation for the dearth of women on boards: 'They have seen the organizations and they have seen their values and they say it's not my style – nothing I want to be part of. Anyone who – like me – goes to board meetings knows it is frigging dull. The board meeting is not the narrative of the business; it is simply financial science. Until they move that financial science away and talk about what the role of business is and bring out personal testimony – who would want to spend time at their meeting?'

This passionate statement probably resonates with many women. In our quest to increase diversity on corporate boards – diversity in all its various dimensions – we open up the opportunity to redefine the role of business.

Career strategy checklist
Accelerating your career

Based on the model of career success that has emerged from the interviews with the award-winning women, discussed in 'Making it to the Top' (see pp. 237–249), this checklist will help women in business evaluate their attitudes and behaviours concerning career success.

Confidence

1 How proud are you of your accomplishments?
2 Do you find it easy to accept compliments at work?
3 Do you worry that you will not be able to meet others' expectations in completing projects or assignments?
4 Do you hesitate to apply for interesting jobs because you feel you do not meet all the criteria?
5 Do you maintain an up-to-date curriculum vitae (CV) which conscientiously records all your career successes?
6 Do you have an appetite for taking on greater responsibilities beyond your boss's job?

Self-promotion

1 Does your manager know how ambitious you are and what positions you are aspiring to as the next steps in your career?
2 If there is an opportunity to get publicity for one of your successful work projects, do you take it?
3 How ready are you to volunteer for assignments beyond the confines of your present job?
4 How often do you put yourself forward to lead a project?
5 In appraisal interviews, do you clearly articulate your achievements and attribute them to your skills and competencies?
6 If someone tries to take credit for your accomplishments, do you tactfully set the record straight?

Risk-taking

1   Have you ever turned down a job because you felt you were not good enough, even though the person offering you the job was confident in your ability to do it?
2   What was your biggest mistake at work? What have you learned from it? What does the sentence: 'I judge my managers on the quality of their mistakes' mean to you?
3   How comfortable are you with challenging other people's views at meetings?
4   Do your colleagues know how you truly think and feel about important issues at work?
5   Does fear of failure stop you from going for challenging projects?
6   How do you respond to behaviour at work that you consider to be unethical?

Visibility

1   Who are the most influential people in your organization and do they know of your work?
2   To what extent do you try to build relationships with people outside your area at work?
3   Are you happy to be interviewed by the press?
4   Do you offer to represent your company in community activities?
5   Would you give a public talk?
6   Do you make an effort to participate with work colleagues in social events?

Career acceleration

1   Do you move positions every two to three years, either within your organization or outside it?
2   Each year do you reflect on what new skills you have added to your CV?
3   How swiftly do your expectations at work change?
4   How often do you benchmark your value in the marketplace by reading job ads?
5   Are you registered with any executive employment agencies or 'headhunters'?
6   Where do women in your organization get stuck (glass ceilings or glass walls)? Are there any women role models you can talk with about their strategies for overcoming these gender-based obstacles?

Mentoring

1 Do you belong to any formal or informal networks that bring you together with other professional women?

2 Who do you most admire in senior management in your organization? Have you ever asked one of these managers to mentor you, clarifying what you would be seeking from the mentoring relationship?

3 Have any senior managers in your organization shown an interest in your work or career? If so, have you thought about how you could make your competencies, achievements and ambitions better known to them?

4 How can you develop the most promising and talented of your subordinates?

5 Do you strive to be a role model for others in the enthusiasm and commitment you bring to work?

6 Do you strive to make work enjoyable, challenging and fun?

Portfolio careers

1 Are you keen to maintain several different strands to your career – for example, combining lecturing with management consultancy and research?

2 Have you ever thought of going freelance or taking a secondment?

3 Do you think of using your managerial experience to become a non-executive director on another company's board? Could you develop a portfolio of such appointments?

4 Is your work experience relevant for appointments to governmental bodies?

5 Can you combine your professional expertise with the media, as Prue Leith did in becoming a food correspondent and a broadcaster?

6 Is your pension portable? Have you thought about how the 'new, implicit psychological contract at work' might affect your career?

International experience

1 Have you ever considered taking an expatriate assignment?

2 Have you undertaken a short-term project abroad?

3 Would you consider working abroad during the week and commuting back to your home on weekends?

4 Would an exchange of jobs with a colleague in another country appeal to you?

5 Would you entertain a management education programme abroad?

6 How do you show your interest in cross-cultural issues?

Positive role models

1   If there are no positive female role models for you in senior management, have you thought about leaving the organization for one that holds more promise?
2   Do you listen to colleagues' career aspirations and strategies to help clarify your own?
3   Do you seek out a senior manager to ask for career advice and inspiration?
4   Do you read business books or the business press, like the *Financial Times*, to stay in touch with issues?
5   Who are the people who have most positively influenced you in your life? How have they done so?
6   If someone were to say to you 'You're a role model for me' would you be embarrassed, or pleased, or both?

A management style compatible with that of male colleagues

1   How would you describe your management style?
2   Do you seek feedback on your management style from your own manager and from subordinates or team members? Have you had 360 degree feedback?
3   When was the last time you went on a management development course? What did you learn about yourself then?
4   How would you describe a successful manager in your organization?
5   How does your management style match that of the successful manager you have just described?
6   Do you think your male colleagues expect you to perform better to win advancement because you are a woman?

Moving forward by action-planning

•   Select three or four of the above issues that would best help you to move forward in your career.
•   For each of these issues, write down one or two actions which you will immediately start to take.

Issue No. 1   _____
Action(s)   _____
Issue No. 2   _____
Action(s)   _____
Issue No. 3   _____
Action(s)   _____
Issue No. 4   _____
Action(s)   _____

References

Asplund, G. (1988). *Women Managers: Changing Organizational Cultures*. John Wiley, London.

Astin, H. S. (1984). The meaning of work in women's lives: A socio-psychological model of career choice and work behaviour. *Counselling Psychologist*, 12(4), 117–126.

Bamford, J. (1995). The Working Woman 50: America's top women business owners. *Working Woman*, 20 (May), 37–45.

Belenky, M., Clinchy, B., Goldberger, N. and Tarule, J. (1986). *Women's Ways of Knowing*. Basic Books, New York.

Bilimoria, D. (2000). Building the business case for women corporate directors. In R. Burke and M. Mattis (eds) *Women on Corporate Boards of Directors: International Challenges and Opportunities*. Kluwer Academic Publishers, Dordrecht, the Netherlands.

Bird, B. J. (1992) The operation of intention in time: The emergence of the new venture. *Entrepreneurship Theory and Practice*, 17(1), 11–20.

Brett, J. L. and Stroh, L. K. (1994). Turnover of women managers. In M. J. Davidson (ed.) *Women in Management: Current Research Issues*. Paul Chapman Publishing, London.

Burke, R. J. (1997). Women on corporate boards of directors: A needed resource. *Journal of Business Ethics*, 16(9), 909–915.

Burke, R. J. and Mattis, M. C. (2000). *Women on Corporate Boards of Directors*. Kluwer Academic Publishers, Dordrecht, the Netherlands.

Catalyst (1998). *Women Entrepreneurs: Why Companies Lose Female Talent and What They Can Do About It*. Catalyst, New York.

Catalyst/Opportunity Now (2000). *Breaking the Barriers: Women in Senior Management in the UK*. Business in the Community, London.

Chell, Elizabeth (2001). *Entrepreneurism, Globalisation, Innovation and Development*. Thompson Learning, London.

Chodorow, N. (1978). *The Reproduction of Mothering: Psychoanalysis and the Sociology of Gender*. University of California Press, Los Angeles.

Compton UK Partners (1970). *If Present Trends Continue . . . .* Compton UK Partners and the Guardian, London.

Cooper, C. L. and Lewis, S. (1999). Gender and the changing nature of work. In G. Powell (ed.) *Handbook of Gender and Work*. Sage, Thousand Oaks, Calif.

Daily, C. M., Trevis-Certo, S. and Dalton, D. (1999). A decade of corporate women: Some progress in the boardroom, none in the executive suite. *Strategic Management Journal*, 20, 93–99.

Davidson, M. J. and Cooper, G. L. (1992). *Women Managers Shattering the Glass Ceiling: The Woman Manager.* Paul Chapman Publishing, London.

Divine, Y. J. (1994). Characteristics of self-employed women in the United States. *Monthly Labor Review*, 117(3), 20–34.

Drucker, Peter (1985). *Innovation and Entrepreneurship.* Harper & Row, New York.

Equal Opportunities Commission (2000). *Management and the Professions, EOC Briefings on Women and Men in Britain.* EOC, Manchester.

Equal Opportunities Commission (2002). *Women and Men in Britain: Management.* EOC, Manchester.

Fierman, J. (1990). Why women still don't hit the top. *Fortune*, 122(3), 40–62.

Fondas, N. and Sassalos, S. (2000). A different voice in the boardroom: How the presence of women directors affects board influence over management. *Global Focus*, 12(2), 13–22.

Gilligan, C. (1982). *In a Different Voice: Psychological Theory and Women's Development.* Harvard University Press, Cambridge, Mass.

Gowler, D. and Legge, K. (1989). Rhetoric in bureaucratic careers: Managing the meaning of management success. In M. B. Arthur, D. T. Hall and B. S. Lawrence (eds) *Handbook of Career Theory.* Cambridge University Press, Cambridge.

Gracie, C. (1998). In the company of women. *Management Today*, 66–70.

Gregg, G. (1985). Women entrepreneurs: The second generation. *Across the Board,* 22(1), 10–18.

Guardian (2000) FTSE 100 directors paid more than £1m last year. 23 August, p. 27.

Hall, D. T. (1976). *Careers in Organizations.* Goodyear, Santa Monica, Calif.

Helgesen, S. (1990). *The Female Advantage.* DoubleDay, New York.

Holton, V. M. (2000). Taking a seat on the board: Women directors in Britain. In R. J. Burke and M. Mattis (eds) *Women on Corporate Boards of Directors: International Challenges and Opportunities.* Kluwer Academic Publishers, Dordrecht, the Netherlands.

Ibarra, H. (1992). Homophily and differential returns: Sex differences in network structure and access in an advertising firm. *Administrative Science Quarterly,* 37(3), 422–447.

Institute of Management (1998). *1998 National Management Salary Survey.* Institute of Management and Remuneration Economics, London.

Institute of Management (2001). *A Woman's Place.* Institute of Management, London.

Kanter, R. M. (1977). *Men and Women of the Corporation.* New York, Basic Books.

Kanter, Rosabeth Moss (1998). Careers and the wealth of nations: A macro perspective on the structure and implications of career forms. In M. B. Arthur, D. T. Hall and B. S. Laurence (eds) *Handbook of Career Theory.* Cambridge University Press, Cambridge.

Kuczynski, S. (1999). If diversity, then higher profits? *HRMagazine*, 44(13), 66–74.

Larwood, L. and Gutek, B. A. (1987) *Working Towards a Theory of Women's Career Development.* Sage, Newbury Park, Calif.

Levinson, D. (1978). *The Seasons of a Man's Life.* Knopf, New York.

Levinson, D. (1996). *The Seasons of a Woman's Life.* Knopf, New York.

McRae, S. (1995). *Women at the Top: Progress after Five Years.* King–Hall Paper, No. 2, The Hansard Society, London.

Mainiero, L. A. (1994). Getting anointed for advancement: The case of executive women. *Academy of Management Executive,* 8(2), 53–67.

Mallon, M. and Cohen, L. (2001). Time for a change? Women's accounts of the move from organizational careers to self employment. *British Journal of Management*, 12, 217–230.

Marshall, J. (1995). *Women Managers Moving On: Exploring Career and Life Choices*. Routledge, London.

Mattis, Mary C. (2000). Women entrepreneurs in the United States. In M. J. Davidson and R. J. Burke (eds) *Women in Management: Current Issues*, vol. II. Sage, London.

Moore, D. (1990). *When a Woman Means Business*. Fontana Paperbacks, London.

Moore, D. P. and Buttner, E. H. (1997). *Women Entrepreneurs: Moving Beyond the Glass Ceiling*. Sage, Thousand Oaks, Calif.

Morrison, A. M., White, R. P. and von Velsor, E. (1992). *Breaking the Glass Ceiling: Can Women Reach the Tip of America's Largest Corporation*. Addison-Wesley, Reading, Mass.

Murphy, A. (1992). The start-up of the '90s'. *Inc.*, 14(3), 32–40.

National Foundation for Women Business Owners (1997). Minority women-owned firms thriving, press release, NFWBO, 25 June.

Parkhouse, S. (2001). *Powerful Woman: Dancing on the Glass Ceiling*. John Wiley & Sons, Chichester.

Pazy, A. (1987). Sex differences in responsiveness to organizational career management. *Human Resource Management*, 26(2), 243–256.

Powell, G. N. (1990). One more time: Do female and male managers differ? *Academy of Management Executive*, 4(3), 68–75.

Powell, G. N. and Mainiero, L. A. (1992). Cross-currents in the river of time: Conceptualising the complexities of women's careers. *Journal of Management*, 18(2), 215–237.

Ragins, B. R. and Cotton, J. L. (1991). Easier said than done: Gender differences in perceived barriers to gaining a mentor. *Academy of Management Journal*, 34(4), 939–951.

Ragins, B. R. and Sundstrom, E. (1989). Gender and power in organizations: A longitudinal perspective. *Psychological Bulletin*, 105(1), 51–88.

Ragins, B. R., Townsend, B. and Mattis, M. (1998). Gender gap in the executive suite: CEOs and female executives report on breaking the glass ceiling. *Academy of Management Executive*, 12(1), 28–42.

Roddick, A. (1991). *Body and Soul*. Ebury Press, Random Century Group, London.

Roddick, A. (2000). *Business as Unusual*. Thorsons, HarperCollins, London.

Roddick, A. (2001). *Take It Personally: How Globalization Affects You and Powerful Ways to Challenge It*. Thorsons, HarperCollins, London.

Rosener, J. B. (1990). Ways women lead. *Harvard Business Review*, December, 199–225.

Rosin, H. M. and Korabik, K. (1992). Corporate flight of women managers: Moving from fiction to fact. *Women in Management Review*, 7(3), 31–35.

Rosin, H. M. and Korabik, K. (1995). Organizational experiences and propensity to leave: Multivariate investigation of men and women managers. *Journal of Vocational Behaviour*, 46(1), 1–16.

Ross, K. (2000). *Women at the Top 2000: Cracking the Public Sector Glass Ceiling*. Hansard Society, London.

Schein, E. H. (1971). The individual, the organization, and the career: A conceptual scheme. *Journal of Applied Behavioral Science*, 7, 401–426.

Schein, V. E., Mueller, R., Lituchy, T. and Liu, J. (1996). Think manager – think male. A global phenomenon. *Journal of Organizational Behavior*, 17(1), 33–41.

Shapiro, E. C., Haseltine, F. P. and Rowe, M. P. (1978). Moving up: Role models, mentors and the patron system. *Sloan Management Review,* 19(3), 51–58.

Simpson, R. (1997). Have times changed? Career barriers and the token woman manager. *British Journal of Management,* 8 (special issue), S121–S130.

Simpson, R. (1998). Presenteeism, power and organizational change: Long hours as a career barrier and the impact on the working lives of women managers. *British Journal of Management*, 9 (special issue), S37–S50.

Singh, V. and Vinnicombe, S. (2001). *Women Directors: Swimming, Sinking or Not Even in the Pool?* Report on Female Directors in the Top 100 Companies Index. Centre for Developing Women Business Leaders, Cranfield School of Management.

Sinclair, A. (1998). *Doing Leadership Differently.* Melbourne University Press, Melbourne.

Sly, F., Price, A. and Risdon, A. (1997). Women in the labour market: Results from the spring 1996 Labour Force Survey. *Labour Market Trends*, March, 99–120.

Stamp, G. (1986). Some observations on the career paths of women. *Journal of Applied Behavioral Science,* 22(4), 385–397.

Stevenson, L. (1986). Against all odds: The entrepreneurship of women. *Journal of Small Business Management*, 24(3), 30–36.

Sturges, J. (1999). What it means to succeed: Personal conceptions of career success held by male and female managers at different ages. *British Journal of Management*, 10, 239–252.

Super, D. I. (1957). *The Psychology of Careers.* Harper & Row, New York.

Tharenou, P., Latimer, S. and Conroy, D. (1994). How do you make it to the top? An examination of influences on women's and men's managerial advancement. *Academy of Management Journal,* 37(4), 899–931.

Turban, D. B. and Dougherty, T. W. (1994). Role of protégé personality in receipt of mentoring and career success. *Academy of Management Journal*, 37(3), 688–702.

Vinnicombe, S. and Colwill, N. C. (1995). *The Essence of Women in Management.* Prentice-Hall, London.

Vinnicombe, S., Singh, V. and Sturges, J. (2000). Making it to the top. In R. J. Burke and M. Mattis (eds) *Women on Corporate Boards of Directors: International Challenges and Opportunities*. Kluwer Academic Publishers, Dordrecht, the Netherlands.

Wall Street Journal Interactive Edition (2001). The Wall Street Journal Europe/Arthur Andersen study, conducted by Lieberman Research Worldwide, 1 March.

White, B., Cox, C. and Cooper, G. (1992). *Women's Career Development: A Study of High Flyers*. Basil Blackwell, Oxford.

Index